WITHDRAWN

Readings in Modern Applied Salesmanship

Contents

Preface

For over fifty-years *Sales Management* magazine (retitled *Sales & Marketing Management* in late 1975), a Bill Publication, with executive, editorial, and circulation offices at 633 Third Avenue, New York, N.Y. 10017, has been generally recognized as the leading American magazine edited and published for men and women who manage sales – at every level and job title.

Over 44,000 such sales executives and sales representatives pay to receive this outstanding publication, and through them much of the helpful information contained in its average thirteen news and feature issues, four survey issues, and four special reports published each year is estimated to reach over one and a half million additional American and Canadian field sales representatives, agents, distributors, dealers, and retailers.

Thanks to the interest and cooperation of Robert H. Albert, Editor of *Sales & Marketing Management*, this collection of readings, a selection of edited and sometimes abridged articles from *Sales Management* issues published during 1973-75, has been compiled by your author and thus made available for the first time in such format, to the thousands of students of salesmanship in universities, four- and two-year colleges, business colleges, and company training programs in the United States, Canada, and the rest of the world.

Organized in six parts to conform to topical presentation in the widely used textbook *Modern Applied Salesmanship*, 2d ed., by Allan L. Reid (Santa Monica, Calif.: Goodyear Publishing Co., 1975), this selection of readings is first and foremost designed for use as a companion volume to that basic text. It can also be used as an effective supplement to any other basic text in salesmanship, or to any text or courses in sales management, advertising, or public relations.

Sales Management magazine was selected as the single source for this collection, because its articles in sum total cover nearly all areas of interest to those men and women contemplating a sales career, or those now engaged in outside or in-store face-to-face with prospect or customer personal selling. Also, the magazine was selected because it approaches the subject in many instances from a managerial point of view (plan your work – work your plan) – a key theme in *Modern Applied Salesmanship*, 2d ed.

Readings from years 1973-75 were selected for a very specific purpose. Sales/marketing executives and millions of individual American sales representatives and salespersons entered into the new 1973 sales-plan year with the generally shared feeling that 1973, like the boom year 1972, would be a very good year. Nearly all economic forecasts and statements by leading economists, both in government and business, backed up this feeling of optimism.

But, as we shall see in the chronological section to follow, "1973-75: Years That Will Long Be Remembered by Sales/Marketing Managers and Sales Representatives," that hope was soon rudely shaken. Commencing as early as mid-February, 1973, as the months wore on, one economic or political crisis or unexpected development after another forced drastic alteration of carefully laid plans, and rapid adaptation of new sales/marketing strategies and tactics at all levels. Not since the Great Depression of the early 1930s had so much happened so quickly to affect sales/ marketing in the United States and Canada. It was not until late 1975 that the marketplace showed signs of returning to normal. During those three tumultuous years, great changes began to occur in consumer attitudes and buying patterns; an indication that the throw-away life style of North American consumers might be changing forever.

We will see, in the readings to follow, how countless American sales/marketing managers, outside sales representatives, and inside salespersons reacted to and coped with these rapid changes that so greatly affected their yearly, quarterly, monthly, and daily sales planning and personal selling. The years 1973-75 were indeed exciting years for those engaged at all levels in sales/marketing, especially for those on the face-to-face with customers' firing line.

Allan L. Reid

Readings in Modern Applied Salesmanship

Introduction

1973-75: Years That Will Long Be Remembered By Sales/Marketing Managers and Sales Representatives

This collection of readings offers a dramatic example of how sales/marketing managers and millions of individual sales representatives faced and reacted to a seemingly unending series of explosive economic and political crises in 1973–75 that buffeted the American economy and caused far greater changes and dislocations in the marketplace than any crises since the Great Depression of the 1930s. These changes greatly affected both large and small businesses and their outside sales representatives and in-store retail salespersons, and, in many cases, called for drastic changes in sales/marketing policies, strategies, and practices.

As background to our readings, let us consider chronologically some of those economic and political events that so shook the marketplace during this period. Since top business management, sales/marketing managers, and managerially-oriented sales representatives and salespersons normally lay their plans and chart their course toward realizing their planned annual sales/marketing objectives program on a quarterly basis within any given calendar year, we shall also chart these events.

As a lead-in to our 1973–75 charting, let us recall that 1972 was a boom year that showed healthy economic gains for the American economy. Auto sales, for example, hit a record high of 13.5 million vehicles, and new starts in private home building reached a new high of 2.4 million. Richard Nixon was reelected president in November, by an overwhelming majority, over Senator George McGovern. While the Vietnam war was still raging, and inflation a major problem, steps had been taken even before the election to cut federal defense and social-program spending, and during his reelection campaign President Nixon promised an early end to the direct American involvement in that war.

1973

FIRST QUARTER (JANUARY–MARCH)

At the beginning of 1973, Herbert Stein, Chairman of President Nixon's Council of Economic Advisors was quoted in the news media as stating that "the prospects are

good for another year combining rapid expansion and a reduced rate of inflation."
Even Senator McGovern's economic advisors acknowledged the economy's strength
and resilience. From all vantage points the economic picture seemed strong; administration economists predicted inflation would be trimmed to about 2.5 percent
annually, and unemployment possibly reduced to 4.5 percent. Auto sales were predicted to reach near 1972's record, and new housing starts to top 2 million.

The president's new budget (for the June 1973–July 1974 period), in an effort
to avoid further inflation and higher taxes, cut back defense spending, offered no
new initiative or programs, and cut deeply into dozens of programs and agencies
designed to achieve President Lyndon Johnson's Great Society.

On the political scene, President Nixon announced to the nation January 23,
"We today have concluded an agreement to end the war and bring peace with honor
in Vietnam and Southeast Asia." Based on an agreement signed in Paris, this signalled the formal end to the twelve-year American involvement in a war that had
plagued four presidents (and driven one from office), cost 46,000 American lives in
combat, and cost the United States $146 billion.

Under the agreement's terms, the United States would immediately stop all
bombing of North Vietnam, the last 26,000 American troops would be pulled out
of South Vietnam within sixty days, and all American POW's would come home.
No provisions were made, however, for withdrawals by North Vietnam of its troops
from South Vietnam.

With a so-called "peace" in Southeast Asia, and a bright economic picture, most
Americans looked forward to a prosperous, normal business year.

There were some dark clouds on the horizon, however! In mid-February a full-
scale monetary crisis exploded across the world, and a growing American energy
crisis had forced the United States to rely increasingly on foreign oil to satisfy an
ever-growing demand at home. The United States announced a ten-percent dollar
devaluation on February 12, but a new international monetary crisis arose in March.

SECOND QUARTER (APRIL–JUNE)

In early April, it still looked like the 1972 American economic boom would continue, but some economists began to see obstacles that might deflate or even end
the boom by year's end—rising interest rates, tightening money supply, and ever-
rising prices that could lead to a new round of inflation.

It was clear, also, that the United States was beginning its third year of horren-
dous deficits in its transactions with the rest of the world. Many foreign political
leaders and business persons had lost confidence in the ability or will of U.S. and
foreign bankers to correct the huge and seemingly unending U.S. imbalance.

THIRD QUARTER (JULY–SEPTEMBER)

The Watergate scandal broke wide open in early July when John Dean, a member of
President Nixon's innermost council, charged before the Ervin Senate Committee

that Nixon had known about the Watergate cover-up as early as September, 1972.

In August, suddenly and shockingly, the U.S. economic picture began to darken. Instead of abundance, there were many shortages: food, energy, paper, and natural resources. The nation's gasoline shortage was getting worse and inflation was starting to rage.

Throughout September, as the Watergate drama unfolded (with Nixon refusing to surrender tapes of White House meetings and phone calls to Senate investigators, and his close aids John Erlichman and H.R. Haldeman on the stand before the Ervin Senate Committee), U.S. inflation reached its worst peak since the Korean War (1950-53), and Americans were beginning to change their eating habits.

With mortgage money increasingly scarce and interest rates at record levels in many parts of the nation, home buying became nearly impossible for many families—especially young married couples. Predictions were now being made that 1973 new housing starts would only reach 1.5 million units versus the earlier predicted 2.0 million.

By late September inflation was beginning to nudge Watergate aside on the front pages of newspapers across the country, and the news media carried stories that Vice-President Spiro Agnew was in deep trouble for allegedly accepting kickbacks.

FOURTH QUARTER (OCTOBER–DECEMBER)

October was a month of new troubles on top of old ones! First, fears of a severe heating oil shortage for the impending winter suddenly thrust aside the gasoline shortage to become the country's chief concern in the energy crisis.

Then the Yom Kippur War exploded in the Middle East, with bitter fighting between Israel, Egypt, and Syria.

By late October, news of Vice-President Agnew's resignation (in a deal with government prosecutors under pressure of kickback investigation), President Nixon's appointment of Gerald Ford to replace him, and a U.S. Court of Appeal's decision that Nixon must turn over his Watergate tapes to Judge John J. Sirica, seemed trivial compared to a sudden announcement from the Arab oil-producing states' Organization of Arab Petroleum Exporting Countries (OPEC).

The OPEC announced to the world they would cut oil production five percent each month until Israel withdrew from occupied Arab territories and some solution was found to restore to Palestinians their "legitimate rights." Enemies (including the United States) would begin getting less oil immediately!

By late November, although the Yom Kippur War had ended inconclusively with a shakey truce, the United States and Holland were under total Arab oil embargo, and President Nixon warned the nation via television that the United States faced the most acute shortages of energy since World War II (1939-45). The administration moved toward the first peacetime rationing of gasoline in history.

As the year ended, to a backdrop of the presidency under siege (Nixon fighting to hang onto his tapes, and his famous "I am Not a Crook" television speech), for the first time in two generations there was widespread fear and talk of economic depression, not just recession, because of continued inflation, poor job outlook, and the ever-worsening energy crisis. Fuel costs rose sharply, administration appeals to motorists to voluntarily conserve fuel weren't working. Truckers reacted angrily to lower speed limits and higher diesel oil prices by halting trucks at key highway spots across the nation and tying up traffic, and gasoline ration cards were printed by the government, ready for use if the situation got worse.

1974

FIRST QUARTER (JANUARY–MARCH)

Since 1973 had been so full of bad news and surprises for economic forecasters and business persons, a pessimism prevailed throughout the nation as 1974 got under-way. And with good reason—the Arab oil embargo was hurting. As auto sales slumped even further, thousands more auto workers were laid off. By late January industrial production was showing significant decline in some areas for the first time in two years. The overall sharp economic decline, coupled with soaring food and fuel costs, had indeed pushed the U.S. economy to the verge of recession.

In February, another major New York brokerage firm went out of business after sustaining months of losses, following the thirty-four such firms that had disappear-ed in 1973—a result of continued falling stock prices and skimpy trading volume.

By March, American consumers as a whole were angry and frustrated at the con-tinued soaring cost of living, as they experienced the most sustained dose of infla-tion in a generation. As prices continued to rise, the economy continued to slow down. This posed a unique new problem for the nation's economic managers—how to control inflation along with recession.

As a Watergate Grand Jury in Washington, D.C., after a twenty-month investiga-tion, indicted seven of President Nixon's key aids on twenty-four counts of con-spiracy, lying, and obstructing justice (H.R. Haldeman, John Erlichman, and ex-Attorney General John Mitchell among them), American consumers entered into a new and, perhaps, permanent change of life style. They began buying smaller cars with less powerful engines, using public mass transit more, and changing their recre-ation patterns. The exodus from urban centers slowed. It seemed that the Ameri-can consumer's throw-away life style might be changing forever.

SECOND QUARTER (APRIL–JUNE)

Bad news came early in April with a government announcement that the actual Gross National Product (GNP), with inflationary elements removed, had declined more than five percent during the first quarter of 1974. This figure was far greater than most economists had expected, and the first GNP slump of any kind since the 1969–70 recession. Although administration spokesmen denied it, most economists and business persons felt it signalled the opening phase of a real recession.

Surprisingly, overall corporate first-quarter profits were high because of higher prices that followed the late 1973 easing of government controls. Some of the biggest profit gains were reported by industries whose products were by now in short supply, such as oil, chemicals, steel, and aluminum.

In May, along with a rapid climb in interest rates that caused a deep slump in new housing starts across the nation, the Judiciary Committee of the House of Representatives began hearings on the impeachment of President Nixon.

In early June, President Nixon forecast some economic progress in the second half of the year, claiming that the economy was moving upward and that it was unlikely we would have a recession.

But by the end of June, as the stock market plummeted, money was so tight that many business firms couldn't borrow enough to pay their bills, and inflation was running at an alarming annual rate of 11.5 percent. These events began having deep economic and psychological effects on millions of Americans. There was a noticeable jump in the number of persons and business firms filing for bankruptcy, and by some estimates 6 out of every 100 American families were in economic trouble.

THIRD QUARTER (JULY–SEPTEMBER)

By July, the major question was, Is the entire world, not only the United States, heading toward a recession? Continued shortages of essential raw materials and fourfold increase in crude oil prices resulting from OPEC actions, both coming on the heels of a worldwide economic boom, had sent prices soaring in every industrialized nation of the world.

In the United States that month, as the House Judiciary Committee published eight volumes of Watergate evidence and scheduled a television debate on "this enormous crime," newly released government figures seemed to confirm officially that the nation had indeed entered into a real recession. The nation's vital housing industry, for example, was in its worst slump in history. New homes cost too much, down payments were too high, and some builders were having to pay eighteen-percent interest if and when they could find money to borrow. The lack of mortgage money was the most serious problem; it simply wasn't available. Revised government forecasts now estimated total 1974 new housing starts at only 1.5 million, versus 2.4 million in 1972 (the all-time high record year) and 2.1 million in 1973.

August was a Big News month! Following an 8 to 0 Supreme Court decision that he must turn over sixty-four more Watergate tapes to investigators, and the voting out by the House Judiciary Committee of a three-count bill of impeachment against him, President Nixon resigned. Vice-President Gerald Ford replaced him.

If August was a Big News month, September was a Bad News month. Along with the "stagflation" (mix of inflation and recession) economy, came a Midwest drought that reduced crop yields and promised still higher food prices.

On the stock market, the Dow Jones Industrial Average (an index of thirty important stocks) dropped below the 700 mark for the first time in four years. As these stocks dropped in price to near book value (considered a distress level), the question nervously asked by investors was, "How much further down can it go?" In just seventeen days of August, the Dow Jones average dropped 119 points. On its worst day it fell by nearly 18 points. This sharp drop—from the all-time high of 1,051 on January 11, 1973, to 697 on August 3, 1974, was indeed alarming.

This bleak third quarter ended with President Ford's pardon of ex-President Nixon for any Watergate cover-up crimes, and widespread alarm at the prospect of a worldwide depression rivalling that of the 1930s.

FOURTH QUARTER (OCTOBER–DECEMBER)

By October, unemployment had jumped to six percent, the highest level in three years, with nearly 5.5 million Americans out of work; some economists predicted it might reach six to seven percent in 1975. The U.S. economy was experiencing its sharpest decline in sixteen years, and fifty-one percent of Americans (according to a Gallup Poll) felt that another depression was on its way.

Auto sales and profits continued to slump—the new 1975 models weren't selling. The airlines were suffering because of increased costs in fuel and other items, plus a sharp decrease in passenger traffic on many routes. In late November, Ron Nessen, White House Press Secretary, obviously speaking for the president, admitted publicly that "we are moving into a recession." With signs of hard times everywhere, it was the dreariest Thanksgiving the nation had experienced since the deep recession of 1958.

Christmas was even drearier! As the slump deepened through December, the Dow Jones average dipped to a twelve-year low and unemployment climbed to a thirteen-year high of 6.5 percent, with six million Americans out of work—an increase of 460,000 in a single month. During Christmas Week, more than 813,000 Americans lined up to file initial claims for unemployment insurance, the largest one-week filing since the program began in 1937.

1975

FIRST QUARTER (JANUARY–MARCH)

The smouldering Vietnam "peace" suddenly flared in January as Communists seized Phuoc Binh, a provincial capital only seventy-five miles north of Saigon. In

Cambodia, Communist troops besieged the capital Phnom Penh. These far-off war news items seemed insignificant to most Americans, who were facing the highest unemployment level (6.5 million) since 1940. Teen-agers were the worst hit by unemployment, with 18.3 percent of them unable to find jobs; 12.8 percent of the black population faced the same bleak situation.

President Ford's budget conceded that 1975 would be the worst year since the Great Depression, with unemployment forecast at more than eight percent, the highest in thirty-five years, and inflation at over eleven percent.

In March, bad news from Southeast Asia filled the front pages of newspapers. As Phnom Penh barely hung on, kept alive only by an American airlift of one plane flying every thirty minutes into the city's airport amidst exploding Communist rocket and artillery shells, President Nguyen Van Thieu of South Vietnam suddenly ordered abandonment of half his country to attacking North Vietnamese, and a great South Vietnamese rout began.

SECOND QUARTER (APRIL–JUNE)

After losing six full combat divisions in just four weeks of April, the end of the Republic of South Vietnam was at hand. As the last Americans evacuated Phnom Penh by Marine helicopter, and the Cambodian government surrendered, Saigon fell under Communist attack.

In early May, President Thieu resigned, and the last Americans evacuated Saigon by helicopter. The long Southeast Asian war was finally over.

But in June, there was some good economic news at least—and at long last! In spite of the worst unemployment in thirty-four years, now at 9.2 percent with 8.5 million Americans unemployed, indications began to show that the worst recession in nearly forty years might be over.

THIRD QUARTER (JULY–SEPTEMBER)

Based on a steady rise of the Commerce Department's index of leading economic indicators for the third straight month, President Ford's chief economist felt confident enough to announce in July that "the recession for all practical purposes is over."

In spite of the near financial collapse of New York City, and continued increase in wholesale and consumer prices (especially food), housing starts were up, corporate profits were up, new orders for durable goods were pouring into the nation's factories, and unemployment declined to 8.4 percent. This good news indicated by late September that the recession really had bottomed, and that the U.S. economy clearly was stronger than other nations in the industrialized world.

FOURTH QUARTER (OCTOBER–DECEMBER)

Although demand for housing was at a near standstill, and most consumers whose real income had been eroded by the inflation spiral were unable to afford the high prices and 9 percent mortgage rates to buy the over 380,000 units available, construction spending was up somewhat. And there were other signs that inflation was slowing and that the economy was on a steady upswing. Car sales were moving upward as they had since October, unemployment dropped to 8.3 percent, and as Christmas shoppers poured into stores, retailers across the nation reported sales gains of from 10 to 25 percent over the same period during the previous year.

Based on these favorable trends, government predictions for 1976, made public at the end of December, forecast an economic growth of between 6 to 7 percent, inflation to decline to near 5 percent by the end of the year, a decline in unemployment to around 7.5 percent, and a steady, normal recovery. Many private economists voiced fears that recovery might not be that smooth, but the general feeling throughout the country at the end of 1975 was that the worst of the bad economic news, and hopefully the bad political news, was over and business would return to normal.

Summary

In retrospect, it is clear that neither economic forecasters nor business persons had adequately anticipated the sudden economic changes that commenced in early 1973, or the depth of the 1974–75 recession, or the extent of the accompanying inflation. The performance of the American economy in 1975 was the worst in nearly thirty-five years; the inflation rates of 1974–75 were the worst in nearly fifty years. Many did, however, predict correctly that the recession would bottom by the third quarter of 1975, which it did, and that inflation, while it would continue high, would start slowing down. Certainly they could not have predicted the Arab oil embargo, Watergate and all its effects, or the sudden collapse of South Vietnam—political events that added to the general economic woes.

With an understanding now of the tumultuous economic and political climate within which American business operated during 1973–75 let us see, via the dated* *Sales Management (SM)* articles in this book, how American sales/marketing managers, sales representatives, and salespersons were affected by all this, and how they reacted to the fast-changing events.

---

*All dates and time references within the articles are as they originally appeared.

PART I What Do You Stand to Gain from Studying Salesmanship?

OVERVIEW

Traditionally, most definitions of *selling* have been in the strictly commercial sense. The American Marketing Association, for example, defines selling as "the personal or impersonal process of assisting and/or persuading a prospective customer to buy a commodity or service and to act favorably upon an idea that has commercial significance to the seller."* *Salesmanship* can be defined as the practice of selling.

Our selected readings in Sections 1 and 2 help answer the question, "What do you (the reader) stand to gain from studying salesmanship?" Please keep in mind that while the readings from *Sales Management* presented in these two sections, and those that follow, are addressed to men and women now engaged in sales/marketing careers, most of the principles and many of the techniques can help *you* achieve success in your own career, whether it be sales or nonsales, or in your nonwork activities that involve close association with friends or other people whom you may wish to persuade or lead.

Section 1 Introduction to Selling and Salesmanship. If you plan to enter upon a sales career, "The Teaching Gap" (p. 10) offers clues to what sales executives feel are the most important areas for you to concentrate on in your study of salesmanship. The term salesman, because of so many women entering the field, is fast becoming obsolete. As noted in "Good-bye Salesman" (p. 11), the U.S. Department of Labor, in its 1976 *Occupational Handbook* now classifies both outside (sales representatives) and in-store (salespersons) as salespersons; but it remains to be seen if it will catch-on in general use throughout business and industry. You may note that "salesperson" starts to appear in a few of the late 1975 readings. The other articles in Section 1 offer an overview introduction to real-life selling and salesmanship.

Section 2 Career Opportunities in Selling. Most of the articles in Section 2 focus on women and illustrate that sales opportunities for women, minorities, and older people are rapidly increasing. As with any career field however, there are both advantages and disadvantages in a sales career. The article "Why Your Salesmen Quit" (p. 23) advances the theme that sales representatives are more likely to stick with smaller companies offering better pay.

---

*From *Marketing Definitions: A Glossary of Marketing Terms* (Chicago: American Marketing Association, 1960), p. 21. Reprinted by permission.

10

Section 1 / Introduction to Selling and Salesmanship

The Teaching Gap [in Sales Training]

Are business schools providing future salesmen with the kinds of skills sales managers want to find in their recruits? To answer that intriguing question, Robert F. Witherspoon, coordinator of marketing programs at Triton College in Illinois, and Gilbert Dobslaw, an instructor there, sent questionnaires to 200 sales managers who are members of the Sales-Marketing Executives Assn. of Chicago. Eighty replied, allowing Witherspoon and Dobslaw to pin down where the schools and the managers differ. "There are 10 major areas that sales managers believe are very important to the success of a salesman's trainee program and should be stressed in a classroom situation," the survey notes. Those 10 areas, in order of importance, are the following:

Time utilization and planning
Customer benefits
Closing techniques
Handling objections
Individual's professional standards
Salesman's self-attitude
Questioning techniques
Listening techniques
Buyer behavior and customer motivation
Change of attitude about salesmen

A major discovery reported by Witherspoon and Dobslaw is that college instructors consider it very important to teach future salesmen how to gain attention and how to build interest, and to give them oral practice in sales techniques. But the sales managers surveyed tended to have a lesser regard for those three—the managers' own training programs put other skills first. One conclusion to be drawn from the survey is that the schools may need to change the training they provide and, in all probability, make it more sophisticated.

Another conclusion is that some of the 80 companies in the survey may be slighting the training they give to new salesmen. The survey notes that most of the companies use either professional trainers working in the field, other salesmen, or general managers to train recruits. It also found that 26 of the firms have no formal training program at all, 46 have classroom instruction that ranges from two years to just a single day, and 56 have on-the-job training ranging from two years to only four weeks.

SM, April 8, 1974, p. 66.

Good-bye, Salesman, Hello Salesperson

The 1976 *Occupational Handbook,* an annual volume put out by the U.S. Labor Dept., nowhere uses the title "salesman." Henceforth, it is "salesperson." Actually, some 3,500 of the volume's 35,000 occupational titles have bowed to unisexism, or whatever you want to call it. Examples: Busboys are now officially known as "dining room attendants," foremen are "supervisors," and bridal consultants are "wedding consultants."

SM, April 7, 1975, p. 86.

Where 1975 Industry Sales Will Be Brightest

Sales managers looking for 1975's high-growth industries should heed the mushrooming popularity of hand-held calculators in the home and school sectors and

1975's GROWTH LEADERS

	1975 Sales ($Mil.)	% Change 75/74	74/73
Consumer Goods			
Calculating, accounting machines	$ 3,100	+61	+134
Shortening	4,588	+20	+ 72
Cane sugar refining	3,192	+20	+ 39
Chocolate, cocoa products	1,936	+20	+123
Mobile homes	3,650	+16	− 30
Frozen fruits, vegetables	5,444	+15	+ 25
Motion pictures	1,975	+15	+ 21
Fresh, frozen seafoods	1,561	+15	+ 15
Health, medical services	125,900	+12	+ 17
Auto rental, leasing	5,390	+12	+ 9
Lighting fixtures	3,200	+12	+ 6
Canned food specialties	2,267	+12	+ 4
Industrial Goods			
Beet sugar	$ 1,966	+30	+ 60
Fertilizer	3,610	+28	+ 33
Oil field machinery	2,528	+21	+ 70
Soybean oil mills	5,352	+20	− 29
Railroad freight cars	1,872	+18	+ 24
Brass mills	4,650	+17	− 2
Plastic materials, resins	7,490	+15	+ 18
Electrical measuring instruments	2,535	+15	+ 20
Computers, related equipment	11,000	+14	+ 55
Prepared feeds	6,498	+13	− 40

Note: Listing confined to industries with $1 billion or more volume.

Source: Commerce Dept., *U.S. Industrial Outlook: 1975. ©Sales Management.*

the soaring demand for sweets. The Commerce Dept.'s annual *U.S. Industrial Outlook* report tabs the calculator industry as next year's fastest-growing consumer goods industry, with sales expected to rise 61%, and beet sugar as the fastest-growing industrial goods industry, with volume up 30%. Other gainers will be mobile homes, motion pictures, auto rentals, fertilizer, and oil industry machinery.

Prepared by the department's Office of Business Research and Analysis, the report includes estimates of 1975 dollar volume for more than 200 industries, along with helpful commentaries on their changes in supply and demand and domestic and overseas prospects, plus the impact of energy problems and materials shortages (making the tome a real bargain at $4). A bonus in this year's edition is a series of flow charts depicting the leading suppliers and customers for selected industries.

Significantly, most of next year's high-stepping industries will grow at a much reduced pace compared with 1974. Thus when you add the inflation factor, the outlook is for very modest, if any, real growth. (SM's *Survey of Industrial Purchasing Power,* due in April, will list the leading countries for the pacesetting manufacturing industries and for many other important industries.)

SM, December 9, 1974, p. 10.

Inter-Continental Hotels [Where Every Employee Is a Sales Representative]

"All the people in my office are considered sales personnel," John Macomber says. "Secretaries are called sales personnel. They take calls from clients. They make sales calls one day a week. And they have business cards that say 'Sales Representative.' "

Macomber, the 54-year-old vice president, marketing, U.S. and Canada, for Inter-Continental Hotels, oversees nine regional offices that handle sales for all 70 hotels in the chain. The offices are staffed by 48 employees, whom he calls "colleagues in selling."

Macomber explains that he began sending secretarial personnel on sales calls during the past year, using the motto "Door to door in '74." To prepare for their new responsibilities, secretaries took a sales training course, visited hotels, and went on calls with experienced salesmen. "A girl who has been called a secretary and is now a member of the sales department is much more interested in her job," Macomber says. "The girls are pleased, and so are the clients."

Furthermore, Macomber says, "any person, male or female, that we hire to do in-office work must have office skills. When they are interviewed, they are also screened for sales ability. The fundamental thing we look for is whether or not *they* sell *us* in the interview." Also important: a good telephone voice. "I use the telephone as an aggressive selling instrument," Macomber says, "but of course nothing can beat the personal call for effectiveness."

Macomber's approach seems to be working. His division, which accounts for 74.1% of total room sales for Inter-Continental, last year had sales of over $41 million. (Inter-Continental is itself a subsidiary of Pan American Airlines.) It has been ahead of forecast throughout 1974. "And in our business," he says, "if you make forecast, you're doing very well."

When Macomber says all personnel are sales personnel, he includes himself. "My lofty title doesn't mean I don't go out and hustle," he says. "I personally handle blue ribbon accounts—and I wouldn't have it any other way."

SM, December 9, 1974, p. 13.

Mogul Treats Salesmen Like Princes

Q.: What do water-treatment chemicals, laboratory tissue cultures, and generic pharmaceuticals have in common?

A: 1. Not much.
2. More than you'd think.
3. They're all sold by Mogul Corp.

The correct answer is "All the above." Mogul, based in Chagrin Falls (near Cleveland), Ohio, sells through three operating groups, which together produced $49 million in sales during the fiscal year ended Oct. 31, 1974. What's more, the combination seems to be recession proof: during the first six months of fiscal 1975, corporate sales rose 22%, to $28 million, and net income went up 19%.

One of the reasons for that success is that each group relies heavily on its salesmen, taking steps to insure that they're more highly motivated and better paid than those of competitors. "Each group is autonomous, selling in its own marketplace," says corporate vice president Charles Clark. "But there is a unifying thread in the way the three sales forces operate."

For example, each operating group sells consumable products, that is, items that are used up and reordered. Individual orders tend to be small (in the hundreds of dollars) and customer bases large (the water-treatment group, for example, has over 30,000 customers, but no one buyer accounts for as much as 1% of sales).

"We've always been marketing oriented," says Clark, "even back when we were just selling boiler compounds. That business is now water-treatment chemicals. Our competitors pay their salesmen salary and bonus; we pay ours straight commission—they even pay their own expenses. As we've gone into other areas, we've kept the same principles: pay your salesmen well, give exclusive territories, and don't slice into those territories."

Within that framework, however, each group has its own compensation plan. The life sciences group (lab materials) pays a substantial draw to attract better-educated salesmen. Their incentive compensation comes from a bonus pot based on the group's profitability and split according to each man's sales. "Before we entered the market," says Clark, "everyone sold through catalogues. Now we're the leader."

Salesmen in the pharmaceutical group don't "detail" physicians; they sell generic drugs to hospital pharmacists. These salesmen are also on commission, but the company pays their expenses and provides them with cars, as other pharmaceutical companies do. However, their commission scale is on a declining basis, with the percentage rates going down as sales increase although total compensation keeps going up.

NO UPPER LIMIT

As a result of those plans, Clark claims, Mogul's 225 salesmen are better paid than those of competitors in each area. There's no upper limit. Many salesmen earn $40,000 to $60,000 and some even more. Territorial integrity is scrupulously maintained: often, if an area has to be split, the existing man becomes the manager of the new man, receiving an override on his commissions.

Such strategies seem to pay off. As the company heads toward another record sales year, all operating groups are participating in the improved performance, perhaps the most rewarding characteristic of all those that Mogul's three unlikely offspring have in common.

SM, September 8, 1975, p. 10.

Total Motivation = Top Performance

At Black & Decker, job enrichment means inspiring salesmen with a careful selection of motivational strategies.

by **John I. Leahy**, Marketing Vice President, Black & Decker Manufacturing Co.

Win a trip to Hawaii or a bonus commission of $499 by increasing sales volume 12% in six weeks!

Popular as such inducements are with some companies, you won't find them being used at Black & Decker. We concluded a number of years ago that they don't bring the kind of effort needed for a consistent, fast-growth business.

We believe that sales executives abdicate their responsibility for planning marketing strategy and directing its implementation when they rely on such devices to motivate salesmen. In addition to creating peak-and-valley sales cycles and diverting the sales force from balanced selling, such inducements tend to motivate salesmen only for a short time.

This is not what we're looking for at Black & Decker. We expect 1973 to be the fifteenth consecutive year in which sales and net earnings have increased. During this span, we've grown at a 15% annual average rate in both these categories. There's no way we could have compiled this record by relying on glamorous trips and commission plans to motivate our sales force.

Our approach to motivation is one of *total job enrichment*. As we see it, this means using the maximum capabilities of an individual by bringing him into the picture with a full range of motivating factors. If total job enrichment is handled properly, the salesman can operate with greater understanding, achievement, and satisfaction. The motivation factors which we consider of primary importance are:
1. Salary
2. Growth potential
3. Self-development
4. Training
5. Communications
6. Responsibilities
7. Recognition

To the experienced sales manager, that list may appear a bit rudimentary. However, when sales management is committed to carrying out the requirements of each of these factors, the results can be most gratifying. Inherent in management's role must be complete conviction that people are the most important asset in selling and that the salesman's job must therefore be totally rewarding. Here's how we approach those seven factors:

1. Salary   This is obviously a prime motivator. We pay higher salaries and provide frequent increases based on performance. This enables us to attract the best people and to set higher performance criteria. Naturally, our sales people must possess the ability to achieve success. It is not realistic to employ a borderline producer and hope he'll improve enough to meet the job requirements. We believe in attracting the top performers and giving them top salaries. Not surprisingly, we also get top results.

2. Growth potential   The company's growth of 15% annually means we double in size every five years. It also means that the company stock has gone up rapidly. Since more than 75% of our salesmen are stockholders through our Stock Purchase Plans, they are able to compile handsome capital gains as the company's stock grows in value.

In addition, the company's fast expansion has resulted in many advancement opportunities. Fifteen years ago, our sales were just over $40 million. This year they will approach $400 million. This growth has resulted in continual opportunities for newer and big responsibilities in the sales force and other areas of total marketing.

3. Self-development   A major portion of sales improvement is self-development. We encourage our sales personnel to improve themselves by providing a complete Educational Assistance Program with no dollar limitations. The company reimburses tuition 100% for anyone who achieves passing grades in subjects related to his job. Participation in the program has almost tripled in the past five years. Specialized development also is provided for those qualified to attend professional association and management seminars.

4. Training   We make available one of the most extensive internal training programs in the world. After a candidate for the sales force is thoroughly screened and hired, he is given a five-day Sales Entry Seminar at the headquarters office. This seminar orients and trains the newcomer in company policies, procedures, and marketing techniques. It is aimed at getting his anxieties down and his efficiency up.

After a year or two on the job, our salesmen return to the headquarters training center for an Advanced Marketing Seminar. This program updates sales techniques, provides insights into management strategies and philosophies, and generates new ideas through peer-group involvement. When salesmen reach mid- to upper-level managerial status they are invited to attend a Management Development Course which provides training in modern managerial skills and the behavioral sciences.

We also provide a comprehensive in-the-field training program for distributors' salesmen who handle our professional products. This two-day ESP (Effective Selling Program) course includes extensive use of the products and how they work. It has proved highly successful in motivating our own salesmen (who also take the course) as well as distributor salesmen.

REGIONAL MANAGERS ARE THE KEY

5. Communications   It is of primary importance that salesmen understand strategies, goals, and the importance of their role in the operation. Twice each year we hold major sales meetings at which the sales force is given complete information on our marketing programs, new product developments, and over-all goals. Regional managers meet more frequently with their salesmen to update sales strategy.

Regional managers have direct profit and loss responsibilities for their areas. They control costs, make profit improvement contributions, and relate these to the goals of their division, operating group, and the total company. We strongly believe in Management By Objectives and feel that it can succeed only if each salesman is fully aware of those objectives and how he can personally contribute toward achieving them.

6. Responsibilities   According to Herzberg and Ford, two authorities in motivational theory, the supreme goal of man is to realize his own innate potentialities—within the limits of reality. Our challenge as managers is to structure sales jobs so that the work itself is a motivator. This doesn't mean that we simply set quotas, provide good working conditions, and then sit back to wait for results.

We must provide challenges for achievers by establishing other performance criteria, such as idea development, managerial potential, willingness to help fellow salesmen work out problems, and a competitive desire to win. If the salesman's job is interesting, challenging, and provides critical responsibilities which he fully understands, then the job itself becomes a powerful motivator.

7. Recognition   Most people work best when their contributions to the company's success are acknowledged with something besides a paycheck. We make sure our salesmen know the importance of their role in the company's success. When they make a sales call they carry the support of everyone in the organization.

Typical of the recognition our marketing effort gets is a statement Alonzo G. Decker, Jr., our chairman and chief executive officer, made at the recent annual meeting of stockholders. Mr. Decker told his audience, "The name of the game now is marketing and you'd better be good at it, regardless of how wonderful your products may be, or the vines will grow thick over your door." Mr. Decker and other senior management people back this view by attending sales meetings frequently and giving commendations to the sales force whenever they are merited. In addition, we make extensive use of our general company newspaper and divisional newspaper to give recognition to exceptional sales performances.

There are other motivators, to be sure, but the seven I've outlined are of primary importance to sales success. Without a doubt, we've achieved far greater sales productivity since adopting them. In the past seven years, our sales volume has more than tripled and dollar sales per salesman also have more than tripled.

We aren't gaining sales by increasing the number of salesmen. What has increased dramatically is sales productivity. We're convinced that our job enrichment approach to developing sales motivation has been a critical factor in this success.

SM, April 30, 1972, pp. 12–13.

Section 2 / Career Opportunities in Selling

"What Would I Tell My Wife?"

Los Angeles personnel recruiters Lear Purvis Walker held a career seminar last month for women interested in sales and marketing. Seventy-two women, ranging from recent college graduates to those wanting to make a midlife career change, listened to seven marketing professionals talk about opportunities in selling. Just about everyone's conclusion: There could be more women in selling if more women knew about the profession.

Lear Purvis Walker specializes in placing women in professional jobs, and executive vice president Archie Purvis says that the seminar was held almost in self-defense. "Over the years," he says, "we have had candidates who were qualified for sales—who were aggressive, persevering, had good communications skills, and so on—but who didn't fully understand what opportunities there are in sales or what the requirements of a selling career are. We just could not take the time on an individual basis to tell them all the things that they were able to get out of this one seminar."

Indeed, the evening event ran over schedule by nearly an hour. Some women were unaware that many salespeople receive a salary instead of just a commission, others didn't realize that there are career opportunities in sales for women, and more than a few were unsure as to what sales and marketing are all about. One woman confessed that the variety in dress, appearance, and attitudes of the panelists demolished her stereotype of a salesman as a hawker of used cars in a bright-checkered sports jacket.

Purvis, formerly national field sales manager of Polaroid, believes that sales and marketing are about to be "invaded" by women. "Right now," he says, "the best opportunities for women are in the big cities on the two coasts, and in consumer products, food products, and pharmaceuticals. Those industries have lots of salespersons. And they are also the ones that generally accept people without prior sales experience."

Still, Purvis says, it's tough for women even to be considered by some companies. "The heavier the industry," he says, "the greater the resistance. Capital goods industries, such as steel and heavy-building products, are totally traditional, and women aren't even in their peripheries." Male chauvinism, Purvis says, is a contributing factor. "One district manager told me he just could not feel comfortable about hiring a woman. And another asked me, 'What would I tell my wife?' "

Such attitudes could deprive companies of above-average sales performance,

Purvis says. "Companies are finding that when they place a woman in the field there is a better than 50% chance of success and that she tends to be more successful than the male." For one thing, he says, because she is likely to be the only woman sitting in a waiting room full of men, she attracts attention. For another, women simply have to be more motivated to overcome the barriers of entry into selling.

Although three out of Lear Purvis Walker's four principals are women, only one out of the seven panelists was—Valarie Eskew, a regional marketing manager for Mattel. The other panelists came from General Mills, New York Life Insurance, Merrill Lynch, Xerox, McGraw Laboratories, and Del Monte.

Purvis says the seminar—which was free to women—may have been the first of its kind on the West Coast. He hopes it won't be the last. "We learned that we have to do this more often," he says, "because it can be very valuable to us from a commercial standpoint. We would like these women to come back and tell us whether in fact they really want to explore sales."

Two already have. Now Purvis must find a sales manager who isn't worried about what his wife might say.

SM, June 2, 1975, p. 7.

The Lady Is a Tiger

American women who are sales engineers have achieved that economic and women's lib rarity: income parity with men. According to a Bureau of Labor Statistics analysis of 1970 population census data, women sales engineers are the highest paid female workers in the country, receiving a median income of $13,181. That's almost what men in those jobs receive.

Elsewhere in selling, however, women's earnings range from 24% to 50% of what males holding the same jobs are able to command:

	Women's Median Earnings	Rank Among Women	Men's Median Earnings	Rank Among Men
Sales engineer	$13,181	1	$13,328	35
Sales manager (except in retail trade)	7,313	40	14,526	15
Stock & bond salesman	5,890	108	13,565	32
Advertising agent, salesman	5,024	173	10,789	84
Sales manager (department head in retail trade)	4,798	189	9,508	134
Sales representative, manufacturing	3,721	271	11,124	77
Sales representative, wholesale trade	3,684	276	9,585	131
Salesman, retail trade	3,092	314	7,839	214
Salesman, services & construction	2,256	350	9,236	151

Source: Bureau of Labor Statistics, *Monthly Labor Review*   ®*Sales Management*

SM, November 11, 1974, p. 14.

American [Airlines] Promotes Its Kiwis

What could be more natural than a former airline hostess talking about flying? Not a thing, in the opinion of American Airlines sales executives. The airline pays 165 of its ex-stewardesses, whose children are grown, $55 to $85 per month, and gives them one flight pass a year, to promote American. The women speak to local social and business groups about such things as travel destinations (American's, of course), how to pack a bag, and aviation history.

American doesn't consider the women, whom it calls Kiwis, mere goodwill ambassadresses. "They sell," convention sales manager Frank L. Svoboda stresses. "They brought in over $2.2 million last year." Svoboda expects them to do even better this year. In January, the airline strengthened the women's ties with its field sales force by having them follow up on sales leads (for no extra pay). They'll also continue to do their usual job of speaking to local groups. Either type of engagement counts toward their quota of 48 presentations per year.

The directive to pursue sales leads is an indication of how successful the Kiwi program is becoming. The airline initially saw it as a way to relieve field salesmen of invitations to explain flying to groups that have too small a ticket-buying potential to justify direct sales coverage.

"Salesmen think the program is the greatest thing we've got going for them," Svoboda says. "When a company with independent agents, or a national organization, such as the American Legion, is planning a major convention, we ask Kiwi speakers to give the organizations' local chapters a presentation on the planned destination. Also, salesmen can ask them to come along on joint calls and help land new accounts." How? Salesmen promise the travel agent or commercial prospect that he too can use a Kiwi to help him promote particular destinations and reassure reluctant fliers.

SM, July 22, 1974, p. 3.

Wanted: Men

When some 300 owners of BMW motorcycles rode through torrential rains to attend a cycle rally near Indianapolis last month, Carol Lumkes biked in too. The 23-year-old sells fairings (windscreens) and other motorcycle accessories for Vetter Fairing, Rantoul, Ill. She was at the rally to make BMW owners more aware of Windjammer II, a $200 plastic fairing Vetter makes, and to promote a new product, a rain fender made for BMWs.

Some of the Indianapolis rallyists were surprised to see a saleswoman, but Ms. Lumkes is hardly a phenomenon at Vetter. The seven-year-old firm's entire sales force—nine sales coordinators, their supervisor, and a service rep—is female. "It just happened to work out that way," says president Craig Vetter, who is now trying to add sales*men* to the force.

Vetter's current all-woman sales team "happened" because the company does most of its selling to 3,000 retail motorcycle dealers by telephone. It insists that its salespeople be able to type orders as well as sell, and sales supervisor Cindi Miller says finding men with both abilities is difficult. Miller hopes experienced male sales help can be found when Vetter sets up sales territories in connection with an authorized dealer organization it is planning. "If someone now on the team wants one of the road jobs, she'll get first choice," Vetter says, but he hopes to be able to hire men also.

The company's unconventionality shows up in another way. It sends two of its production line workers to each of the four national motorcycle shows held each year. "Our workers profit from this close contact with our customers," Vetter says. *SM*, July 22, 1974, p. 3.

Swingline Fastens onto Women

With do-it-yourself home decorating growing increasingly popular, it would seem impossible to overlook that market. Swingline missed it for a time—but not any longer. "Just 15 months ago, homemakers thought our staple guns looked dangerous and difficult to use," says Ernest M. Raasch, executive vice president of Swingline Div., a part of Swingline, Inc., the American Brands subsidiary. "Now, unit sales have more than tripled, and even *Seventeen* and *Woman's Day* do stories on staple gun decorating.

"Women like to decorate, but they hate to hammer," Raasch continues, explaining that a staple gun is as good as a hammer—if not better—for upholstering and putting up wall coverings. "With the staple gun, there's no danger of smashing the thumb or marring the materials with dents and holes," he claims. The trouble was, research showed that women didn't associate staple guns with decorating, and there was nothing in the way of packaging, promotion, or distribution to spark their interest.

To appeal to women without weakening sales to traditional customers such as serious handymen and professional builders, Swingline swapped its hardware sales approach for a segmented selling effort focusing on three markets: handymen, women, and gift givers. Separate packaging, sales promotion materials, and ad campaigns were developed.

But the coup responsible for bringing women into the Swingline fold was hiring a designer to decorate a room, using the staple gun as his fastening tool. He came up with fabric-covered walls and furniture. A women's magazine editor decided the result was sensational, and the magazine gave the room feature treatment. Homemakers' demand for staple guns has been growing ever since.

To meet that demand, Swingline had to extend distribution from hardware and specialty stores to mass-merchandising outlets and catalogue stores. Again Raasch decided to segment—he split the sales force.

The office products division, consisting of a national sales manager, four regional managers, and 35 salesmen, continues to sell to wholesalers and large office stationery retailers. The new consumer products division, whose sales manager and 21 salesmen report to a marketing vice president, sells to distributors and large chains. Salesmen in both groups have been retrained to sell a complete program, including point-of-purchase literature that gives consumers new ideas for using their tools— thus creating demand for refill staples.

"Hardware stores sold an average of 17 staple guns annually before the change," Raasch says. "Now they do at least three times that business, and the chains do even better." Raasch claims that a mass merchandiser sold 5,000 units in 10 days, and that one cataloguer will sell 20,000 units this year. And if the TV ad campaign and the new products that Swingline begins testing this month pan out, he figures he'll really have the market stapled down.

SM, April 8, 1974, pp. 3–4.

Rivella: Going My Whey?

Last summer, Fred Kulow paid a sales call on Bob Tobin, a buyer for the Stop 'N Shop supermarket chain in Connecticut. Kulow told Tobin, "I'd like you to carry Rivella. It's a whey-based, nonalcoholic drink from Switzerland."

"Sounds like corn squeezin's to me," Tobin replied, recalling his boyhood farm days. "I don't think it'll sell." But Kulow, president of Rivella Imports, Waltham, Mass., prevailed, and Stop 'N Shop became Rivella's first supermarket outlet in the U.S. Kulow now claims his drink is in most of the major chains in Connecticut and western Massachusetts.

Kulow was formerly group vice president, marketing and sales, for Fairmont Foods, where he helped introduce Apple Beer (dropped last year by the company). And sales manager Stephen Tomasino last year was hired away from Arnold Bakeries, where he, too, had a selling job. The Rivella recruiting effort doesn't stop there. "We thought this product would take a lot of missionary work because it doesn't fit into any of the standard product categories," Kulow says. "So we've hired women, who can be more enthusiastic and more convincing, to help with promotion."

For his director of merchandising, Kulow picked Jane Fuller, a highly photogenic, 25-year-old blonde with no sales or marketing experience. "I was an actress and model who had made appearances for Rivella at trade shows and other events," she says. "They asked me to work for them full time." In addition to her promotion work, she's helping train two women as area merchandising managers and hopes to recruit even more belles for Rivella. The company will add other area merchandising managers and some part-time demonstrators, all female, as distribution expands—negotiations are now going on to bring Rivella into five midwestern states.

For the uninitiated, Rivella is the No. 2 nonalcoholic drink in Switzerland (Coke is first). In the U.S., it's usually sold in the fruit juice section of food stores, packaged in ½-liter (16.9 oz.) bottles priced at 39¢ apiece or $1 for a three-pack. Slightly carbonated, with a taste that hints of ginger ale and cider, it's promoted as a thirst quencher, especially after sports. "It's more isotonic than Gatorade," Kulow says— meaning that Rivella is more quickly absorbed, and thus works faster to kill thirst.

Other Rivella boosters tout its nutritional benefits, its compatibility with meals, and its value as a mixer. "I drink it with Scotch," Ms. Fuller avers. She calls it a "Heathcliff."

Another bit of Rivella lore: it's said to be terrific for a hangover.

SM, April 8, 1974, p. 10.

Why Your Salesmen Quit

Sales executives who still believe that one way to keep sales force turnover down is to offer quick career development opportunities will find *Sales Force Performance and Turnover,* a study just published by Marketing Science Institute, alarming. The study, which is based on statistics from 1,029 U.S. companies, was written by Prof. Derek A. Newton, of the Univ. of Virginia's Graduate School of Business. Prof. Newton says that his statistics show that companies offering fast promotions actually have a higher turnover rate. The study also knocks holes in what Prof. Newton calls other sales management "myths."

One of these is the belief that a certain amount of turnover is needed to keep selling performance high. Another is that high performance is partly a function of low turnover. Neither theory is supported by what Prof. Newton turned up; his study found no relationship between performance—defined as the productivity of a sales force—and turnover. (The survey contacted companies selling all kinds of products; also studied were trade selling, missionary selling, technical selling, and canvassing.)

THOSE BIG LOSERS

What does have an important effect on turnover, the professor found, is the size of the sales force. "Simply stated, the turnover rate tends to increase as the size of the sales force increases," he says. That is because the larger organization may strike a salesman, especially a new one, as impersonal.

Another reason why bigger sales forces lose more men is that they contain more younger men, who are by nature more "job mobile." Another factor in turnover is that "many of the larger sales forces which promise a good chance for advancement may have made a policy decision to use a salesman's job as a training ground for marketing management careers. "These firms," Prof. Newton believes, "seem to be willing to tolerate high turnover in exchange for the opportunity to develop future management."

The study shows that the sales force likely to have the lowest turnover is smaller, older, better paid, and offers somewhat fewer chances for promotion. Managers, the professor says, should realize that applicants drawn to sales forces that offer them a good chance for fast promotion may quit shortly after they get passed over, "particularly if 'the money isn't there.'"

Because his findings show that performance and turnover do not affect each other, Prof. Newton suggests that sales managers view each separately. "Once an executive has achieved a desirable level of turnover (less than 8% to 10%), he can turn his attention to improving performance, being fairly certain that these improvements in themselves will not produce skyrocketing turnover."

But once a manager sets about making improvements, the professor cautions, the way he implements them is far more important to salesmen's performance than the practices are.

SM, April 8, 1974, pp. 9–10.

PART II Concepts of Modern Selling

OVERVIEW

The readings presented in Sections 3 to 9 delve into the concepts, economic and business foundations, nature, development and functions of modern sales/marketing. Knowledge of these concepts and foundations is essential in order to understand the evolving nature and role of modern personal salesmanship, one of the four (and in our eyes the most important) functions of marketing. (The other three functions are advertising, sales promotion, and public relations.) Sales representatives and salespersons of the future, as illustrated by these selections, will be far more than mere sellers of goods and services. As fully integrated members of the marketing management team, their role will be that of a true consultant to their customers.

The topics developed, which cover a wide range of concepts, practices, problems, and responsibilities are presented in the following order:

Section 3 – How Companies Organize and Plan for Selling in a Changing Market Environment

Section 4 – How Sales Force Helps Management in Forecasting, Planning, and Goal-Setting

Section 5 – How One American Went About Selling Successfully to Eastern European Countries

Section 6 – How Advertising, Public Relations, and Sales Promotion Personnel Learn to Better Support Sales Representatives and Salespersons

Section 7 – Sales Training Methods

Section 8 – Buying Behavior and Psychology of Selling

Section 9 – Social, Legal, and Ethical Issues in Selling

Section 3 / How Companies Organize and Plan for Selling in a Changing Market Environment

For Selling, There's No Shortage of Challenges

What changes are in store for the sales function during the crunch? To find out, *SM* polled some top marketing authorities.

The sales function will experience more pressure to increase productivity. That doesn't necessarily mean working faster or harder, but instead, working more efficiently. The salesman will have to plan better and make more efficient use of sales aids such as direct mail and the telephone. He'll have to screen prospects more carefully. He may find that, in the long term, the adjustments he makes will be personally beneficial.

Bert E. Phillips, President, Clark Equipment

The sales function will become more difficult in respect to account servicing and the equitable distribution of scarce merchandise. Materials shortages that may occur will require a great deal of tact and fairness in merchandise allocation. We plan to allocate mostly on the basis of previous purchases, and we won't take advantage of tie-in sales that have given many suppliers a questionable reputation in times of previous shortages.

Plans have been developed that will enable our sales people to devote part of their time to regular mail and telephone solicitation if travel restrictions become severe. We have even discussed the possibility of car pools with salesmen of competing companies. Certainly, it's not the most desirable operation, but it is one way to maintain account servicing.

Morgan Lefferdink, Vice President, Menley & James's Love Cosmetics

One thing facing all sales forces is a reduction in face-to-face selling because of travel restrictions. Hence there will be an increase in other forms of communication: telephone, letter, and various forms of sales promotion. Where personal sales calls are made, preplanning will be needed to make each call more productive. For those industries where demand exceeds supply, the selling function will concentrate on assisting customers through the emergency period with service, fair allocations, tips on efficient use of existing supplies, troubleshooting, and maintenance of communications. Buyers, as well as sellers, must become conscious of the need to conserve salesmen's time and to reduce sales costs.

Victor P. Buell, Associate Professor of Marketing, Univ. of Massachusetts School of Business Administration

The shortages problem provides an opportunity for the salesman to build long-term relationships with customers by helping them in a difficult time. He does that by satisfying their needs and by advising them on programs for minimizing or solving shortage-caused problems. For example, we're providing buyers with technical assistance and recommendations for conservation programs, substitute materials, and methods for improving yield. We're also encouraging our salesmen to concentrate on the capital goods industry, where enormous expenditures will occur in the next decade to meet energy and other shortage problems.

Internally, the sales function is also changing. We'll coordinate sales, production, purchasing, and marketing more closely to factory inputs from the field into manufacturing and marketing planning.

George M. Hohmann, Vice President, Gases and Related Products Group, Chemetron

The challenge that confronts us today will bring out the best in the real salesman, who always finds a way—or makes a way—to get the job done. Communications between sales people, manufacturers, and suppliers of raw materials will become more important. Sales managers will have to concentrate more on long-term projections and determine what substitutes they can use in the event of supply shortages. Inability to deliver will probably be a problem for everyone. It will require great finesse on the part of the salesmen to keep customers happy, but one of the traits of a good salesman is that he enjoys challenge.

A. W. Elzerman, President, Stanley Home Products, Sales Div.

The anticipated economic slowdown will present a strong test of salesmanship. The basic function of salesmanship—serving customers' needs—will not change, but it will compel far more thought, efficiency, and effectiveness than are required when the economy is flourishing. It's a challenge most would prefer not to face. It's also an opportunity to come up with innovative sales techniques.

Van B. Phillips, Vice President and General Manager, Marketing Div., Eastman Kodak

Making more efficient use of time on the road will become a top priority for sales people. One way to achieve this is for salesmen who might ordinarily return home in the evening after a day of selling to remain on the road overnight in order to get an earlier start the following day. Sales executives and their field forces will also conduct more business over the telephone.

Stuart Better, Marketing Vice President, Keystone Div., Berkey Photo
SM, January 12, 1974, pp. 16–17.

Curtis Addresses the Big Time

Curtis 1000 is the key marketing arm of American Business Products (ABP); its sales of envelopes, forms, and related supplies make up about 80% of the Atlanta-based parent company's total revenues. . . .

ABP likes to bill itself as "the steady growth company," proudly pointing to 36 straight years of record sales. But for most of that time, corporate growth came at tortoiselike speed: by concentrating on sales to banks in medium-sized and small markets, the company had nudged annual sales up to $38.3 million by 1971.

Then ABP decided to aim for major metro areas, obviously the big market for office supplies, and to diversify its customer base even further. Since then, sales have nearly doubled (to $69.6 million in 1974), and earnings have risen even faster. The recession is slowing things down this year, but record sales year No. 37 should still be attained as the company continues to introduce new products and expand its sales area.

Helping to make the shift from country boys to city folk are a constantly growing sales force and several sophisticated marketing strategies. Curtis has 430 salesmen and saleswomen in the field, a number that increases by about 10% each year. The chain of responsibility begins with salesmen reporting to some 65 district sales managers, who report to 20 division sales managers. These, in turn, answer to division managers, who have profit-and-loss accountability and who report to six regional managers.

Marketing vice president [Jack] Holloman began selling for the company 29 years ago, working his way up through a series of sales management positions. He now has a staff role and is responsible for coordinating most aspects of Curtis's sales efforts:

Recruiting   "At least half of our new salespeople have never sold before," Holloman says. "We like to get men and women with some business experience, usually those who are used to dealing with the public. Bankers, teachers, and accountants, for example. We never hire salesmen away from competitors because they've already picked up too many bad habits."

Training   Holloman requires that all new hires spend two weeks at Curtis's headquarters in Smyrna, Ga., near Atlanta, which has a training center replete with modern audio-visual equipment. Then they spend a week at their new division headquarters and a week on the road with a district sales manager. After another month on their own, they come back to the divisional base for a refresher course.

"Our salesmen are never finished with training," says Art Kerrigan, a division sales manager based in West Hartford, Conn. "There's a manager with them once a month for the first year, once every other month for the next four years, then once a quarter—forever." Holloman says that turnover among new salesmen is exceptionally low and is virtually nil for salesmen who have been with the company for five years.

Scheduling   Each salesman is assigned an exclusive territory. He must, in fact, sign an agreement that bars him from selling competitive products in that area for two years after he leaves Curtis. Holloman notes that each territory is subdivided into 20 zones, and a salesman is expected to visit one a day, so that he covers his entire account list once a month.

Compensation   Salesmen begin on salary plus commission, then go on straight commission when *they* decide they're ready. "Most of them are in a hurry to make the switch," Holloman says, "because they make more money that way." Of course, if a man is content to live on his salary, Curtis usually has other plans for him anyway. The average Curtis salesman earns about $20,000, with some top men going over $50,000 a year.

There are also constant incentive programs in which salesmen can win additional money. There are six "clubs," based on income level, so that Curtis salesmen across the country compete with others who have a comparable sales base. Within each club, bonus points are given each month to those who exceed their quotas by the largest percentage, and a running tally for the year is kept in each club.

But why all the special training and motivation for men selling envelopes and forms, products not much different from those a competitor could offer? "We don't sell strictly on a price basis," Holloman states. "We go after specialty business, trying to show that our products are different and that they can help a customer save time and money."

His sales managers echo that theme. Kerrigan likes to tell how he sells one type of air mail envelope that's $100 per thousand more expensive than standard models. "I call on multi-national companies based in New York City that do a lot of international air mail," he says. "I show them that our envelope is an ounce lighter and point out that with international rates 28¢ per half-ounce, they save 56¢ an envelope in postage, or $560 per thousand. That helps close the sale."

SM, August 4, 1975, pp. 41–42.

Champion Spark Plug's Charles A. Schwalbe, Jr.

Sales vice president Charles Schwalbe has a big job. He's in charge of all domestic OEM (original equipment manufacturer) and aftermarket sales for Champion Spark Plug, whose 1973 sales were $419.2 million, up 14% from 1972's $367.4 million. Earnings in 1973 showed a 20% gain, from $39.8 million to $48.5 million.

But the job is in capable hands. Schwalbe has been with Champion since 1945, most recently as director of sales. And he has 320 men in the field seeing to it that the sales dollars keep coming in. "We're unique," the 53-year-old Schwalbe says, "in that we probably have the largest sales force in the automotive industry devoted to a single product."

The organization is divided into two broad categories: the regular force, which contacts dealers, and the OEM salesmen. Schwalbe says, "Our OEM salesmen are specialized; they're really more like sales engineers. Their contacts run the gamut from manufacturers of small engines, such as those for lawn mowers, right up to automobile manufacturers."

About 90% of Champion's spark plug sales come from the aftermarket, and the emphasis seems to be in the right place. Figures from the Motor Equipment Manufacturers Assn. show that aftermarket sales in January 1974 were 11.1% higher than those of January 1973. And Schwalbe says there is tremendous potential: "Our market research department has found that about 60% of the automobiles in the U.S. need some form of engine maintenance, and the energy crisis has made motorists more keenly aware of the need for tune-ups. That will certainly benefit the spark plug industry."

Schwalbe thinks the switch to smaller cars will also be a plus. "Tests we've conducted show that the average driver can't detect early signs of misfiring in an 8-cylinder engine," he says. "But with a 4-cylinder engine, one plug is 25% of your power. If it's misfiring and needs replacement, you can't help but notice."
SM, March 18, 1974, pp. 11-12.

One Raytheon Division Prefers Selling through Independent Sales Representative Organizations

There are plusses and minuses in working with sales reps, but Walter Curran thinks the plusses have it. As national industrial sales manager for the Distributor Products Operation of Raytheon, Lexington, Mass., he's in an unusually good position to know. Curran, 48, is responsible for U.S. and Canadian sales of a broad line of industrial electronic components, ranging from entertainment semiconductors, which are used in TV sets and radios, to the power tubes used by TV stations. He oversees 19 independent rep organizations that deal with some 1,200 distributors. The reps also sell knobs and switches to OEM (original equipment manufacturer) accounts.

An advantage of using rep organizations, Curran says, is that "they are in-place professional selling organizations. If we set up our own sales force, we would have to go into training in salesmanship per se, plus product training. But training in basic salesmanship is the business of the rep principal. Also, we have an intermixture of types of customers, and that requires organizations that are fairly flexible. Rep organizations can offer us, for example, a man who is technically trained but can talk to purchasing agents as well as engineers."

The problem, of course, is that reps handle other lines: "We have to struggle for a share of their time," Curran says. "And today's situation requires a lot more scrambling to get the business."

One way Curran tries to get a larger share of his reps' time is through incentive programs. "For our small industrial accounts, for example," he says, "we gave prize points for any account under $15,000 that doubled its business from 1973 to 1974." Points were given to the rep organization, which was then responsible for rewarding the individual salesman.

Curran, who joined the $1.6 billion company only last June, sees his own role as a key to strengthening the performance of the reps. "I want them to have a much clearer idea of our philosophies, procedures, and policies," he says. "My biggest challenge is to develop a closer working relationship with them." Considering that his background includes 12 years in marketing communications in GE's power tube and semiconductor divisions, Curran shouldn't have any trouble getting his message across.

SM, December 9, 1974, p. 13.

Fuller Revives That Old-Time Religion

People who have witnessed the travail of Fuller Brush in recent years tend to sound as if they are just back from an archaeological dig.

First there was the Old Fuller civilization, founded 68 years ago. Then came dissension among the king's heirs, setting the stage for a takeover by the Consolidated Foods tribes in 1968. The chieftains installed priests from their holy-owned temple of Electrolux, who were thrown to the crocodiles when they foundered building a pseudo-pyramid sales organization. Finally, there were the vestal virgins of the goddess Avon, who tried to get the magic scent of their previous incarnation to rub off on the homespun threads of Fuller's 13,500 women and men dealers (the ratio is now about three to two).

All that ended abruptly last spring, when Consolidated Foods dispatched Walter Freedman to head the faltering division. As part of his plan to pick up the shards of the Old Fuller empire, Freedman promoted 33-year-old L. Scott McKnight to vice president, household sales and marketing. "It may sound hokey," the plain-spoken McKnight says, "but what we're trying to do is reestablish the principles of Dad [Alfred C.] Fuller." Contrary to those foot-in-the-door stories, the founding Fuller saw his salesmen not as aggressors but as missionaries come to save the housewife from a purgatory of dirt and grime.

In the process of getting back to principles, the two executives have made a number of hardheaded managerial decisions in a hurry. In April, Freedman ordered the sales effort curtailed in no fewer than 20 states, leaving sales managers free to concentrate on key territories in the West, Midwest, and East. A month later, McKnight began testing telephone selling in Philadelphia and New England to gain greater penetration in urban markets. Division headquarters were moved from East Hartford, Conn. to Niles, Ill.

Most important, McKnight drew on his 16 years of Fuller experience to continue pruning the managerial empire that even the previous regime admitted was unwieldly. Less than two years ago, for example, there were 864 field managers; now there are 317. "The difference," McKnight says, "is that most of the people we have now are there because they can recruit and manage. Before, many were interested only in selling their own accounts."

If all goes well, Freedman and McKnight hope to develop an organization that resembles the Fuller Brush Co. of yore, although it doesn't matter to them that brushes account for less than 25% of sales (two current bestsellers: Stain Spray and a nonslip suit and pants hanger). Restoration doesn't come easy, though. In the mid-1960s, Fuller's sales were over $100 million; McKnight's goal for the fiscal year ending next June 30 is only $39 million. Still, McKnight does expect the company to turn a modest profit, which hasn't happened in years.

Meanwhile, he claims to have more than doubled sales per dealer and hopes that by the end of the fiscal year his personnel turnover will be down from a massive 400% to a tolerable 140%, about average for home-to-home sales companies. McKnight sums up modestly: "If our whole trip is to be, say, two feet, then we may have gone an inch and a half."

SM, October 14, 1974, p. 3.

AIC's Miranda Decision

Walter Director finally fulfilled his nomenclature promise last year, acquiring the title of vice president and sales director, but he found himself in a situation that would certainly have shaken the self-confidence of the remote ancestor who first had his surname. Director's company, Interstate Photo Supply, is the U.S. sales arm of AIC Photo, Carle Place, N.Y., which imports camera equipment from Europe and Japan under the brand names Miranda, Bauer, Soligor, and Ultra-blitz. "With currency fluctuations and dollar devaluation, our costs were constantly changing," Director says, "and price controls kept us from doing very much about it."

Thus Director turned to sales force innovations. He instituted quotas with incentive pay for his 35 salesmen, organized clinics for retail salesmen of Interstate's 4,000 dealerships, put color into the company's consumer ads, and began installing field supervisors to act as liaisons between the salesmen and the four regional managers. Perhaps most important, he stepped up customer service as a sales tool.

"We've always been strong on service," Director says, "especially on Miranda products, where we extend the one-year factory warranty to three years on our own plan. Last year, we sent trained servicemen to key dealerships and advertised that they would inspect and adjust Miranda cameras free of charge. In that way, we attracted all the Miranda camera owners in a given area to our dealer, which gave him a chance to sell more and us a chance to build our relationship with him."

Miranda sales rose "dramatically" last year (AIC corporate sales rose 20%, to $28 million, but worldwide inflation depressed profits sharply) and Director plans a similar customer service campaign this year for Bauer motion picture cameras. Instead of servicemen, this time he'll send a professional cinematographer to his dealers in a drive to reel in the movie buffs.

SM, July 22, 1974, pp. 8–9.

How Sycor Programs Selling

Computer terminal marketer Sycor, Ann Arbor, Mich., is giving its salesmen a new tool for entering orders: Sycor computer terminals. It plans to equip its 24 branch sales offices with terminals linked to the main office computer, to speed ordering and cut paperwork. The move lets the salesmen take advantage of a product benefit—quick transmission of data— they always include in their sales presentations. It is also a sign that Sycor's domestic sales team is coming of age.

The company, founded in 1967, initially sold only in the less competitive overseas market, with most of its output going to Olivetti. (In 1971, it added another foreign distributor, Mitsui in Japan.) In 1970, it began building a domestic sales force for its first try at markets in the U.S. and Canada.

Sycor now has 42 salesmen and three regional managers under national sales manager Robert Roth. Ten systems engineers and 70 field engineers back up the sales team. The result is that 40% of its $31.7 million sales last year (a 100% sales increase over 1972) were domestic.

Marketing vice president Paul C. LaVoie, who joined Sycor in 1969 as its eastern regional sales manager, and then held Roth's present job, notes that most companies Sycor's size hire beginning salesmen because their salaries are lower. Sycor, in contrast, looks for men in their mid-thirties with about 10 years' experience. The lower rate of turnover and the savings on training costs, he says, more than make up for the higher salaries the experienced men command. LaVoie says that the company also tries to hire locally because "it's an unusual salesman who can move to a new territory and be as successful as he was at home."

Another Sycor practice that LaVoie credits with keeping its turnover low is its sales quota plan. Sycor divides the year into two quota periods. "Even a very successful salesman has times when he sells less because he is installing equipment and hand holding," LaVoie says. "If he has to meet a single, annual quota, that can kill his motivation. He feels he's not going to be able to sell enough in remaining months to make quota and qualify for lucrative bonuses. When he has two shots at quota, he's less likely to sandbag and coast." LaVoie adds, "Our quota is about double that of our competitors, but almost 50% of our men make it and earn $35,000 to $40,000 a year with bonuses."

To goad them to even greater achievement—Sycor's current objective is 50% compound annual growth—the three regional managers spend 70% of their time on the road in close personal contact with salesmen and customers. They also help salesmen close all sales approaching a quarter of a million dollars (the average sale is $100,000).

To help salesmen land those bigger sales, Sycor recently put more muscle into its customer servicing by adopting—what else?—a computerized reporting system.

SM, June 24, 1974, pp. 7-11.

Warner-Lambert Tastes Trouble

Listless Listerine profits are weakening the entire Consumer Products Group. Here's what its sales management is doing about it [and how the sales force is affected].

by **Don Korn**, Associate Editor

After a recent lunch date, Bob Spessard's companion mentioned that Warner-Lambert had just acquired Tetra Werke, a West German fish food company. Spessard, director of broker operations for Warner-Lambert's Personal Products Div., brightened visibly. "That's great," he said. "Maybe I'll have another product to sell."

His enthusiasm is more than admirable; for Warner-Lambert, it's vital. Spessard is charged with selling Listerol, a product that represents the giant drug company's attempt to enter a new market through a new sales channel. Its success could do much toward restoring Warner-Lambert in an area long regarded as its principal strength: consumer products marketing. Fighting a profits sag there, the Morris Plains, N.J., company is also juggling management, reorganizing and shifting sales forces, stepping up new product introductions, and changing ad themes (possibly ad agencies as well).

This agitation is not apparent from a cursory examination of the annual report. Last year, corporate sales ($1.67 billion) rose 12% and earnings 13%, both reaching record levels, and pace continued during the first half of 1974. But nearly all that success came from the company's Professional Products (Parke-Davis, Warner/Chilcott, American Optical) and International groups. . . . Consumer products sales, however, rose only 2% last year, to $407 million, and pretax profits dipped nearly 13%, to $77.2 million from $88.6 million the year before. This year's results appear to be similarly depressed.

You have to peel a few more layers off the onion before you get to the real eye-stinger. Within the Consumer Products Group, two of the three main revenue-producers—American Chicle and Schick Safety Razor— had strong years in 1973, with American Chicle "increasing its sales and overall market share" and Schick having a "record year."

What's left? The recently renamed Personal Products Div., the foundation of Warner-Lambert's success. This division has one 1970s success story: the Efferdent-Effergrip denture products line. Then there's a nostalgia sector that would delight trivia buffs with the likes of Bromo-Seltzer, Anahist, Pristeen (which became an instant "oldie" when the hexachlorophene scare hit), Corn Huskers Lotion and Sloan's Liniment. The biggest seller, though, is the company's perennial money-making machine: Listerine antiseptic mouthwash.

But Listerine is now in the unenviable position of losing its share of a stagnant market. It still holds nearly 50% of the $275 million (at retail) mouthwash market, but it has been giving ground to Proctor & Gamble's Scope (approximately a 20% share), as well as to private label brands . . . . "Listerine is a downsale product, with a lot of appeal to older people," a product manager for a competitor says. "Many of its buyers are literally dying off."

FLANKER CANKER

To halt the attrition among the living, Warner-Lambert has tried to take advantage of the Listerine name with an ever-proliferating family of flanker products, some of which can still be found in stores: Listerine toothpaste, throat lozenges, cold tablets, children's throat lozenges, breath spray, cough-control lozenges, breath drops, and cough syrup. Many marketers contend that those products cannibalize the original (because consumers will substitute a breath drop or throat lozenge for mouthwash) and thereby blur its identity. Indeed, Listerine mouthwash sales did go down last year.

In 1973, when Warner-Lambert introduced more new products than in any previous year, the Listerine siblings were given some first cousins. Listerex, an acne scrub, went national; Listermint, a Scope-type mouthwash, went into test market in Atlanta, Denver, and Indianapolis, and has not been heard from since; and Listerol, a spray disinfectant, was test marketed and turned over to Spessard to sell nationally.

"It's the division's first move beyond the health and beauty aids area," Spessard says. "But we feel it's a natural product for us because the consumer is familiar with Listerine's 'germ-kill' claims." It may be a natural, but not for Warner-Lambert's existing consumer products sales force. "As a household product, Listerol is sold through a different type of distribution system, to different buyers," he says. "We thought we should start out in a new area by using food brokers." Spessard, a Bristol-Myers sales veteran who had worked with brokers, was hired away from a small Kansas City chemical company and brought into corporate headquarters in the summer of 1973 to direct operations.

"Because of a deadline that had already been set, I had to move quickly," he says. "I hired six area managers—four from outside the company, two from within—and in less than two months we lined up 71 brokers across the country. By the time the product was rolled out nationally, in the late fall, we had sold all but five major accounts."

An incentive program for brokers and cash refund coupons for consumers helped push initial sales, and Spessard says he's well satisfied with Listerol's performance to date (it's estimated that Listerol's market share is 10%; market leader Lysol has over 80%). "We've held onto all those major accounts and even picked up the ones we didn't get the first time around," he says. "Consumer repeat purchases have been excellent."

SALES FORCES COMBINED

While Spessard and his brokers are trying to gain a foothold in the household products sector, Warner-Lambert's regular sales force will soon be getting some reinforcements in health and beauty aids. As of the first of next year, there will be more salesmen, and they'll have another line to sell: Schick razors, blades, and shaving cream. The company is moving the Schick Div. (acquired in 1970) from Milford, Conn., to its headquarters in Morris Plains and consolidating it with the Personal Products Div. "Schick salesmen and Personal Products salesmen often call on the same buyers. By combining them we'll get better efficiency," Howard Bloomquist, president of the Consumer Products Group, predicts. "Sales calls could increase and coverage will be better."

Greater efficiencies may be realized, but the company could be more efficient about informing its own salespeople. "I don't know anything about it," Ms. Gerry O'Hara, who works northern New Jersey for Schick, said two weeks after the realignment was announced. She agrees that she could probably sell Listerine, Efferdent, and the like as well as Schick, but declines to comment further. "Call me in a couple of months, when I know if I still have a job."

Ed Werner, Schick's sales vice president (he'll have the same position in the consolidated division), says that he hopes to keep on "as many of the existing salespeople and sales managers as possible from the Personal Products and the Schick divisions. We've stopped hiring, and have lost a few men through attrition," he says. "For those who won't fit into the new division, we'll try to find jobs elsewhere in the corporation, perhaps at American Chicle. It might be a step down for some," he admits.

Werner will have his work cut out for the next couple of months: territories must be realigned and all the salesmen retrained to handle the additional product lines. But it should be worth it in increased sales calls, he says, because more people will be selling the various products.

Contemplating the change in sales force organization is Warner-Lambert's plan to consolidate shipping for Schick, Personal Products, and American Chicle by setting up five master distribution centers, which will stock all product lines. The object is to enable the company to guarantee retailers 48-hour delivery. "We should have done this a long time ago," says a Personal Products salesman who works in the Midwest. "I spend at least 15% of my time chasing down lost or delayed orders."

Two distribution centers, in Dallas and Anaheim, are already operating, and a third will open in Chicago next March.

Shaking up sales force responsibilities and ad messages may help, but it won't correct what appears to be a more serious Warner-Lambert flaw: the lack of internal management development. For a company that prides itself on its sales training program and its modern Manpower Development Center, there seem to be few case histories of salesmen and sales managers rising through the ranks.

Can Listerol put a dent in Lysol's market dominance? There's ample precedent, to be sure. If Spessard wants to find out how an aggressive competitor can cut into the No. 1 brand, all he has to do is walk down the hall and ask his colleagues, at Listerine, who have learned the hard way.

SM, November 11, 1974, pp. 27–30.

Xerox and IBM Tango Again

Word processing is the buzzword for the automated office setting where tomorrow's sales executives will toil. In brief, it means an integrated system for converting ideas, words, and data into information via interrelated automatic dictating, typing, test-editing, computing, and display services. It's also the market where Xerox and IBM will meet head-on in a broad-scale confrontation.

In the mid-1960s, the strategy of IBM's office products division called for touting the information-handling capabilities of the company's magnetic tape Selectric typewriters. In 1970, IBM made another word processing thrust, invading Xerox's heartland with its own line of copiers. Last month, Xerox made a long-expected countermove by entering the automatic typewriter field with an electronic version, the Xerox 800, that executive vice president Raymond A. Hay insists is twice as fast as the Selectric, mainly because the Xerox machine types right to left as well as left to right.

Xerox considers the 800 typewriter as more than just another new product. The machine will be sold by a new sales force and service support group with its own branch sales managers. Initially at least, they will be free to sell wherever they can find customers instead of aping the copier sales force's assigned-industry approach. Key customers are expected to be the legal, banking, and insurance concerns because of the amount of paperwork they generate. Xerox's electronic typing system operates from magnetic tapes or cards and leases for $210 to $310 a month, a spokesman says.

Shelby H. Carter, Jr., vice president, systems marketing, won't talk about the size of the final sales force but says he intends to have all major metro markets covered by the end of 1975. It is known that the sales force will be a blend of in-house transfers and salesmen from other office equipment firms. "Emphasis will be on men used to thinking in terms of systems solutions to customer problems rather than in terms of a product," Carter says.

Nevertheless, Xerox product marketing manager Donald P. Roth confirms that the typewriter salesmen will not do team selling with Xerox's copier or computer salesmen. This is because Xerox marketers believe the shift from stand-alone office equipment to integrated systems won't occur until the end of the 1970s or early 1980s. IBM's office products salesmen now do team selling with the firm's data processing division, but only in a few special instances "because some people are beginning to think of links between typewriters and computers."

Right now, Roth's big job is getting a foothold in a market dominated by IBM. He estimates that 150,000 automatic typewriters are currently installed and that the number will increase 20% to 25% a year. IBM it is believed has as much as 95% of that market.

A number of small companies, such as Lexitron and Vydec, now sell ultra-electric typewriters but most observers say the word processors will be like the computer mainframe industry—dominated by a few giant companies. In-depth commitment to sophisticated technology on a broad front, the need for large marketing support groups, and the desirability of leasing instead of outright selling require substantial capital, which only the biggies have.

SM, November 11, 1974, p. 14.

Gruen Industries' Edward M. Miller

"The men who do well in this economy will have to be out looking under rocks to sell their product," says Edward M. Miller, who in January became vice president, marketing, for Gruen Industries. "That's the type of men we have. Our policy is to eliminate any weak links, and as a result we have a sales force of professionals." Miller, 35, is counting on those professionals to help Gruen break into new sales territory: department and jewelry stores.

Since the 1940s, Gruen watches have been sold through discount stores and through catalogues prepared by independent coordinators. "We're No. 2 in catalogue watch sales," Miller says. And he considers the strong catalogue business to have been a major factor in the company's dramatic turnaround from an operating loss of over $1 million in fiscal 1972 to a profit of $318,000 in 1973. Net sales grew from $11.6 million to $14 million.

Gruen hopes to boost sales even more by using its digital watch to move into the retail jewelry market now dominated by HMW Industries and others [*SM,* May 14, 1973]. Miller says, "We've come out with a full-priced line headed by Teletime, a liquid crystal digital watch." Teletime, he explains, has two significant features:
(1) Constant readout—the wearer doesn't have to push a button to see the time.
(2) Low price. Miller says, "We're looking for the blue-collar worker, someone who can spend $150 on a watch, not $500."

Miller is confident that his sales force can make Teletime succeed. "In a bad year, you have to work much harder," he says. "This year our salesmen will all be travelling more, not less. And we've expanded their territories, rather than cutting back, the way some companies have. Our salesmen will probably make more money this year—we hope they'll all produce over $1 million—but they'll have to work harder for it. But I feel that it's better to have a few great salesmen making a lot of money, than to have a lot of salesmen making a little money."

SM, February 18, 1974, pp. 10–14.

Britannica's Key Word: "Sell!"

Any third-grade teacher knows that knowledge has to be sold, and nowhere is that tenet preached more enthusiastically than on the 5,000-person sales force of Encyclopaedia Britannica. In recent years, however, the army of in-home representatives and their Chicago-based overseers have watched sales falter because of two hard facts: (1) Unrevised since 1929, except for annual updates, the *Britannica* was losing its reputation among scholars; and (2) because of its highbrow image, it had limited access to the family market, which was being eaten up by Field Enterprises' *World Book Encyclopedia.*

The answer, naturally, was to streamline the product, which is exactly what EB has done with its fifteenth edition, dubbed "Britannica 3." Still on press, the 30-volume work is already being promoted by salesmen, and the tempo will pick up early this month with an ad campaign choreographed to tie in TV and newspaper plugs with an eight-page insert running in *Newsweek.* Official publication date for the 42-million-word encyclopedia is March 1. Price: $550 to consumers, $298 to schools.

As in all door-to-door ventures, the ads are intended partly to buck up the sales force and attract recruits. That's important to Eugene D. Sollo, EB's executive vice president for sales, who expects to increase his force of regulars and part-timers by 50% in the next three years. For the past year, the 42-year-old Sollo has been paving the way for expansion by increasing the number of divisions from 15 to 45 and slicing up districts into smaller units. The result is that Sollo now has 175 district offices, up from 125 a year earlier, and intends to raise the number to perhaps 300 by year-end.

As the name implies, Britannica 3 comes in three sections, each with a specific function. Though EB likes to talk about the intellectual reasons for the format, it can't do the company's marketing any harm. For example, the 10-volume Micropaedia has short articles suitable for those junior high schoolers who have been curled up with the *World Book.*

Britannica, by the way, has taken care that its Greek subtitles—Micropaedia, Macropaedia, and Propaedia—don't intimidate its customers. The actual volumes are labelled "Ready Reference and Index," "Knowledge in Depth," and "Outline of Knowledge." Snorts Sollo: "If you ask me, those Greek words are confusing to customers—and to my salesmen." Well, they could look them up.

SM, February 4, 1974, pp. 3–4.

Putting Fight into Paper Tigers

Profits are great, but shortages pose special problems for sales executives in the paper industry. One solution is "selling for the future."

by Don Korn, Associate Editor

Next Monday, July 1, is D-Day for paper companies. "D" in this case stands for Decontrol, as the last shackles of Phase Umpteen are removed from most paper products. And in the words of more than one industry insider, "there *will* be a price increase."

As top executives of those companies cheerfully fiddle with their Bowmars, figuring out how much each cent-per-hundredweight rise will mean to the bottom line, another group is girding itself for the first day of July: paper salesmen. They're the ones, in most cases, who'll have to notify customers of the price increases and explain why paper users will have to pay more, yet still contend with limited stocks and delayed deliveries.

Next Monday's events will symbolize the current situation in the paper industry: difficult for salesmen, bountiful for their companies. Last year, Alexander Calder, Jr., chairman of Union Camp, prophesied that "prospects for the paper business are better now than at any time I've seen them." Sure enough, in 1973 industry profits shot up 53%, to $1.4 billion on $26.5 billion in sales, and so far 1974 results have maintained the upward momentum.

WORLDWIDE PAPER SHORTAGE GOOD FOR PRODUCERS

Part of that increased profitability is attributable to a worldwide paper demand that threatens to outstrip supply—last year U.S. mills operated at 96% of capacity. Paper industry spokesmen shy away from the term "shortages," preferring to talk of "tight supply," but there is no doubt that the companies are selling all they can produce, and then some.

In addition, the companies are taking advantage of the heightened demand to shift into faster-growing markets and more profitable weights and grades of papers. "We've switched from certain periodical publication grades to carbonless business forms, web offset papers for commercial and book printers, and bond grades for the office copy market," states Jim Becher, a Mead vice president with sales force responsibility. "The reason was simple: magazine publishing papers show a growth rate that's marginal at best, while the others are increasing 7% to 19% a year."

BUT HARD ON MANY CUSTOMERS
[The paper shortage and switch by producers to more profitable grades has made supplies uncertain and costs a problem for many buyers.]

Other woes facing paper buyers include late deliveries and the practical necessity of accepting slightly damaged goods because a returned shipment might not be replaced for months. All of this hasn't exactly improved the disposition of customers, who are waiting patiently for the demand-supply situation to reverse itself. "Some of the salesmen we see are very helpful," says the purchasing manager of a major midwestern bank. "Others are out to get us. This paper shortage isn't going to last forever, and we're going to remember the good guys and the bad guys."

These "good guys" and "bad guys," the paper salesmen, are the ones caught in the middle. Because most of them are on allocation, with only a certain amount of product available, there is little real selling to do. Instead, they've become company apologists, explaining to their customers why certain paper grades and weights aren't available and why prices keep rising when paper industry profits are so high. Often, they have to tell old, once-valued customers that their supply of paper is being cut down, or eliminated altogether. "Some of my men get a bit frustrated," admits Jack Clifford, general sales manager for printing papers for St. Regis, "because they're not able to grow with their accounts."

SALESMEN'S DILEMMA

That attitude has also become apparent to Bill Shaughnessy, of the Great Northern Paper Div. of Great Northern Nekoosa, who is vice president of the Sales Assn. of the Paper Industry. "There is a feeling among salesmen now that there is no room for them to advance," he says. "I don't know how many times in the past few months somebody has said to me over a lunch, 'It's no fun any more.' " In fact, Shaughnessy's career path has been redirected by the situation. Great Northern is streamlining its sales organization to enhance customer service, and he has been given line sales responsibilities, a switch from his former role as manager of coated products.

For John Coutu, a salesman for Rising Paper, Holyoke, Mass., the current tight supply situation means he has to work harder than ever. "I'm more involved with all aspects of the business," he points out, "from learning about raw materials to evaluating the profitability of different orders." On the other hand, a salesman for one of the major mills, operating out of Atlanta, admits he sometimes feels as if he has nothing to do. "It's a bit disillusioning, not being able to go out and stimulate new business."

CHANGE FROM BUYER'S TO SELLER'S MARKET CREATES PROBLEMS FOR SALESMEN

"The difference between a buyer's market and a seller's market is one ton of paper," says Charles Beall, vice president, marketing development, at International Paper. "It can turn around that fast. We insist on keeping our sales effort sharp, and we insist that our salesmen keep calling on their customers. Now is the time for them to add value to their accounts."

Most salesmen for the larger paper companies are on straight salary; so the limits to product supply haven't dried up incentive compensation plans. Still, there is a feeling of insecurity: a product that doesn't have to be sold may not need salesmen, either. Robert Powers, sales manager of fine papers for Westvaco, says his sales force has been reduced 10%, by attrition, and Mead's Becher adds that attrition and shifts to other parts of the corporation have cut his force about 20%. "Eliminating various paper grades has narrowed our account list," he explains, "so we need fewer salesmen."

Salesmen's morale, therefore, is bound to slump, and sales executives at the major companies have instituted various plans to keep their men on the job and in good spirits. At Westvaco, Powers insists his men keep their call frequency up to preshortage levels. Charles Beall heads a special task force established to improve International Paper's position with its major corporate accounts: when he and his task force visit those accounts, he makes sure that the local sales manager is involved in both the planning of the call and the call itself.

NEW SALES TECHNIQUES CALLED FOR

Of course, just having the salesmen show up isn't enough—they must have something to do once they get there. Phillip Morris's Nicolet Paper Div. has turned its salesmen into account managers. "We tell our men the straight truth about supplies and deliveries, then leave it to them to work out a schedule with their customers," says customer service manager Claude Crawford, a former field salesman himself. "It's enhanced our credibility tremendously, and our salesmen seem to be overjoyed."

Another sales executive who believes in telling it straight is Bill Thompson, sales vice president of Bergstrom Paper. "Some paper salesmen are hiding these days, but not our men," he asserts. "If the customer calls them, they show up." Thompson urges his men to think about what will happen when the capacity situation changes. Will customers look for fewer suppliers? Will you be among the chosen ones? "We're selling now for the future," he reasons, "and the best policy is to tell our salesmen, and our customers, the truth."

To keep their salesmen better informed, most of the major companies are stepping up their sales training programs, with trips through paper mills and outside courses often included. Now, the men are told, they must become advisers as well as salesmen. "We want our salesmen to convince their customers to weed out specialty weights and grades and stick with the standard items," says Jim Cummings, sales manager for reproduction papers at International Paper. "In that way, we can increase total output."

AND OLD SALES TECHNIQUES SHARPENED UP

Sales executives also want their men to maintain the old virtues, even in these prof· itable times. "We stress humility," says Oxford's Chambliss. "We'll need all those customers someday." At St. Regis, Jack Clifford is quick to point out that the company is standing by its traditional product mix, even including lightweight pub lication papers. "We're not exploiting the current situation," he avers.

Indeed, throughout the industry the tendency is to soft-pedal the good times and explain that the mills really aren't taking unfair advantage of paper users. American Paper Institute officials are defensive about changes in product mix; officials are unavailable for interviews unless a public relations man is sharing the speaker phone. Top paper industry sales people, such as Al Fortune, of Consolidated Papers, would rather not talk about the tight supply situation at all. And the companies that used to turn out slick calendars and posters to demonstrate their wares have now switched to booklets and copies of speeches on the general topic "Why there is a paper shortage," carefully pointing out that the industry's return on investment, which rose from 5% in 1971 to 12.5% in 1973, is still below the 14% of 1951.

When prices go up again next week, it's likely that even more companies will come forward with new capacity plans. And as the machines come onstream in a few years, paper salesmen just might find themselves with some real selling to do. In that case, salesmen and sales managers now "selling for the future" or practicing "humility" will get a chance to show that they're more than run of the mill.

SM, June 24, 1974, pp. 19–23.

It's Time to Do Something About Salesforce Turnover

by **Mack Hanan**, Contributing Editor

"My company has a philosophy," the district sales manager says sarcastically, "and we're very proud of it: If a man has been on his present assignment a year and a

Mack Hanan is managing director of Hanan & Son, management consultants in business growth and diversification, and president of The Greenhouse Group, an institute of teaching practitioners in management growth.

half, he's a veteran. The trouble is that just as he begins to get his veteran's rights, he's gone. He's handling a different set of customers. Or he's out of the territory altogether."

"It's the fault of the recruiters," another DSM charges. "The promise-them-anything boys go around talking about rapid promotions and lateral moves for well-balanced experience. So when the young salesmen come here, the company gets itchy about leaving them in one spot too long."

Those district managers are talking about one of the most serious problems they face in managing their businesses: salesman turnover. As one of them says, "With all the shuffling that goes on, sometimes I think I'm in business to keep Allied, North American, and the Mayflower van people going."

There is little doubt that, in the last couple of years, salesman turnover has accelerated in many companies. Most sales managers can point to a number of changes in just the past six months. "Last year," one DSM recalls, "my company ran salesmen through my territory like they were going through a tin horn. This has created confusion among my customers about what in the world is going on with us in the field."

The confusion is threefold, says the manager. "First, our customers are upset because we put in a man and withdraw him. He starts a policy and then it's changed. Second, the salesmen themselves become confused. I don't give a darn how good a man is; when you move him into another territory, it takes time for him to get oriented and find out what's going on. While he's learning—you should forgive the expression—he isn't earning. Third, the district sales managers themselves are confused. Our business is managing people. How can we manage people when they go by like a parade?"

As companies compete for the brightest candidates who both deserve and desire fast promotions and the transfers that go with them, the problem will probably worsen. Most district managers agree that turnover is good. But it must be done the right way, or it becomes detrimental.

HOW TURNOVER AFFECTS SALESMEN

District sales managers see policy-directed turnover affecting their sales forces in three ways. First, they believe that few men can learn a customer's business in less than a year or two. After that, they can begin to get the job done. If there is no "after that," the salesman suffers because he lacks authority.

Second, salesmen can't identify with the companies they handle. "We used to have something I called 'my account,' " says one manager. "Now. who's going to feel proprietary about a customer he may never see again?"

A third problem affecting salesmen is the temptation—even the necessity—to sacrifice long-term account-building practices for short-term rewards. Their attitude: Why build an account for the next man? Managers fear their men may over-sell today and let the next man worry about the inventory problems that overselling may create. They also worry about key account relationships. "What am I supposed to tell a disgruntled customer? 'Don't worry about it. You'll never see that man again'?"

THE CUSTOMER: NEVER HAPPY

Rapid turnover of salesmen creates doubts in the customer's mind as to who is calling the shots. If the salesman is really going to act as the customer's representative back at headquarters, how can he fill this role with minimal knowledge of the customer's business?

The problem can be even broader than that. "One of my customers asked me for a fee," a DSM recounts. "He said that as long as he was going to be used as a tryout camp for our sales force, he wanted to be compensated for it. He asked me, only half kiddingly, if I had any idea how much it was costing him to train my men. How do you argue that one? When I started to tell him there were benefits, he cut me off with, 'Sure, for the next customer.' I'll admit he had a point."

Salesmen and their customers find it difficult to enter into a solid relationship. "It takes a customer a while to observe how a salesman operates with him," says one manager. "If you move him away too soon, no confidence has been built up in the customer's mind. Then the customer goes through the process of evaluating a new man all over again. As a result, he's always confused and never happy. A competitor can come in at any time and promise better service just by leaving the same man against the business longer than we do."

MANAGERS: OPERATING BY HUNCHES

"I feel very much like my customers," a DSM beset by salesman turnover says. "I'm always training. Yet I never see a payoff. I'm like a football coach who develops great freshman teams but loses them to someone else just when they learn how to play the game."

The major problem faced by DSMs is their inability to know which of the men can be depended on. A typical comment: "I have no book on my men. When I come into a territory, there's never any guide that spells out in my own terms who the dependables are. I can see who's been producing. But what can I really count on from a man? Is he steady, flashy, trustworthy, or what? Then after I get some of these inputs into my head, the whole scene changes. I'm always operating by hunch. And it's the same with every other manager I know in my company, which, incidentally, prides itself on planning."

"If you think that's bad, and it is," another DSM says, "what about the cumulative effect on you? Because you don't know what to count on, you try to play the position yourself. More often than not, you end up playing field salesman over and over again just to protect a situation you're unsure of. Now that you're a manager, you've earned the right to be a salesman 10 or 12 times over. Congratulations."

SOLUTIONS, ANYONE?

Managers agree that it takes up to six months in the field in a specific area for a salesman to develop any significant ability to influence the business. Then after three to five years, a man may top out and feel he is getting nowhere. So, somewhere between one and three years seems to be the optimum length of time for a man to serve a specific group of customers.

From the standpoint of the company and the customer, managers feel that they would be about right. From a salesman's personal perspective, however, they can see that there might be some misgivings. A man might well feel his career objectives had been compromised by an overlong commitment to one phase of his development

DSMs generally would like a policy to provide for a one- to three-year minimum before a salesman can be turned over to a new territory, or even to a new customer category. One DSM proposes a third-year bonus on a man's sales to keep him involved at the point when he starts to look ahead to his next move.

It may be possible to rely more on distributor salesmen when their turnover is small. Suppliers also can run training programs to help distributors with their sales and service staffs.

Such remedies are only stopgaps, however. The main solution must come from company policy. "If the men at the top keep changing every couple of years, and the senior division managers are only on the job a few years or so," says one DSM, "who's going to get excited about salesman turnover? When everybody's in motion, nobody seems to be in motion."

The issue cuts deeper than mere personnel policy, too. "What we need to do is stop and figure out what our priorities are: to serve customers or provide careers for bright young men," a disgruntled manager observes. "If we're going to be a career academy, that's one thing. But if we're going to be a service business, that's another. Somebody has to find a way to bring the two together better than it's being done right now."

SM, February 4, 1974, pp. 47–51.

Sharp Contrasts in Metro Growth
SM's projections of U.S. metropolitan markets to 1980

The slowdown in metropolitan growth rates, and the parallel pickup in nonmetro growth rates, will continue through the balance of the 1970s, *Sales Management's* projections indicate. Total U.S. population will increase 4.7%, to 222.5 million, by 1980, or only 0.7% a year. Population in *SM's* 300 metro areas will grow at an even

SURVEY HIGHLIGHT

Ferment At The Top: Shifts Among Biggest Markets

Rank 1980	1970	*SM* Metro Market	1980 Population (Thous.)	1970 Population (Thous.)	% Change 1970–80
1	1	New York	9,415.3	9,973.7	– 5.6%
2	3	Chicago	6,976.8	6,977.6	0.0
3	2	Los Angeles–Long Beach	6,786.6	7,042.0	– 2.0
4	4	Philadelphia	4,769.8	4,824.1	– 1.1
5	5	Detroit	4,425.1	4,435.1	– 0.2
6	6	Boston	3,472.6	3,376.3	+ 1.5
7	8	Washington, D.C.	3,253.7	2,909.4	+ 5.6
8	7	San Francisco–Oakland	3,222.9	3,108.8	+ 3.7
9	9	Nassau–Suffolk	2,840.4	2,555.8	+ 5.6
10	12	Dallas–Fort Worth	2,680.0	2,378.4	+ 6.2
11	16	Houston	2,436.9	1,999.3	+21.9
12	10	St. Louis	2,316.5	2,410.5	– 2.3
13	11	Pittsburgh	2,282.0	2,401.4	– 5.0
14	13	Baltimore	2,179.5	2,071.0	+ 5.2
15	15	Newark, N.J.	2,089.2	2,057.5	+ 1.5
16	17	Minneapolis–St. Paul.	2,052.6	1,965.4	+ 4.4
17	18	Atlanta	2,008.0	1,595.5	+25.9
18	20	Anaheim–Santa Ana– Garden Grove	1,951.3	1,421.2	+37.3
19	14	Cleveland	1,859.2	2,063.7	– 9.1
20	23	San Diego	1,768.0	1,357.9	+30.2
21	30	Tampa–St. Petersburg	1,678.4	1,088.5	+54.2
22	24	Miami	1,618.5	1,267.8	+27.7
23	27	Denver–Boulder	1,604.5	1,239.9	+29.4
24	35	Phoenix	1,457.2	969.4	+50.3
25	21	Milwaukee	1,440.9	1,403.9	+ 2.6
		25-Market Total	**76,585.9**	**73,679.9***	**+ 3.9%**

*Based upon top 25 markets as of 1970.
Sources: *Sales Management's 1975 Survey of Buying Power–Part II,* Census Bureau's
*Estimates of the Population of Metropolitan Areas and Components of Change Since
1970* (P-25, No. 537). Further reproduction strictly prohibited. ©*Sales Management.*

Market rankings, like the times, are always "a-changin'." This table, a sort of advance look at what the 1980 decennial census will reveal, suggests the dramatic differences that will occur among the leading markets between 1970 and 1980. Three new markets will join the list of 25 biggest metros–Tampa-St. Petersburg, Denver-Boulder, and Phoenix. To make way for them, Seattle-Everett, Cincinnati, and Kansas City will drop out. The most startling shift among the remaining metros will see Houston climbing five notches to eleventh place.

slower pace, 4.3%, to 166.5 million, while in the nonmetro counties it will increase a brisker 5.9%, to 56.0 million.

However, although it has become the vogue in some quarters to chatter about Americans turning their backs on the nation's metropolises, sales executives are well advised to ignore that kind of trendy conjecture. Although it is true that deep-seated changes are taking place in the social values people rely on in deciding where

to live, the phenomena of slower metro and faster nonmetro growth are too recent
for any hard-and-fast conclusions about the durability of the trend.

OLDER, BIGGER MARKETS HURTING

As sales executives pore over [reference] data for the [nation's] 300 metropolitan
[market areas], they will quickly perceive that there are many metro areas that in
the years ahead will enjoy substantial growth rates.

What is happening, as the table on this page makes clear, is that the metro slowdown is largely limited to the older, bigger markets in the Northeast and Midwest.
Metro markets in other areas of the country will continue to expand at an above-
average rate. Whether or not this big-market deceleration trend will trickle down to
younger, smaller markets is one of the great unknowns that cloud the near-term
future.

In any event, the trend is not a universal one yet, and differs radically from one
region to the next. Metro population in the Northeast will remain flat in the fore-
seeable future, increasing only 0.8% between 1974 and 1980, while nonmetro population will enjoy a 6.4% gain. The same contrasting pattern is expected to prevail in
the Midwest, where a metro gain of 1.2% will trail the nonmetro gain of 4.6%.

However, just the opposite will occur in the South and West, the nation's two
fastest-growing regions. In the South, where metropolitanization started much later
than elsewhere, metro population will increase 8.5% in the 1974–80 period, topping
the nonmetro's 5.6% gain. And in the West, the rush to the big cities will continue
as metro population increases 9.1%, or almost four times faster than the nonmetro
gain of 2.5%.

There is some evidence that even if people don't want to live in the core of a
metropolitan market, they will want to be close enough to enjoy its pleasures.
Calvin L. Beale, leader of population studies at the U.S. Dept. of Agriculture, notes
that in the 1970–73 period the population of those countries immediately adjacent
to metro market boundaries increased 4.7%, somewhat faster than the 4.2% increase
shown by all nonmetro counties. However, he adds, a more significant finding is
that "the net migration pattern of nonadjacent counties has shifted more than that
of the adjacent counties, going from a loss of 227,000 annually in the 1960s to an
annual gain of 130,000, a shift in the annual averages of 357,000 persons. On a
slightly larger base, adjacent counties have shifted from an average annual loss of
72,000 persons in the 1960s to an average gain in 222,000, an annual shift of
294,000 persons." Only 600 nonmetro counties lost population in the 1970–73
period, vs. 1,300 in the 1960s.

ATTITUDES SHIFTING

Decentralization of manufacturing, the development of recreation and retirement
activities, and the rise of nonmetro state schools have been key factors in the come-

back of the nonmetro counties, Beale concludes. Paralleling this is a shift in attitudes, he says. "The environmental-ecological movement, the youth revolution with its somewhat antimaterialistic and antisuburban component, and the narrowing of traditional urban-rural gaps in conditions of life all seem to have contributed."

Changing attitudes may get a stimulus from problems in the international area. George Brown, former head of the Census Bureau and now Secretary of The Conference Board, thinks worldwide food shortages and energy costs will in time influence the flow of people on the move. He speculates that the "rapid growth of the U.S. as a supplier of food" to the rest of the world will enhance the importance of farming and stop the out-migration from the agricultural heartland. He also notes that "energy costs, which include costs of travel as well as heating and cooling, tend to be minimized by high-density living, which benefits the central city and penalizes the exurbs."

Even Beale, too, is aware of the latter point. In conceding that it could retard future growth of nonmetro counties, he says, "Inasmuch as rural people travel a greater average distance to work or for goods and services than do urban residents, and do not usually have public transportation alternatives, the higher costs of personal transportation could have a depressing effect on the future trend of population dispersal." Wherever the shifts take the people, the sales and marketing executive will be able to track them through the *Survey*.

SURVEY HIGHLIGHT

Fastest-Growing Metros In The Last Half Of The 1970s

SM Metro Market	1980 Population (Thous.)	% Growth 1974-80	SM Metro Market	1980 Population (Thous.)	% Growth 1974-80
Fort Myers, Fla.	192.7	31.4%	Anchorage, Alaska	190.1	21.7%
Sarasota, Fla.	198.1	26.0	Phoenix, Ariz.	1,457.2	21.4
Orlando, Fla.	745.1	25.6	Austin, Texas	472.8	20.0
Fort Lauderdale-			Tallahassee, Fla.	160.8	20.0
Hollywood, Fla.	1,002.2	25.1	Gainesville, Fla.	151.4	19.4
Fort Collins, Colo.	143.9	24.8	Daytona Beach, Fla.	244.3	19.1
Killeen-Temple, Texas	257.8	24.2	McAllen-Pharr-		
Tucson, Ariz.	550.4	23.4	Edinburg, Texas	262.2	18.6
West Palm Beach-			Pascagoula-Moss		
Boca Raton, Fla.	545.0	23.4	Point, Miss.	123.2	17.2
Tampa-St. Petersburg, Fla.	1,678.4	22.6	Las Vegas, Nev.	378.2	17.0
Colorado Springs, Colo.	374.0	21.7	Reno, Nev.	166.3	17.0

Source: *Sales Management's 1975 Survey of Buying Power—Part II.* Further reproduction prohibited. ©*Sales Management.*

Metro growth in the latter part of the 1970s will have a strong southward tilt. Nine of the 20 fastest-growing markets are located in Florida, another five in Texas and Arizona. This is a continuation of a trend that dominated the 1960s, when sun-blessed states were a strong attraction for retirees seeking to escape the rigors of northern winters, and young adults looking for locales whose climates favored year-round leisure and recreational pursuits.

A more recent trend, which surfaced in the early 1970s, is the increased popularity of smaller markets: 14 of the above markets have a population of less than 500,000. Interestingly enough, only half of the markets shown here were among the 20 fastest-growing markets in the 1960s, demonstrating once again how each decade puts its own stamp on population shifts.

SM, October 20, 1975, pp. 57–58.

Section 4 / How Sales Force Helps Management in Forecasting, Planning, and Goal-Setting

Salesmen Speak, Syntex Listens

Syntex Laboratories' product managers have long yearned for closer ties to field salesmen, and now they're getting their wish. The Palo Alto, Cal., drug maker has formed three Salesman Advisory Boards headed by the divisional product managers for oral contraceptives, dermatologics, and nutritionals. Each board includes five field salesmen—one from each of the company's regional sales districts. They meet in the winter to help plan promotions for the next fiscal year (beginning in August) and again in the fall shortly after the programs are in full swing.

The benefits are mutual, says market planning director Ray E. Wrigglesworth, who conceived the idea. "Product managers," he says, "had to rely too much on market research and personal experience for their marketing data. The field force, a primary source of marketing intelligence, tended to be used the least. Also, salesmen find that having an extra line of communications to product managers can really get things done for them."

At the first board sessions last winter all three product managers learned that salesmen very much wanted what Wrigglesworth calls "a basic visual aid portfolio" for each Syntex product—something the company had 10 years ago and dropped. It's now being revived. The product managers also listened to rumbles over the company's traditional product sampling methods. "Our practice had been to give each of our 300 field salesmen the same standard shipment of samples," Wrigglesworth says. "The men on our Advisory Boards convinced us that our salesmen's needs vary greatly. So we've decided to develop an individualized sample program." That means salesmen send in their own sampling requirements, observing a specified budget, and the lists are fed to a computerized ordering system, just as is the case with Syntex's customers.

A major reason for the new program's success to date, Wrigglesworth says, is that it operates outside the usual chain of command. "But this doesn't denigrate sales managers," he insists. "It helps them."

SM, May 14, 1973, p. 8.

Honest Salesmen, Honestly

For some sales managers, the height of folly is asking a salesman to participate in sales forecasting and quota setting. The "Don't Ask" school of managers argues that no customer ever experienced flimflam like the kind that salesmen practice on superiors who ask them to estimate their future sales. But research by a San Diego State Univ. graduate student, Michael Thurlow (he now works in Del Monte's marketing department), offers proof that managers who solicit such information from salesmen invariably like the data they get, praising its honesty and, hence, its value in planning.*

Thurlow's special interest was the effect compensation has on salesmen's participation in both forecasting and quota setting—is a salesman who receives one kind of compensation more likely to manipulate his estimates than a man receiving another pay package? Thurlow sent questionnaires to sales managers at consumer and industrial goods firms in the Los Angeles and San Francisco metropolitan areas.

More than 200 replied, three-fourths of them responsible for outside salesmen. Seventeen percent of those salesmen, Thurlow notes, worked for commissions only; 21% for straight salaries; 10% for commissions plus guaranteed draws; the rest—52%—for salary and commission and/or bonus.

Thurlow found that more than 8 out of every 10 of the 200-plus managers asked their salesmen for an estimate of their future sales as an aid in sales forecasting. Although such participation in the forecasting process occurred in all kinds of companies at about the same rate, sales forces on straight salary and straight commission tended to participate more than sales forces working under other types of compensation plans.

"Nearly 40% of the respondents," Thurlow says, "indicated that their salesmen forecast 'just about right,' [and] had a formal policy towards soliciting forecasting information from their salesmen." He notes that "managers of sales forces working on straight salary were most likely to say their salesmen forecast 'just about right'."

Only 5% of the managers believed that their salesmen forecast low in order to earn more money, Thurlow says. Of those managers, 80% led salesmen who were paid a combination of salary with commissions and/or bonus. Also, those managers "were likely to have a less formalized policy towards their salesmen participating in forecasting, or no policy at all," he says.

Other findings were the following:

One in four of the managers indicated their salesmen forecast too high because of overoptimism. Especially prone here were salesmen on commission plans.

One in five of the managers said their salesmen were inaccurate forecasters because they lacked information. Salesmen were most in need of facts about (1) company plans that might affect sales and (2) needs of customers for the products and services the salesmen sell, Thurlow says.

---

*Full details of the study appear in Thurlow's unpublished master's thesis, Salesmen's Participation in Quota Setting and Forecasting, San Diego State Univ.

Three out of four of Thurlow's respondents used quotas and a majority asked their salesmen for independent estimates of what they felt their quotas should be. Companies that paid salesmen straight salaries or straight commissions were most likely to involve salesmen in the quota process.

The managers told Thurlow that salesmen's quota estimates were just as likely to be too high as too low. Most managers put the degree of error at 5% to 10%—only 7% of the respondents thought that the error was greater than 20%. Accuracy, or the lack of it, Thurlow found, had nothing to do with the compensation plans paid.

"The respondents from companies which do not have a policy of asking salesmen for an independent estimate indicated, by a two-to-one margin, that, if they did ask, the salesmen would underestimate," Thurlow says. "These responses are significantly different from what was indicated by managers who do ask."

SM, November 11, 1974, pp. 7-9.

Section 5 / How One American Went About Selling Successfully to Eastern European Countries

Between the Caviar, a Job of Selling

by Bob Inman

This month, in his office in Gastonia, N.C., Al Bohanan will attempt to close a sale with a buyer who has come 5,100 miles for the event. The sale is just one of a number Bohanan generated in September when he went to the Soviet Union and Eastern Europe bearing goodwill and good ideas. He heartily recommends such a trip to other Americans.

Bohanan, 36, is president of Bohanan Industries, a textile machinery firm. He was part of a North Carolina trade mission to Europe and Russia, the first from southern states since the new U.S. Soviet detente took shape. Thirty-five executives and state officials went to Moscow, then split up to cover the Continent.

Ironically, Bohanan almost backed out the night before the trip was to begin. He had, after all, plenty of work at home in his thriving precision machinery plant. Too, he was concerned that he did not have a specific product line to offer—only technical skill and craftsmanship. As it turned out, that was an asset, not a liability. He learned that Eastern Europeans want U.S. technology more than they want U.S. products.

"Those governments have tremendous pressure on them from consumers," he says. "Most of their effort goes toward improving their own standards of living, and they don't have the resources to put into technology. They have to buy it." And buy they did.

Bohanan left this trail of successes across the region:

In Rumania, a firm deal to set up a $6 million synthetic fiber plant, supplying both machinery and the know-how to operate and maintain it.

In Yugoslavia, a request for proposals on two complete plants, a $15 million sale scheduled to be further developed and possibly closed this month when a ranking Yugoslav trade official visits Bohanan in Gastonia.

In Poland, a request for pro forma proposals on supplying machinery for Poland's synthetic fiber industry (meaning, says Bohanan, that the Poles have money in hand to buy if foreign salesmen persevere).

And in Russia, inquiries about licensing Bohanan's specialized textile machinery for manufacture or sale in the Soviet Union.

At the first stop, Moscow, Bohanan didn't stick with the three or four meetings a day set up by the American Embassy. He saw the possibilities for more, and pressed for a broader itinerary. The result: seven or eight business calls per day with representatives of Russia's textile, paper, shoe, woodworking, and food production ministries. He developed extensive contacts by courting the Soviet Chamber of Commerce, a group which has far greater influence over Soviet industry than does its American counterpart.

Still, Bohanan found his Soviet experience—and that at the second stop, Poland—frustrating. "In these countries you're dealing with government ministries that are made up primarily of politicians," he says. "You have to work hard to get past the politics and down to the people level where you can talk shop."

One tool he used throughout the tour was his visual sales presentation, mainly pictures of his parts and subassembly works and manufacturing facilities. "It's something they can see and start asking questions about," he says. "If you can get them talking and asking questions, you know you're making headway. And it begins opening doors to plant people and project engineers."

However, it was on the third stop, Rumania, that Bohanan's "personal touch" began to work to his satisfaction. There, he found that because government ministry officials had worked their way up through the ranks, they were knowledgeable about the industries they represent.

Bohanan urges Americans who would sell in Eastern Europe to "get to know your interpreter." He credits one in particular with much of his success. Twenty-two-year-old Sorin Ignat, a bright, ambitious Rumanian, took Bohanan under his wing and opened doors that otherwise might have remained closed.

"You have to remember that your interpreter can help you get your point across or he can kill you," Bohanan says. "You should get to know him on a person-to-person basis. Be interested in his background, his family, his point of view."

The friendship paid off the second day in Bucharest, when Ignat pressed hard for contacts in the Rumanian textile industry. The interpreter lined up appointments for a Friday morning and the Rumanians invited Bohanan back for an afternoon session. Their keen interest in his technical background was clearly evident. By mid-afternoon, Bohanan knew something big was up: the country's minister of foreign trade, Dumitru Butnaru, joined the discussion. After hearing more of Bohanan's presentation, Butnaru said, "Let's take a trip."

Early Saturday morning, they did. In Butnaru's Mercedes, they drove north to the Rumanian mountain city of Brasov, where the government had built a prototype synthetic fiber plant. They toured through the day, Bohanan asking and answering questions, impressing the Rumanians with his knowledge of textile production.

At day's end, Butnaru popped the big question: "What will it cost to set up an entire plant to produce our own synthetics on a large scale?" Bohanan started figuring, and 30 minutes later handed Butnaru a $6 million proposal. "You've got it," said his host; "go to work." An initial agreement was signed on the spot and Bohanan was given detailed specifications and drawings to take home.

Bohanan is convinced that much of his success was due to his broad background— enough to give the Rumanians a package deal. They were struck by the fact that he was the top man in his company—someone with both technical knowledge and the ability to make deals and sign contracts. "These people had seen nothing before except American engineering firms," he says. "They were delighted to talk to somebody who had actually been banging out equipment—a manufacturer."

Bohanan's advice: Include the front office in the initial visit. Then let lower-echelon people take over.

Yugoslavia, he found, is more like America than any of the other countries he visited. Businesses operate on a profit basis, independent of the government, and are interested in joint ventures with U.S. firms. Here, as elsewhere, the idea is to import technology and produce goods for home consumption, thus keeping hard currency within the country.

Bohanan is convinced that Eastern Europe is a fantastic opportunity for Americans who don't mind working hard to get the business. Throughout, he found government and industry officials tough, firm bargainers—not much different from Americans. However, "Be sure you're getting a good deal for yourself," he advises, choosing in his own case to make a return on his investment in five years.

Actually, U.S. government officials predict an excellent market in Eastern Europe for U.S. salesmen for 25 years or more. Bohanan says U.S. embassies in Russia and Eastern Europe can be a tremendous help to American businessmen, setting up initial itineraries and advising on accommodations and transportation. But the embassies are only a starting point.

No one in Gastonia, N.C., is surprised at Al Bohanan's success. After high school, he worked his way through a local machinery company—from shoveling sand at the foundry to the top sales and marketing job. Through technical school training and practical experience, he gained an ICS equivalent mechanical engineering degree.

In 1965, with $16,000 he had borrowed on his home, he founded Bohanan Industries. Today, it has 120 employees and $5 million annual sales. New business brought home from Eastern Europe means an immediate expansion of 30 people and corresponding production space. The credit goes to Bohanan's luck or personal diplomacy or hard work—or to all three.

SM, November 12, 1973, pp. 35-36.

Section 6 / How Advertising, Public Relations, and Sales Promotion Personnel Learn to Better Support Sales Representatives and Salespersons

Who's That Suave Stranger Calling on Your Customers?

by Dr. Conway L. Lackman, Assistant Professor, Rutgers University

Sales managers are showing considerable interest in having their advertising agency personnel gain selling experience by calling on customers.

Direct selling activity by agency account men is especially useful in marketing managers' execution of their own jobs, especially in product adjustment and purchase motivation. In these two steps, both of which are often troublesome for marketing managers, the ad agency's contributions may in fact be extremely valuable in that the agency "shortens the feedback link" for marketing management.

[This article represents surveys of ad agencies involved in both industrial and consumer goods areas. Agency executives of several ad agencies of different size (small, medium, and large) and types of customer were interviewed. Here are highlights of some of the findings:]

SMALL AGENCIES

Consumer Products   Within the framework of the current marketing–advertising environment, small agencies most benefited by this type of activity, specifically in the consumer goods accounts, for example, drugs, financial institutions, and new products in general. Chart 1 shows small agency account men with the heaviest involvement (50%) in direct selling of clients' products. Chart 2 shows the products where activity was most concentrated and gives the reasons.

In the drug industry, a problem for the advertising agency is that of consumer reaction to side effects and dosages. Direct field participation (30% of the activity— Chart 3) enables more direct feedback and measures the consumer's reactions directly instead of indirectly through the client. For financial institutions, direct selling involvement (40% of the activity) by the account executive can more clearly define

Chart 1 / Percent of Account Executives Having Client Product Sales Experience*

Firms	1	2	3	4	5
Percent	40%	95%	50%	50%	50%

*Participating more than once per year in selling of clients' products.

**Chart 2 / Current Involvement of Ad Agency Account Men in Client's Direct Selling–
by Product Type**

Size Of Agency	Percent of Involvement by Product Type			Percent of Total Time Involvement		
	Consumer[1]	Industrial[2]	Services Financial[3]	All Products	New Product[4]	Old Product
Small	30%	30%	40%	50%	75%	25%
Medium	40%	55%	–	95%	80%	20%
Large	35%	40%	25%	40%	85%	15%

[1] Direct selling experience gives a direct measure of consumer reactions to "side effects" of drugs.
[2] Direct selling experience gives insight into technical features and specifications that would promote product sales.
[3] Direct measure of most misleading copy.
[4] Facilitates needed product adjustment before marketing.

Chart 3 / Percent of Involvement by Marketing Management Functions*

Size Of Agency	Market Delineation	Purchase Adjustment	Product Adjustment	Distribution	Follow-Up And Control
Small	15%	25%	40%	5%	15%
Medium	10%	20%	50%	10%	10%
Large	10%	20%	50%	4%	10%

*Participating more than once a year.

the constraints on advertising appeals placed by government regulation.

New Products   With respect to the introduction of new products (accounting for 75% of the involvement—Chart 2), direct selling activity in test marketing offered the best opportunity for the account man to (1) measure consumer attitude toward the product before it went to the market and use that information as leverage, if necessary, to induce product adjustment by the client before he incurred further cost; and (2) elicit a more candid response from not only the consumer but the retailer.

The retailer would tend to be more honest with a representative from the advertising agency than he would be with the supplier. All agencies interviewed felt this was an important source of information in the marketing of a new product that is often ignored, but can be obtained by having the account men participate in direct selling.

Industrial Products   The small agencies held unique views on the role of the account men in the selling of industrial goods. The specific products mentioned were tools and equipment, machinery, transformers, and farm equipment. They stressed the importance of the account men's finding the actual technical features and specifications that would promote sales of the product. The general feeling of the smaller agencies was, however, that this activity was less important in the industrial goods than in consumer goods because most sales in the industrial market are made through channels of distribution, making personal-selling study less meaningful.

Marketing Functions   Product adjustment (40% of involvement—Chart 3) and purchase motivation (25%) were the steps in the marketing process most enhanced by direct selling activity. Market delineation (15%) was relatively more important than for larger firms (Chart 3), possibly because of the generally less sophisticated marketing research done by smaller clients.

MEDIUM-SIZED AGENCIES

Consumer Products   The specific products named by medium-sized firms interviewed were retail gasoline and general merchandise. In the gasoline industry (retail outlets), it was felt that direct selling (studying station operations) would be useful as a credibility check. Claims made by the client could be verified (for example, windshield cleaned and oil checked). With respect to general merchandise, a handle on on competitors' strategy could best be achieved by observing that strategy in the marketplace itself.

Industrial Products   In the industrial goods market, filing systems, adding machines, and calculating machines were considered areas where direct selling by the account men would allow the agency to get a better feeling for consumer satisfaction and complaints with respect to the clients' product. The features that most appealed to the consumer could be recognized and the negative features as well could be isolated. In general, the more sophisticated the selling process, the less likely is direct participation by account executives or their counterparts.

Marketing Functions   Product adjustment is a step where more concentration of this type of activity takes place (50% of the involvement—Chart 3). Purchase motivations (20%) and market delineation (10%) become less important, again possibly because of the clients' relatively greater resources in research compared with small agencies.

LARGE AGENCIES

Consumer Products   The large agency felt that direct selling activity was indeed necessary and mentioned basically the same products and reasons as those already mentioned by small firms. In the consumer area, these are (1) importance of showing interest in their clients and (2) obtaining new product information.

Industrial Products　　In the industrial market, the importance of attending clients' trade shows to get technical information for ads in trade journals was emphasized.

Marketing Functions　　The same pattern by function existed as for the medium-sized agency (Chart 3), with the exception of a decline in activity in the distribution step.

What about the future of ad agency personnel involvement in selling clients' products? Small agencies feel that the future marketing environment will call for less emphasis on consumer packaged goods and show a trend toward stressing services. An example was given of an account man going to a travel agent and observing his sales methods. This would allow him to see firsthand the service he was to promote, and he would not have to rely mainly on the client. The rationale for this trend is that advertising dollars are shifting from volume to fewer and more expensive ads.

Medium-sized agencies feel that the future, influenced by consumerism, implies more government regulations and controls placed on advertising. As a result, the agencies will be forced more and more into direct sales activity for account men. This, the respondents feel, would give the account man a good understanding of the mechanics of sales and give him specific ideas about appeals for ads.

The large firm is convinced that the future will call for fewer salesmen in the field. Hence, "compensatory" activity on the part of agencies will be required. It is also felt that ad personnel will have to participate in the sale if they are to understand shelf-space competition in the future, electronic shopping, and new uses of credit. Product adjustment and purchase motivation are expected to become even more the central steps in the managerial marketing process and ad men, it is felt, will need to concentrate their selling involvement on them.

Currently, regardless of agency size, direct selling activity is essential for ad agency personnel. Over 50% of all agencies' account men are involved, affording the account men an opportunity to (1) evaluate the marketing environment directly, (2) obtain the client's confidence, and (3) let the client know the agency is thoroughly involved. It also provides information to the account men that they simply could not get by other methods.

It is quite clear, especially as agency size grows, that new product marketing strategy captures most of the involvement in direct selling. Large and medium-sized agencies report this activity to be equally important with respect to both consumer and industrial products; small agencies concentrate this activity in consumer products (70%), with consumer services composing 40% of that category.

As noted, direct selling activity by agency account men is especially useful in marketing managers' execution of their functions, particularly product adjustment and purchase motivation. Direct selling activity of this type improves the agencies' comprehension of the market and the client's execution of these two steps of the marketing process.

In the future, increasing government regulation, the rise in consumption of services, and the relative increase in direct response (electronic) buying will foster more short-run involvement by account men. For the long run, agency involvement in the selling of your products and services will have different goals, but it will not decline. Far from it.

SM, May 5, 1975, pp. 56–60.

How Public Relations Helps Sales
"Why bother with PR at all!"

by **Richard R. Conarroe**, Contributing Editor

George Franklin, the marketing vice president, had called a meeting of some key men at Fowler Equipment Co. to discuss next year's proposed marketing budget. Everyone agreed on the proposed advertising budget, but when the subject of public relations came up, it set off a verbal explosion of clashing opinions.

"Why bother with public relations at all!" said Bill Fox, the sales manager. "Let's put the money where it counts—in some extra incentive pay for the sales force."

Not surprisingly, Charlie Jacobs, the ad manager, claimed the PR budget would do more good if used to beef up the company's advertising. Harry Schwartz, in charge of research, chimed in. "With the kind of money you're thinking of dumping down the drain to get the company's name in the paper, I could buy an important piece of test equipment that would really do some good around here."

And so it went. Shirley Adams, who handled what little PR activity the company indulged in, wasn't even invited to the meeting. The result was that only a token sum in the proposed marketing budget was earmarked for publicity activities. It was just enough to keep a so-called public relations program alive, but not enough to do any good.

By strange coincidence, at exactly the same time, a similar meeting was being held in another city by the marketing group of one of Fowler Equipment's chief competitors, Equipment Dynamics, Inc. Fowler Equipment and Equipment Dynamics were almost identical in many important ways: size, share of market, management caliber, and growth rate. One very definite difference between them, however, was that Equipment Dynamics had a positive attitude toward the value of PR as a sales tool. Where Fowler Equipment took the "Why bother!" stance, Equipment Dynamics viewed PR as a strong, economical, uniquely useful marketing tool able to produce results often unattainable in other ways. Because of this philosophy, Equipment Dynamics earmarked a reasonable percentage of its total marketing budget for public relations activities—and set specific goals to be accomplished with this budget.

Dick Conarroe, who has enjoyed an extensive career as a business journalist, heads his own public relations concern, The Walden Co., Westport, Conn.

A year passed. Now the similarities between the two companies were fewer. Because of its imaginative, even aggressive, use of public relations as a sales tool, Equipment Dynamics enjoyed several advantages over Fowler Equipment: better credibility, better customer awareness of products, bigger share of market, and greater recall of its advertising. In short, there was less sales resistance for its sales force to overcome. The reason for these advantages was that Equipment Dynamics had new product stories popping up in the trade press consistently, along with by-lined articles by salesmen and other members of the marketing team that appeared frequently in various business publications. Equipment Dynamics had established itself as a spokesman for its industry.

SM, January 22, 1973, p. 40.

Section 7 / Sales Training Methods

AV Plays a Leading Role [in Sales Training for Many Companies]

Mike Yaffe is playing doctor. Not in the sense that some of us might remember, but in his professional capacity, as training director for Endo Labs, Garden City, N.Y. He's taking the role of a physician while a new salesman shows how he would make a presentation on behalf of Endo's products. It's a typical role-playing situation, commonly used in sales training, but with several important differences. For one thing, the entire performance is being recorded on videotape, for later review by the salesman. For another, the camera is not in the position used by many trainers for role-playing—directly in front of the trainee. Rather, it is off to the side and slightly behind him, so that the man won't be distracted by the equipment.

Yet another difference is that Yaffe and the trainee are alone in the room, without other salesmen or managers to make the man nervous. For that reason, Yaffe conducts his training sessions at Harrison Conference Center, Glen Cove, N.Y., where there are several rooms with videotaping equipment. Yaffe and other experienced Endo salesmen conduct simultaneous role-playing sessions, then play the tapes back to the entire group in the afternoon for criticism. "This helps new salespeople feel more comfortable," Yaffe says.

Endo, of course, is but one of many companies that rely on audiovisual equipment to enhance their sales training programs. With the cost of hiring a new man and sending him on calls continuing to grow, it's increasingly important that he be fully informed and skilled. Thus sales managers are using every means at their disposal, which naturally includes AV equipment and programs. The traditional AV media, such as films and slide presentations, continue to get widespread use, both because they're effective teachers and because they provide a refreshing change of pace in training sessions. But coming on strong is the powerful video medium because many people, especially young sales trainees, are used to getting their information from a TV set.

ROLE-PLAYING WITH AV

Role-playing is probably the most common use of video in sales training, for experienced salespeople as well as new hires. For example, Inland Steel decided it wanted its salesmen to sell coil-coated products, which were formerly sold by specialists. This required not only extensive product knowledge but training in sales techniques different from the ones they were used to. So Inland brought its entire sales force to a motel in suburban Chicago for a two-day training session. One day was devoted to role-playing, with instant reply available on a Sony video-cassette recorder. The salesmen could see, instantly, just what they were doing wrong.

Often, role-playing situations stem from real-life applications. The Missouri Pacific railroad, for example, has its salesmen come to training courses with descriptions of tough selling situations they have faced. These become the basis for role-playing. After the training, MoPac salesmen get to take audiocassettes of their own role-playing efforts with them, to play again on automatic tape recorders.

AV USED IN TRAINING DISTRIBUTOR SALES FORCES

For many companies, sales training must extend beyond their own sales forces, to distributor, dealer, and retail salespersons. These people, after all, are responsible for selling the product at one stage or another. Toro, for example, sells its distributors a complete kit that includes a film and slides to show the line to dealers, as well as a training film for retail salespersons. This year, that film is also available on cassettes for portable Technicolor and Fairchild projectors.

Other companies use AV to help train distributor and retail personnel out in the field. Amway, a supplier of household cleaning products and cosmetics, uses Eva-Tone Soundsheets—flexible records that can be mailed and played on a standard phonograph—to send monthly training and motivation messages to its distributors. Similarly, retailers such as Montgomery Ward and Belk use these soundsheets to train retail sales personnel.

Other types of new equipment are continually coming onto the market, helping the sales manager with his training activities. General Electric, for example, has introduced its PJ5000, a large-screen color projector designed for front- or rear-screen applications and computer-generated displays. It's priced at $41,500, but such customers as Ford Motor, American Airlines, and Braniff have found the investment worthwhile. . . .

PICKING THE RIGHT SITE

Many companies prefer to consolidate all their AV equipment into a corporate training center, with sales training one of the main uses. One such facility occupies a floor of American Republic Insurance's headquarters building in Des Moines. Designed by New York City AV consultant Jerome Mennell, it has two classrooms, projection and storage areas, and its own production studio. Sales training director Fred Lloyd says it was designed so that trainers could use a wide variety of AV equipment with a minimum of mechanical distraction. Companies without their own training centers can use one of many "conference centers" now being built that are designed specifically for business meetings and fully equipped with AV equipment. Endo Labs, which uses Harrison Conference Center, is one example; larger companies, such as Procter & Gamble and British Airways, also use Harrison for sales training. And, of course, most hotels provide AV equipment for group meetings.

SM, August 4, 1975, pp. 55–62.

66

Section 8 / Buying Behavior and Psychology of Selling

How Much Do Salesmen Know About Key Accounts? Listen to Them Tell All

by **Mack Hanan,** Contributing Editor

Squeezed by both the rising cost of sales and pressure from top management to improve profits on every sale, more and more sales managers are becoming keyed up about key accounts. In other words, they are rediscovering the "80-20 rule." If as much as 80% of profitable sales volume comes from as little as 20% of all accounts, alert sales executives are saying, the customers who make up that 20% should become the bull's-eye of our sales target.

As soon as this fact is out on the table, the next question is, "How well do we know our key account customers?" The first answer, the easy one, is almost always wrong: "Like the backs of our hands." The second answer comes a lot harder but it is a good deal more correct: "Not nearly well enough, if we really want to zero in on these accounts and base the achievement of 80% of our sales goals on them."

One of the most instructive exercises a sales manager can put his field force through is a Key Account Needs Inventory. This makes clear just what each salesman knows and doesn't know about his key accounts and the major decision-makers in their midst.

WHAT SOME SALESMEN "KNOW"

A short while ago, a 25-man industrial division's sales force went through what experience has shown to be a typical inventory. The salesmen were told to "let it all hang out," and that produced some absorbing dialogue. First, look at the questions posed to Salesman A and see how he answers:

Q. *Who is the key decision-maker on the account?*
A. Mr. Fred Smith, the purchasing agent.
How long have you called on him?
Four years plus.
What are the main subjects of your conversations with him?
The Little League baseball team he manages.
What does he reveal as his primary needs?
He wants me to act as his warehouse. And keep the price down.
What unfulfilled expectations of you does he seem to have?

He wants more service than I can give him. Just to provide what I do is at
times difficult.
How do you plan to increase this account's profit contribution?
My overriding goal is to hang on to our current position.
Now Salesman B speaks out—in terms that are all too familiar to anyone who's
been in sales management for a while:
Who is the key decision-maker on the account?
Mr. Bob Jones, director of corporate purchasing.
How long have you called on him?
Five, six years or so.
What are the main subjects of your conversations with him when you call?
He is a home gardener. His great pride in life is his green thumb.
What does he reveal as his primary needs?
He wants economy. Savings, savings, savings. Price, price, price.
What unfulfilled expectations of you does he seem to have?
He wants assurance all the time that I am giving him the greatest savings pos-
sible. Every time he signs an order, he feels he is laying his career on the
line.
How do you plan to increase this account's profit contribution?
By acting with extreme caution, inch by inch.
Finally, let's hear from Salesman C, who is quite frank about the sales problems
he faces every day:
Who is the key decision-maker on the account?
Mr. George Brown, general manager and head buyer.
How long have you called on him?
Ten years.
What are the main subjects of your conversations with him when you call?
Women, horse racing, golfing, and new drinks.
What does he reveal as his primary needs?
To be able to assure his plant superintendents that they will never be out of
stock on our items.
What unfulfilled expectations of you does he seem to have?
He always is interested in testing and evaluating new products. He wants me
to pick up every new competitive product I can and bring them to him, like
I was his comparison shopper.
How do you plan to increase this account's profit contribution?
By killing myself to insure delivery within 48 hours, seven days a week, and
eating the cost of the secondary stock warehouse I have to keep to do it.
It doesn't take an in-depth analysis of these salesmen's reports to realize several
things. First, the business they are in is apparently a commodity business. Few, if
any, competitive product differences exist and buying is often based on price and
delivery considerations. Second, the salesman–customer relationships seem to have
become perfunctory. Little if any need-prospecting is going on. Nor does there
seem to be much penetration of accounts to reach a full roster of decision-makers or

buying influences. Third, no true penetration planning that could increase profitable sales is going on. All these factors can be found in any business. They are especially common to commodity businesses. Unfortunately, they also act to insure that a commodity business remains that way.

CENTRAL NEEDS-AUDIT

Sales managers are coming to realize that the knowledge their sales forces have about key account needs can be the most important aspect of information resources. The problems are twofold: what the information should consist of and how it can be obtained.

Some companies are setting up a central audit of key account needs. Each need is carefully spelled out and evaluated for its intensity and potential growth. It is then restated in terms of the way the customer views this particular problem. A recommendation is made on how to solve each problem by prescribing the remedy of equipment and services that will yield an optimal profit for the supplier.

The key account audit is run like a blood bank. Only salesmen who deposit information can draw from it. "We treat it like blood," one sales manager says, "because knowledge of key account needs is our lifeblood." The bank contains information on key decision-makers' hobbies and personal interests, of course. This is regarded as the "small change." The "big bills" are in the form of valid customer problems. These are the inputs that pay off.

INFORMATION PIPELINE

In another company committed to systems sales, a four-source pipeline for key account information has been set up to keep its needs inventory well stocked. The sales force is required to file a monthly intelligence report on key customer needs that can lead to equipment sales and service sales or to systems sales, which combine both equipment and services. Another report provides an opportunity for the sales force to file information on customer needs gathered from competitive sources, trade shows, and exhibits.

Finally, each salesman must file a monthly reading of customer-need information gathered from the general press, his own trade publications, and customer industry publications.

A company that takes its key accounts seriously is committed to maintaining a key account needs inventory as its most important product. The buyer's traditional question, "What's new?" for the first time may provoke a substantial answer. "These are the new key customer needs I am anticipating," a salesman may say. "These are the problems they can be translated into. And these are the new solutions I can prescribe to solve them and, in that way, earn more profitable sales volume for us."

Only when his men are capable of this sort of response can a sales manager say with assurance, "Yes, we know our key accounts."

SM, May 14, 1973, pp. 44-47.

Section 9 / Social, Legal, and Ethical Issues in Selling

Salesman George Wingfield's Day in Court

What salesmen say is being used against them more and more in courts of law. The latest illustration of how vulnerable the verbal promise is becoming happened last month when the District of Columbia Superior Court rescinded an automobile sales contract and ordered the full $2,470 purchase price refunded to a couple who charged the salesman with "fraudulent and deceitful" promises.

By now George Wingfield probably wishes he had never walked into Dale Morton's pharmacy that December day in 1970. Since Wingfield, a frequent customer, is a veteran salesman with Wilson-McIntosh Buick, Inc., Morton asked his opinion as to whether the dealer's Opel compact might make an economical runabout for his wife. Wingfield quite naturally sang his product's praises and soon had the Mortons in the showroom ready to sign.

There was only one hitch: a General Motors strike had whittled dealer inventories. Rather than the orange, factory-air-conditioned model the couple wanted, would they settle for a green, un-air-conditioned station wagon they could drive home immediately? Mrs. Morton's old Peugeot had gasped its last that week, so they took the deal—but only on condition that custom air conditioning could be arranged later.

NOT SINCE 1965

Thereupon ensued a familiar tale of woe: sparks and sputters on the first drive home, a gas tank that bled mysteriously, and diseases pronounced incurable after long stretches in the repair shop. Still, it was air conditioning that riled the Mortons into filing suit. After a Sears-installed unit literally fell out of the car, the couple learned that GM itself hadn't air conditioned Opels since 1965 and recommended against custom installations for this model. This, charged the Mortons, had been misrepresented by Wingfield.

Last month, Judge Joyce Hens Green agreed. "It is well settled that material misrepresentations, even though innocently made, may be sufficient to warrant rescission in a court of equity," she said. Her written opinion also touches on these other key legal points:

"Concealment or suppression of a material fact is as fraudulent as is a positive direct misrepresentation," wrote the judge.

Even though the salesman's statements may have reflected his personal opinion, "they were made under such circumstances and in such manner as to lead any reasonable person to believe the salesman knew what he was talking about."

In what could be the lawsuit's most significant aspect, the judge totally ignored an Opel warranty which contained the familiar language disavowing "all terms, conditions, statements and misrepresentations" not included in the written statement. "The plaintiffs did not lose their rights by failing to investigate warranty terms before signing the contract," said Judge Green. "They obviously relied on the salesman's statements, and it is clear they had a right to."

If the latter point holds up in other courts, a salesman's verbal word will be as binding on an agreement as a written contract.

SM, January 22, 1973, p. 3.

Case of the Battling Salesman

Turbulence seemed to surround Ronnell Lynch, a salesman for Nabisco in Minneapolis: he was constantly scolded by grocers for being overly aggressive and for poaching on shelf space reserved for his competitors' cookie and cracker products.

Things finally exploded in May 1969, when Lynch called at Jerome Lange's grocery store to service the snack rack. As court records tell it, "An argument developed between plaintiff [Lange] and Lynch regarding Lynch's servicing of plaintiff's store. Lynch became very angry and started swearing. Plaintiff told Lynch either to stop swearing or to leave the store, as children were present. Lynch then became uncontrollably angry, saying, 'I ought to break your neck.'"

Which, as court records show, he almost did. After "viciously assaulting" the owner, Lynch "proceeded to throw merchandise around the store and then left."

Lange decided to throw his counterpunches in court. His strategy was so unusual that it was not until a few weeks ago that the case was finally resolved by the Minnesota Supreme Court. The grocer, angling for a high damage-payment, had sued Nabisco instead of its salesman. Lange's action conflicted with hundreds of state and local statutes that make only employees liable for their own rash acts during business hours unless specifically "motivated" by their employer.

The Minnesota high court, however, in a statement written by its ruling judge, declared, "An employer is liable" for an assault by his employee when the source of the attack is related to the employee's duties and "occurs within work-related limits of time and place."

Minnesota's decision is the latest in a trend toward finding management responsible for the behavior of workers. Alabama, California, Illinois, Kentucky, and Montana have all ruled against companies in such cases.

As Nabisco will rediscover when a lower court gets around to assigning an expected five-figure damage settlement due grocer Lange, the customer is always right.

P.S. Salesman Lynch doesn't work for Nabisco anymore.

SM, February 4, 1974, p. 10.

Salesmen are Monsters

Salesmen in most industries think of pens, paperweights, and other door openers as common and usually innocent. But in pharmaceutical selling, they're payola, insists Sen. Edward M. Kennedy (D.-Mass.). And if Congress backs his view, as expected, drug detail men will find themselves selling under a tighter rein.

The alleged side effects of overpromotion held the spotlight last month during hearings in which Kennedy's health subcommittee grilled four former detail men and eight company presidents. Chairman Kennedy, flanked by longtime industry nemesis Gaylord Nelson (D.-Wis.) charged that "a system of hard sell" leads to overprescribing, which, he says, contributes to the estimated 30,000 deaths a year from adverse reactions to prescribed drugs.

Dipping into a stack of promotional aids, Kennedy had caustic comments for everything from a phonograph album touting Parke-Davis, to a "How to Sell Doctors" manual (Kennedy blasted it for "appealing to fear and vanity"), to a contest in which physicians were awarded appliances and vacations depending on the number of prescribing "points" accumulated. Kennedy argued that such promotions reflect an "encounter . . . where gifts and gimmicks are used to win the physician's favor . . . where samples are given freely as an inducement . . . and where side effects are downplayed in favor of benefits."

None of the industry witnesses denied the existence of such practices, but all took issue with claims that they are widespread. The four ex-detail men praised their companies (Eaton, Ortho, Pfizer, and Merck, Sharp and Dohme) for stressing the importance of balanced sales presentations. They were backed by Pharmaceutical Manufacturers Assn. president C. Joseph Stetler, who called salesmen "our most vital communications and educational link to doctors."

With Kennedy promising a formal proposal by May and Stetler willing to negotiate for "proper company advocacy of its products," some sort of regulatory prescription seems to be in the making. Possibilities: licensing detail men, publishing a federal drug compendium stripped of ad claims, imposing patient drug use review, requiring federal clearance for all leave-behind sales material, or forbidding salesmen to examine a doctor's prescribing records.

Of those, the last got the most support during the Senate hearings. Several witnesses were indignant because many pharmacies now allow salesmen and market research firms access to prescription orders from physicians. Pharmaceutical marketers may soon lose one of their major tools for sales reporting and forecasting.

SM, April 8, 1974, p. 3.

Remember This Number: 301-496-7631

The scene: An appliance salesman takes his wife shopping at a local department store and stops to show off his company's latest clothes dryer. But something's not right. The door handle is sharp and jagged—obviously a production flaw. He asks to check others in stock and finds them equally unsafe. What does he do?

Under tough regulations effective this month, he or his company has 24 hours to tell the Consumer Product Safety Commission (CPSC) about the flaw in writing or by phone (301-496-7631). If one or the other doesn't make the report and CPSC later decides negligence is involved, they face civil penalties of up to $500,000.

The unprecedented rules cover toys, appliances, household cleaners, aerosol containers, and some 10,000 other products under CPSC's jurisdiction. . . . The product defect notification regulations, effective March 21, apply to any retailer, distributor, and manufacturer—and their salesmen—who come across information that "reasonably supports the conclusion" that a product has a defect that could present a safety hazard.

Once the initial report is filed (it need only describe the product problem and known distribution points), the reporting party must follow up in 48 hours with an "exhaustive" written report answering no fewer than 23 questions. Besides pinpointing the number and location of defective products, the report must describe any injuries to users incurred to date, what quality controls have been devised to avoid future defects, and how the company intends to make refunds to customers. Retailers and distributors who file such reports are excused from questions only a manufacturer can answer, but must still furnish such data as product model numbers and plans for notifying customers.

The above rules come hard on the heels of an equally tough proclamation on what's to be done when the commission bans a product. Effective March 6, the rules now require retailers to display two large signs (22″ x 28″ minimum) together in a "conspicuous place." The first is a "Banned Articles or Substances List" naming such products and warning shoppers not to buy them. The second is a "Notice of Refund Procedures" telling prior purchasers they are entitled to their money back plus "reasonable and necessary transportation charges incurred in return of the product."

CPSC leaves it up to marketers to work out how they will reimburse their distributors and retailers for *their* purchase price. The new rules also leave undiscussed the problem of the strained relationship between salesman and account certain to result from the CPSC move. Example: Who will pay a retailer for hunting down banned products or for figuring who gets what refunds?

That, the commission seems to be saying, is one of the few remaining elements in product safety that should be a matter of laissez-faire.

SM, March 18, 1974, p. 3.

PART III Organizing, Prospecting, and Planning for Personal Selling

OVERVIEW

The modern customer-oriented, problem-solving outside sales representative needs to know a great deal about his or her industry, company (its products and policies), and the competition before making sales calls. This is essential if he is to truly become a diagnostician, able to discuss intelligently all aspects of his prospects' or customers' businesses, and advise solutions to their problems in the form of the products or service offered, which he will present in terms of user-benefits.

In most areas of outside selling, considerable attention has to be paid to building up lists of firms or individuals who may need the products or service being offered, and then qualifying or checking them out to see whether they have a need, the authority to buy, and the money with which to make the purchase. This procedure is called prospecting, and it is most often done face-to-face, by mail, or by telephone. Constant, systematic prospecting helps provide what every top sales representative needs—an endless supply of potential customers.

Since two-way communication is so important to a successful understanding between a sales representative or salesperson, and his customer or prospect during a sales presentation, prior planning for the presentation is essential. This prior planning involves thinking points through carefully, and putting thoughts into words that will persuade and motivate. The representative's first step in planning an orderly presentation around benefits that will arouse interest, create conviction, and motivate action (to buy) is to prepare a structured outline of the presentation. This outline can then be developed into a more or less detailed, planned presentation or into a highly detailed, word-for-word, canned presentation. This same approach also applies to developing effective sales letters.

The term *preapproach*, as employed in selling, involves (1) finding out as much as possible about the prospect prior to the interview, and (2) determining how to get the specific interview, with or without an appointment.

All these points, and others, are covered in the following readings under these headings:
Section 10 – Know Your Company—and Know Your Competition
Section 11 – Prospecting and Organizing Your Prospect List
Section 12 – Planning Your Sales Presentation
Section 13 – The Preapproach: Getting in to See the Decision-Maker

Section 10 / Know Your Company—and Know Your Competition

Pan Am's 32,500 New Sales Representatives— Its Employees

[Note: During 1974, in face of rapidly rising fuel costs, increased air fares and a worldwide slump in international air travel, Pan Am applied for a subsidy from the U.S. government that was denied. Pan Am employees, unsupported by their company organized themselves to help boost sales (and save their jobs) as this article notes.]

Pan Am employees are growing increasingly bitter over the company's refusal to lend its support to their "Support America—Fly Pan Am" drive. And except for allowing employees to use its ticket offices to disseminate their literature, the company reportedly will continue to stand aloof. Undaunted, leaders of the 32,500 employees are launching a new sell: travel agents are being asked to "think Pan Am." A spokesman says, "If each would sell just one more Pan Am ticket a month, it would mean $10 million in added sales monthly." Which is almost the amount of the federal subsidy the airline wanted but was denied.

SM, November 11, 1974, p. 13.

Facts Are Where You Find Them

It will be a warmed-over dish for statistical gourmets, but others will find helpful the U.S. Commerce Dept.'s just-released *Measuring Markets: A Guide to the Use of Federal and State Statistical Data.* The 71-page primer, compiled by the agency's Domestic and International Business Administration, shows in a single package how various federal and state reports on population, income, employment, and sales can be used in sales forecasting.

Some of the listed sources are well known (examples: The Census of Business, The Annual Survey of Manufacturers), but many marketers may not be aware of other, less publicized reports, such as the Census Bureau's Advance Monthly Retail Sales and the Product Class Value of Shipments. The guide cites statistical contributions from the states, ranging from California's quarterly Taxable Sales to the annual product sales breakdowns compiled by Wyoming's Board of Equalization.

The publication also offers seven how-to-do-it sections using "case histories" of fictitious firms in manufacturing, wholesaling, retailing, and market research.

Copies are available for $1.35 each from the Supt. of Documents, U.S. Government Printing Office, Washington, D.C. 20402.

SM, December 9, 1974, pp. 10-13.

Section 11 / Prospecting and Organizing Your Prospect List

Business Publications: How to Make Them Work Harder for You

Jack Campbell had a problem—and an opportunity. Campbell is sales manager for Bird Machine, South Walpole, Mass., which recently introduced a Pannevis horizontal vacuum filter, a product with many industrial applications. Campbell's salesmen were capable of selling it to existing customers, but they were not familiar with the mining and metallurgical market, a potentially lucrative one for the filter. "Rather than hiring new salesmen," says Campbell, "we decided to reach buyers through $25,000 to $30,000 worth of ads in business publications. We'll screen the inquiries that result and pass the most promising ones on to the sales force for follow-up."

Campbell is far from alone in using his business publication advertising in a new way to enhance his company's total selling effort. As sales budgets get tighter, buyers harder to convince, and selling costs more astronomical, sales and marketing executives are working hard at making their business ads an even more effective selling tool. Not everyone is substituting ads for new salesmen, but rare indeed is the manager who is not taking steps to get a bigger sales bang from every advertising dollar he spends. Here, based on the results of nationwide interviews conducted last month by *Sales Management* editors, are what sales executives are now doing or plan to do to achieve just that:

1. Setting specific objectives for their business publication ads. Most marketing departments spell out the goals they want their ads to attain. "We give our agency, Campbell-Mithun in Minneapolis, specific objectives," says Dick Yakel, general sales manager for 3M's Decorative Products Div. "Then we have final approval over their plan. In general, we don't expect our ads to produce leads, but we want them to condition the buyer so that when our salesman calls, he'll say, Oh, yes, I've heard of you people."

More business publication ads are being written and placed to answer specific customer objections about the product or service being sold. Caterpillar Tractor, for example, is running ads to convince price-conscious customers that Caterpillar equipment, though initially expensive, will save money in the long run because of low maintenance costs and high trade-in value. "It's a major selling problem in certain markets," admits dealer promotion representative Greg Towles. "The ad campaign we're running in industry magazines, based on 'total cost evaluation,' helps to tell the customer that there's more to costs than the purchase price."

2. Building flexibility into ad programs to meet those objectives. Sales Management's survey also shows that most companies are pegging their ad expenditures to a percentage of sales. Often, companies try to avoid placing a rigid limit on ad spending to gain greater flexibility. Clayton Ryder, marketing director of Allen-Bradley's Electronics Div., explains his division's attitude: "We try not to put too tight a straitjacket on our advertising. If we think it will be worthwhile to spend more to achieve a certain goal, we'll do it."

Today's economic conditions are also prompting many to change their ad plans. "If our sales were to be seriously affected by the recession, we might spend a higher percentage than normal to stimulate new business," says John Reick, marketing manager for Hillyard Chemical. (Table 1, on page 78, from *Sales Management's 1975 Survey of Selling Costs,* shows some typical advertising/sales ratios.)

3. Using ads to cut their selling costs. The expense of adding a single salesman, says *SM's Survey of Selling Costs,* can be as high as $32,000. Once the salesman is in the field, his cost per call can reach $56 (see Table 2, page 79). Up against that kind of outlay, companies are discovering that it does indeed pay to advertise.

Marketers also report a new willingness to test a market by advertising in it *before* adding men to the sales force, thereby easing the strain on the sales budget. Bird Machine's Campbell says, "We may find we'll eventually need more salesmen if we are to sell customers in our new mining and metallurgical market. Right now, we want our ads targeted at that market to tell us how much demand there is."

There is, however, a danger of doing too much advertising before a sales force is in place to handle sales. "If you're advertising to arouse interest, that's one thing," says Guy Shelley, market operations manager for 3M's Decorative Products Div. "But if you want to close the sale, you'd better have salesmen available to follow through. You don't want to create an appetite that you can't satisfy."

4. Playing a more active role in selecting media. As part of their closer vigilance of all phases of their advertising, most sales executives require ad agencies to submit proposed media schedules for approval. With that increase in media scrutiny, companies are becoming more inclined to add or delete specific publications. "We want to be certain that we're reaching the right people with our ads," says Allen-Bradley's Ryder. Often, advertisers rely on the business publications they advertise in to help them get to the "right" people. "Many publishers can now satisfy all of their customers' needs for sales-prospect lists, to be used for direct mail or for salesmen's routing," says James Mulholland Jr., president of Hayden Publishing.

5. Playing a more active role in deciding ad themes. Meetings between sales and advertising personnel—previously a rare event in many companies—are becoming common. Their purpose is usually twofold: to help ad men "speak the language" of the marketplace and to suggest to them what must be in an ad if it is to catch the attention of buyers. In addition, many companies like their ads to be built around case histories that show how customers have prospered by using the advertiser's products or services. The necessary details most often are supplied by the sales force.

At Dorr-Oliver, Stamford, Conn., product manager Bob Honeychurch recently

Table 1 / Advertising As A Share Of Sales By Size Of Firm

Industry	Companies Grouped by Size of Total Assets ($000)					
	Under $10,000	$10,000-$24,999	$25,000-$49,999	$50,000-$99,999	$100,000-$249,999	$250,000 & More
	Advertising as a Percent of Sales					
All-Manufacturing	0.70%	1.10%	1.54%	1.38%	1.82%	1.46%
Food	0.09	1.49	1.33	2.36	2.41	3.68
Tobacco	0.43	3.05	6.97	0.97	4.71	4.77
Textile mill products	0.26	0.40	0.50	0.47	1.42	0.97
Apparel	0.45	0.91	1.63	1.21	1.25	2.35
Lumber & wood products (exc. furn.)	0.04	0.28	0.57	0.41	0.71	0.56
Furniture & fixtures	1.00	1.01	2.66	1.46	4.06	—[1]
Paper	0.25	0.48	0.65	0.95	0.29	1.22
Printing & publishing	0.63	1.39	1.22	0.91	1.88	0.91
Chemicals	1.63	2.58	6.26	2.65	5.47	3.96
Petroleum refining	0.54	0.41	0.09	2.21	1.07	0.43
Rubber & plastics	0.53	0.75	0.78	0.95	0.91	1.67
Leather	0.59	2.21	2.27	3.06	3.86	1.49
Stone, clay, & glass	0.35	0.42	0.97	0.50	0.49	0.81
Primary metal	0.15	0.16	0.03	0.29	0.25	0.38
Fabricated metal	0.46	0.72	0.65	0.79	0.64	1.41
Nonelectrical machinery	0.84	1.13	0.89	0.96	1.03	0.71
Electrical equip. & supplies	1.09	1.12	1.03	0.91	1.54	1.56
Motor vehicles & equipment	0.05	0.57	0.75	0.77	0.95	0.68
Trans. equip. (exc. motor vehicles)	0.64	0.49	0.52	0.91	0.43	0.24
Scientif. inst., photo., & watches	1.84	1.37	1.64	0.98	3.26	3.09

[1] No company in this category.
Note: Data cover corporation income tax returns with fiscal periods ended July 1971 through June 1972.
Source: *Sales Management's 1975 Survey of Selling Costs.*

suggested that the company promote its new exchange program whereby customers can replace centrifuges without suffering downtime. Honeychurch's idea pleased Tom Bier, the firm's centrifuge marketing specialist. "There are five companies in our industry selling good products," Bier says. "But we are the only one with this kind of an exchange program. It's a valid sales assist."

6. *Telling salesmen more about ads.* Sales meetings agendas more frequently include time for showing salesmen the next ad campaign. Companies are also soliciting salesmen more often for their reactions to *future* ads—and listening to their reactions. Also, more salesmen are being supplied with ad schedules to ensure that they can tailor their presentations to the ads.

"We send advance copies of all ads to our salesmen and we tell them where they'll be appearing," says Ed Roth, marketing development manager for FMC's Industrial Chemical Div. "They may not be excited by some of the ads, but if it's one telling about a new product or a new process, it's a different proposition. Our salesmen will then even call the advertising staff, encouraging it to 'Keep it coming.' "

Table 2 / Direct Cost Per Salesman's Call

Type Of Salesman		Direct Sales Cost	Average Calls Per Year		Cost Per Salesman's Call[1]	
			Territory A	Territory B	Territory A	Territory B
Account	R*	$15,000-$24,000	956-1,434	478-717	$10-$25	$21-$50
Representative	M*	$19,500	1,195	598	$16	$33
Detail	R	$14,000-$20,000	1,434-2,390	956-1,434	$ 6-$14	$10-$21
Salesman	M	$17,000	1,912	1,195	$9	$14
Sales	R	$23,000-$32,000	760-1,330	570-760	$17-$42	$30-$56
Engineer	M	$27,500	1,045	665	$26	$41
Industrial	R	$19,000-$26,000	1,434-1,912	717-1,195	$10-$18	$16-$36
Products Salesman	M	$22,500	1,673	956	$13	$24
Service	R	$17,000-$26,000	1,912-2,390	956-1,434	$ 7-$14	$12-$27
Salesman	M	$21,500	2,151	1,195	$10	$18

*R Range of calls.
*M Mean number of calls.

Note: [1] Direct cost per salesman's call $= \dfrac{\text{direct sales cost}}{\text{average calls per year.}}$

Source: *Sales Management's 1975 Survey of Selling Costs.*

7. *Providing more support materials to back up the ad message.* In addition to informing salesmen about what their advertising will be saying and when, most companies provide salesmen with preprints or reprints of the ads to give to their accounts. Some companies give their men specially designed sales promotion aids that complement the ad message.

"If you can get your advertising, your sales promotion literature, and your salesmen all saying the same thing, you have a better chance of being heard," says 3M's Shelley. Accordingly, his division will often take a magazine ad and make it the center spread of a four-page salesman's handout. Similarly, Caterpillar provides its dealers with a series of direct mail pieces that they send to prospects; the material is based on, and thus augments, the "Total Cost Evaluation" theme Caterpillar uses in its ads.

8. *Following up ad leads more selectively.* Nearly every sales executive that *Sales Management* editors talked with reported that reforms are underway, accomplished, or planned in their handling of ad-inspired inquiries. The problem is a universal one: how to spot the genuinely interested buyers among the "literature collectors" and "thesis writers." Compounding it is, once again, the growing cost of sending a salesman on a follow-up mission and the sheer volume of inquiries that business publication ads generate, a figure estimated in the millions annually.

FMC's Industrial Chemical Div. now has a lab technician either telephone or personally visit likely prospects who respond to printed material that the division routinely sends out each time a coupon or bingo card is received. Only if the prospect "passes" the technician's screening is a salesman dispatched, armed with a history of everything that has transpired in the follow-up before he was called in.

At Techbuilt, Spring Valley, N.Y., marketing vice president Gerald Cutler re-organized the sales force when he discovered that 50% of inquiries, most touched off by ads in consumer magazines, were not being followed up.

SM, June 2, 1975, pp. 39–42.

How to Organize Yourself for National Accounts Selling

by J. H. Morris, Jr., Merchandising/National Accounts Manager, Advanced Drainage Systems

A tailored national accounts program for selling to the mass merchandisers is vital for anyone with consumer-oriented products who expects to achieve maximum growth in the 1970s and beyond. It is not news that accounts like Lowe's, Moore's, Wickes', etc., in the building materials market, and J. C. Penney, K Mart, etc., in the general merchandise category, are big—and determined to get still bigger. You could well find yourself reading about your competition if your company doesn't have a coordinated selling-and-servicing approach for such corporate accounts. Yet few firms have a national accounts approach.

Let's assume that you have decided to commit yourself to developing—or up-grading—your own national accounts program. How do you proceed? Before doing anything else, make a firm commitment to provide the full support needed by an operation that may one day be one of the largest profit-producers you have. For example, don't name a national accounts sales manager, only to hamstring him by having him work under a divisional sales operation. He will need to be autonomous, free to work directly with all line and staff personnel in order to coordinate and direct the most effective sales and support program possible. He should also report directly to the president or marketing vice president of your company.

Once you've committed yourself to providing all the necessary support, you're ready to embark on the following program.

1. PICK YOUR ACCOUNTS

Make up a list of the target accounts you can most effectively service. It goes without saying (although I'll say it) that you should sell only what you can deliver. Remember that your performance will be judged by the client, starting with his initial order.

J. H. Morris, Jr., joined Armstrong Cork as a salesman soon after his military service. He be-came the company's first national accounts executive and was instrumental in winning such national accounts as J. C. Penney and K Mart. Morris's operation became a multimillion-dollar sales producer in less than a year. He is currently merchandising/national accounts manager for Advanced Drainage Systems, Columbus, Ohio, the nation's largest supplier to major building material chain accounts.

Your account-selection list should be based on, among other things, your production capabilities, the size of the account, the geographical area involved, your dominance in the marketplace, the account's payment record, the amount of merchandising required, your current sales commitments, and the cost to you of doing business with the client.

You no doubt already know the key national accounts in your markets; so you can formulate a list immediately. If you don't, *Chain Store Guide* (2 Park Ave., New York, N.Y. 10016) publishes a directory of department, discount, and general merchandise stores, plus home centers and hardware chains. *Building Supply News's* "Top 500 Report" (5 S. Wabash Ave., Chicago 60603), published each January, is an excellent source for the building materials industry. Other publications cover other markets, among them *Chemical Engineering's Equipment Buyers' Guide,* the *Thomas Register,* and numerous specialized Chilton buying guides. Your field salesmen will also be able to supply valuable information.

2. RESEARCH ACCOUNTS THOROUGHLY

Before a national accounts presentation is attempted, or even considered, the national accounts sales manager should be thoroughly familiar with the client, from top to bottom, side to side. One of the best ways I know of to achieve that is for the national accounts manager to get out of his office and call on as many retail locations as possible, listening to what the store manager, retail salesmen, warehousemen, and others have to say about the account you're trying to sell. Some of the questions on his list should be as follows:

How does the company operate? What are its problems? How does it view his products?

Does it central warehouse or take direct shipments?

Do the store managers have any buying authority at all or is that function left to a central purchasing office at the headquarters level?

What is its breakout of sales builder/contractor vs. consumer trade?

It is essential for the national accounts manager to discover personally all he can about the client. D&B reports, *Standard & Poor's,* articles appearing in business publications, and annual reports will help him supplement his knowledge of the prospect. Also, he should never pass up opportunities to talk with other national accounts managers who you know have good programs with the account you plan to approach. You'll discover that most will be eager to talk about their successes. If you're willing to listen, you'll get information that can be priceless in setting up your own program.

3. CREATE YOUR PROPOSAL

Let's assume that you're the new national accounts manager at your company and that you've done your homework—you've selected the top potential accounts in your markets and know all there is to know about how they operate. Now comes the part that can make or break you—the properly constructed, specific proposal that is the heart of your sales presentation.

Many of us still enter the buyer's office with a sample, a smile, a price (not always in that order), and a "walk him around, talk him to death" presentation. Managers who enter that way usually leave the same way they came in: minus anything even resembling an order.

Here are some of the elements you should consider when putting together your national account proposal:

Give the buyer information about your company. Tell him who you are and what you have accomplished in your industry. Be brief, but be specific. Give your national distribution and the number of your distributing points. If you're one of the largest advertisers, say so. If you're the biggest in your industry, say so. Put all your plusses into a three- or four-sentence opening.

If you're going in with a product not now stocked by the account, describe the industry, the growth potential of the product, and the profitable growth that other, similar accounts have experienced. Any pertinent information you have obtained from your marketing research people should be included here.

Explain the terms, the F.O.B. point, and current shipping schedules. *Be realistic.*

From your homework, recommend from national and local best-selling items the products the account should stock. Go with proven winners and don't expect the large chain to pioneer any product test program. . . .

At this point, review all the retail support you can provide to the individual retail outlets. Include the following elements:
   a. Display assistance—setup and maintenance
   b. Local sales training meetings
   c. Product literature, product information sheets, and promotional aids
   d. Local market knowledge and merchandising help
   e. Assistance to retail salesmen with contractor and builder calls
   f. Consumer do-it-yourself clinics, etc.

If there is to be an advertising and promotion allowance (usually 2%-3% of sales) as part of your total program, outline all the specifics in this section of the proposal. Also, indicate or give suggestions on how this money can be most effectively spent in promoting your product. Remember, you're the expert.

Prepare this section as a separate page in your proposal; entitle it "Account Custom Service Program Information Sheet." Under this section list this information:

The name, address, and any flattering information on the account

The name and address of the national account executive in your company responsible for the total sales coordination between your firm and the account

The approved products on the national account basis

Name and address of the order department contact for the account

Name and address of the local sales contact for the account

Any additional information directly related to the sales and service of the
   account
Note: Be flexible. Design your proposal/presentation to fit the requirements of
the account. Don't expect the large mass merchandiser to adjust his buying methods
to meet your selling procedures.

As a final section of your proposal, you may consider adding the following
   material:
   a. List of distribution points
   b. Map showing manufacturing locations, regional offices, sales routes, etc.
   c. Display illustrations
   d. Pictures of products being recommended
   e. Any additional information about advertising, promotions, product knowl-
      edge, etc.

Now you've made your presentation and sold the program. At this point, I want
to add one last piece of advice. Your entire program, from initial sales presentation
to local support and training, should be company owned, operated, and directed.
Don't go to all the trouble of formulating an effective national accounts program
and then expect your independent distributors' salesmen to provide the retail support necessary to make the program go at its most important point—where the consumer meets the retail salesperson selling your product.

If you don't sign the paychecks for all involved, you don't have control of your
whole program. The retail support function must be controlled by your own marketing representatives. When volume and profits permit, initiate your own national
accounts sales force under national accounts executives responsible for a selected
number of chain accounts and charged with accomplishing all retail support.

National accounts selling is the most sophisticated sales challenge of all. It
requires the most thorough preparation and the most detailed followthrough. It's
also most rewarding.

SM, December 9, 1974, pp. 29–31.

Section 12 / Planning Your Sales Presentation

Hasbro Plays to Win

[An *SM* report on Hasbro Industries, a company whose sales and earnings are improving, despite the economy, because of innovative sales/marketing.]

Most American families may not have been forced to fill the kiddies' stockings with coal last Christmas, but they definitely trod more cautiously in toy departments than in the past. Not only did that put a lot of elves on the unemployment line but it dampened holiday spirits for toy marketers because anticipated fourth-quarter reorders never materialized. The glum look in fun and games still continues, with retailers sitting on carry-over inventory and the weak economy slowing the rate at which those stocks diminish.

But Hasbro Industries, Pawtucket, R.I., which shared the industry's fate last year, is determined to bounce back. "Our sales are up 8%-9% for the first quarter," says sales vice president Jack McCrory. "From the way future orders are coming in, we'll be up 15% to 20% for the year, definitely outpacing our competition."

Hasbro (Hassenfeld Brothers until 1968) gets virtually all its revenues from sales of toys (about 80%) and school supplies (20%). McCrory is concerned strictly with toys (school supplies are a separate operation, sold through manufacturers' representatives) and he has had cause for worry. Last year, corporate sales dipped to $86.6 million from $92.5 million in 1973. Toy sales slid from $75.9 million to $67.4 million, toy profits from $427,000 to $218,000.

To brighten this year's results, McCrory is counting on a strengthened marketing effort. Hasbro, which until recently relied on reps for toy sales as well, finished the conversion to a direct sales force in 1973. Now, there are four regional managers and 31 salesmen. "We're going back to basics," McCrory says, "and concentrating on the fundamentals of selling. For example, we're insisting that all our salesmen, no matter how experienced in the industry, carefully prepare for each call in advance."

If the call is likely to result in writing an order, Hasbro salesmen must make up a suggested order beforehand. "You have to present it tactfully," he cautions, "so that the buyer doesn't feel that you're telling him what to do. But if it's presented as an aid to the buyer, a recommendation as to which items are best for him, it's very effective. Our salesmen are then on the offensive, and the buyer is talking about what might come off that list, rather than what should go on."

McCrory also requires his salesmen to turn in their precall lists along with the actual orders. In that way, regional managers can (1) be certain that salesmen are truly preparing for calls, (2) see if there are many items salesmen aren't emphasizing enough, and (3) learn which items seem to be encountering buyer resistance.

To spur his salesmen on, McCrory has two incentive compensation plans for 1975, which he calls short-term and long-term. The first is based on a salesman's total volume each month, from February through May, when most toy orders are written. "We do it month by month so that a man who falls behind early won't give up on the whole thing," he says.

The long-term plan is based on total volume for the year, plus increased distribution—the number of items a man actually puts on retail shelves—for each account. That, McCrory says, keeps his salesmen servicing their accounts all the way through Christmas. With both of those plans, a successful salesman will be able to earn 15%–20% of his salary in bonus money.

Backing up the sales effort is an ad budget increased 15% over 1974, to $9 million. Most of that is destined for TV, with emphasis on children's shows. But the current uproar over "kidvid" advertising isn't forcing Hasbro to change its pitch. "We made the big move in the early 1970s," McCrory explains, "when we took G.I. Joe—our leading line—out of the military and made him into an adventure character. Now he goes on safaris and so on. Benton & Bowles, our agency, has been tremendously helpful in implementing this." Hasbro runs only "clean ads," he says, approved by the National Assn. of Broadcasters.

The switch apparently has bolstered G.I. Joe's sales as well as his image. Sales of Joe and his "Adventure Team" have shot up from $7 million in 1970 to $22 million last year. G.I. Joe and Hasbro's Romper Room line, the second biggest seller, together account for nearly 60% of corporate toy sales.

Now McCrory and his sales force are out to achieve similar results for the entire toy line. If, meanwhile, they're seeking new adventure situations for Joe, they could consider making him a true hero: a salesman winning out against the recession of 1975.

SM, May 5, 1975, p. 23.

The tough economy and a market that's ripe for consultative selling
are just two reasons they're
Selling Smarter in Incentives

by Sally Scanlon, Associate Editor

A band welcomed the Million Dollar Leaders as limos carrying them and their wives pulled up in front of Jurys Hotel in Dublin a few weeks ago. During their stay, the couples wined and dined from crystal and china in candlelit Irish castles. They rode chauffeured limousines to and from shopping and sightseeing activities. Tasteful little gifts sometimes surprised them in their hotel rooms. And before flying back home to another year of selling, each salesman and manager on the trip received a plaque recognizing his achievement: selling over $1 million in business for Maritz, one of the country's top incentive companies.

[This salesman's contest] is but one example of how most leading companies in the $2 billion sales and dealer incentive industry practice what they preach. Sperry & Hutchinson recently took its top 15 incentive producers and their wives to Puerto Rico. E.F. MacDonald has two honors clubs, which pay off in merchandise and travel as well as recognition. Carlson Companies' Performance Incentives Corp., Minneapolis, and Top Value Enterprises, Dayton, run year-long point programs for their account executives with both merchandise and travel awards. Maritz, St. Louis, and Business Incentives, Minneapolis, have separate merchandise and travel programs for their account executives.

BI, for example, awards merchandise for increased sales, travel for increased bookings. Top merchandise prizes this year included installation of a complete home stereo system for one winner and the privilege of driving a Cadillac Eldorado for a year for another. In addition, 28 sales leaders and their wives went on a week-long trip to Mexico earlier this month.

"Our salesmen are probably even more receptive to incentives than our clients' salesmen because our men believe in incentives so strongly," says BI president Guy Schoenecker, voicing the opinion of most top executives in the industry. Also, as Top Value regional manager George Glaskin puts it, "We'd be hard pressed to convince prospects of our belief in the value of incentive programs if we didn't use them ourselves."

INCENTIVE USAGE GROWS

The top practitioners' faith in incentives obviously has paid off in market share. Edwin P. Johnson, vice president, incentive operations, Sperry & Hutchinson, estimates that as in most industries, 20% of the companies in incentives do 80% of the business. E. F. MacDonald, Maritz, and S&H lead the parade along with other full-service incentive houses and leading premium reps. Scrambling for the remaining business are manufacturers, smaller premiums reps, airlines, hotels, sales promotion agencies, and just about any other company that has the slightest hope of grabbing a piece of the incentive action. . . .

How fast the action is these days is difficult to determine. Since 1967, sales of incentives have doubled, . . . but there's no question that product shortages and inflation have affected the growth rate this year. That doesn't keep incentive men from being optimistic, of course. "A lot of users are coming back on-stream," says Rutgers G. Van Brunt Jr., vice president and director of marketing for Maritz. "Next year will be outstanding for us, and 1976 will be even better unless something unforeseen crops up on the economic and political scene."

Industry leaders are also confident about the long-term prospects for incentives.

George C. Gilfillen Jr., chairman of E. F. MacDonald, told stockholders earlier this year: "Incentive programs have become as firmly entrenched within the budget structures of modern marketers as advertising and sales promotion. . . . They will continue to play an ever more important role in individual and corporate growth."

THE STRATEGY OF CONSULTATIVE SELLING

One strategy that is paying off for incentive companies is the increasing use of consultative selling. Hardly a new idea in the industry, it is nevertheless winning a lot of converts during the present period of economic uncertainty. Many clients of incentive suppliers feel the change is long overdue. For instance, Donald Borgwardt, West Bend's communications and sales promotion manager, complains that he used five different full-service houses in as many years in search of one that's "truly interested in our corporate goals." Says Toro's senior product manager, Gary Holland, who runs his company's incentive programs: "If you don't know what you want, you can really get hurt. The supplier is likely to slip something off the shelf and hand it to you. It may be a great program, but not for *your dealers.*"

CONSULTATIVE-ORIENTED SALESMEN NEEDED

Robert B. Nagel, manager, distributor markets, Owens-Illinois's Lily Div., agrees. Says Nagel, "We're looking for a supplier who will be a consultant: look at our business, talk with our field sales managers and salesmen, then present a program that will help us solve our sales problems. Often supplier salesmen just want to hand you a stock program."

Jogged by such complaints and faced with intensifying competition, incentive industry sales executives are reexamining their salesmen's approaches to prospecting, probing, and presenting programs. Hyatt Hotels, for example, is setting up a corporate incentive group separate from its meetings and conventions staff to give incentive users better service. Waltham has just given its 29 watch salesmen special sales aids to make them more effective in the incentive area. Bulova is preparing specific presentations for its premium reps. Performance Incentives Corp. took its 40 field salesmen and managers to Florida last year to train them in consultative selling. The agenda included an eight-step selling format, which PIC salesmen use as a guide from initial contact with prospects through post-program evaluation.

The change in PIC's approach is a good example of the way incentive companies are rethinking their sales activities. Plagued three years ago by low profits, PIC decided to study the attitudes of both its own salesmen and top decision-makers in user industries. "We discovered," says president William F. Penwell, "that our salesmen saw no difference between us and our competitors—and maybe they even felt a bit inferior."

CUSTOMER SURVEY RATES INDIVIDUAL SALESMEN AS KEY TO SUPPLIER SUCCESS

The study of users, though not as simple, was even more revealing. Penwell hired a consultant to find out what decision makers in about 40 large companies thought of (1) the incentive industry as a whole, (2) specific incentive companies, and (3) premium and incentive salesmen. He found that the industry had a fairly good reputation, but no single company stood out in interviewees' minds. More important, they told him that their opinion of the individual salesman, rather than of the company, was the key to selecting a supplier. Many interviewees complained that incentive salesmen waste their time. Like Owens-Illinois's Nagel, they said they wanted salesmen who would become part of their marketing team and help them solve problems.

To satisfy them, PIC is upgrading its sales force. After the Florida training session, it began recruiting men with more education and broader business experience, especially in marketing. It also changed its compensation program to get the men to call on only large accounts. Says Penwell, "We no longer pay a commission on small business."

FOR SUCCESS—SALESMAN MUST KNOW HIS PROSPECT'S INDUSTRY AND SALES PROBLEMS

To be consultative, the incentive salesman has to broaden his perspective. If he hopes to sell an entire program, rather than just a bushel of prizes, he must find out about the prospect's industry and sales problems. Says BI's Schoenecker: "If you want to provide a successful program for the client, it's essential to have your salesman do his market research and help the client set realistic goals." Before he gets very far, he must know the prospect's distribution system, sales goals, and how much the company can spend to attain them. He also must have an accurate reading on the size of the sales force and on the age and sex of its members.

The usual probing technique, especially among large companies, is to have salesmen follow up promising leads gleaned from advertising and trade show contacts, in-house research, selective direct mail, and word-of-mouth recommendations. During the call, a salesman will describe his company, perhaps relate success stories, and try to find out more about the prospect's needs.

If the incentive company has a showroom or a headquarters staffed with creative and administrative experts, the salesman probably will invite the prospect to visit it. Then, if the prospect is sufficiently interested, the salesman will complete his research and, with in-house help, prepare a custom presentation of the program he thinks will help the prospect reach his sales goals or solve specific problems.

When a key account is involved (big incentive companies like to talk in terms of six figures), a good salesman's research can involve a lot of legwork. At Top Value, for example, Robert H. MacKay, assistant to the Incentive Div. vice president, says the account executive often goes out and talks with the prospect's sales managers and distributors. He may even travel with its salesmen to find out what objections they get from buyers and what the competition is doing. "That way our marketing team can put together a very specific presentation," MacKay says, adding that his company closes "a high percentage" of such sales.

At S&H, after an account executive does his initial calling and market research, he confers with the company's task force group. The group, which sets priorities on programs, includes national sales manager Merritt Anderson, marketing services manager Richard Shea, the account executive's regional sales manager, and, usually, a market researcher. It evaluates the salesman's information and decides what type of presentation the company should give. If the prospective account is large, S&H, like Top Value, makes a team presentation. The object, of course, is to convince the buyer (and his management) that the supplier has the resources to provide a successful program and is willing to put them to work.

HANDLING OBJECTIONS THE CONSULTATIVE SELLING WAY

One of the key areas where consultative selling comes to the rescue is in handling the objections of a potential client. If the prospect is new to incentives, he may object that he's afraid an incentive will become a crutch that he can't discard without alienating salesmen or dealers. "I tell him, So what if your men get hooked," says William G. Christophere, incentive marketing director, EGR Communications' Travel International Div., New York City. Says Christophere, "If the program is properly structured, it's geared to the user's profits, and it's also giving him residual benefits, such as goodwill." Thus Christophere tells the prospect that if his first program is a success, it is true that he'll have to top it next year. "But I show him that it won't have to cost him more," he says. "It'll just have to be more creative. And that's our job, not his."

Business Incentives' top account executive, Dick Metzger, says, "I answer objections in terms of return on investment. What the buyer spends is in proportion to the profits he makes. Also, if he ever has to turn it off, it's easier to take away a merchandise or travel incentive than it is to stop paying a cash bonus. A salesman gets to thinking of a bonus as part of his salary."

AFTER SALE FOLLOW-UP AND FOLLOW-THROUGH

After he's closed the sale and a program is in the works, the salesman's job is to keep track of promotional mailings and to check for hidden weaknesses that could undermine its success. For example, Top Value's MacKay says that a change in the competition's sales practices could put a crimp in a client's incentive plan. The alert incentive salesman, MacKay says, might help circumvent the problem by working with the client to make a few changes in the program's structure.

It's also up to the salesman to keep users informed of any problems with the pay-off. For example, until the middle of last month, B. F. Goodrich planned to take its top dealers on a cruise of the Mediterranean and Black seas this fall. The political crisis in Cyprus scuttled that plan, causing Goodrich and its supplier, PIC, to change course and use a previously arranged Plan "B," which called for cruising friendlier waters. Goodrich sales promotion manager Larry Schrader says he and PIC regional vice president Richard S. Sowerbutt were in constant touch on political developments. Together, they made the decision to switch plans.

Most alternatives are less dramatic. They involve substitution of merchandise or changes in delivery dates. Nonetheless, buyers complain, this is the area in which incentive salesmen fail them most frequently. A typical comment: "Salesmen won't level with you about the supply and delivery situation. They're continually over-optimistic and their record doesn't justify it."

SALES SUCCESS DEPENDS ON SERVICE HE PROVIDES

A few buyers say they have gotten so disgusted with the lack of follow-up from salesmen that they now do all incentive work themselves, including negotiations for merchandise and travel. Most, however, try to solve the problem by sticking with salesmen who come through for them. Usually, this means dealing with from one to four firms on a fairly consistent basis. As Harry Klemm, marketing director, Jafra Cosmetics, Malibu, Cal., says, "The salesman's greatest asset is the service he can provide. I haven't time to follow through on all the details; I expect him to do that."

Numerically, of course, the majority of sales and dealer incentives are sold by the industry's smaller suppliers, most of which do not provide the full-line services of the large houses. Their customer is the man who either prefers to dream up his own programs or whose budget is too small to interest the big companies. In-depth consultative selling is practiced by relatively few of the smaller suppliers for the obvious reason that they have neither the time nor the manpower to do it.

SALESMEN'S COMPENSATION

The typical premium rep's salesman works on straight commission and sells 10 to 20 product lines or more. He often turns to manufacturers for help in putting to-gether proposals and closing the sale.

In contrast, an account executive for an organization such as Maritz is paid salary and commission, is offered incentives from his own company, and handles three or four major accounts at most. The company has three or four creative people to back up each man in the field. Nonetheless, buyers say smart manufacturer and rep salesmen are probing more than before and offering better service.

"More and more of our clients are becoming interested in the collateral service we can provide," says A. Rick Kash, president of Roberts Incentives, a small Chicago promotional agency. Kash's company handles incentive sales for six national apparel companies and sells through 28 manufacturers' rep organizations. He offers buyers a standard package of 15 mailing pieces that they can use to promote their sales and dealer programs.

PLANNING THE PRESENTATION AND SALES STRATEGIES STRESSED IN TRAINING

Like Kash, Bulova's Earl C. Lynch, national director, Presentation and Incentive Div., identifies a trend to more professional, specific, and creative presentations by industry salesmen. He says Bulova, which depends on reps for 95% of its incentive sales, now is writing presentations for them on a selective basis. "We approach it in one of two ways," Lynch says. "Either we make the initial call with the rep or he sends us the information he gathers." In either case, Bulova then writes up the proposal that the rep presents.

Manufacturers also help reps with leads and case histories, and, generally, make some attempt to train them in the most effective strategies to use in selling their lines. Joint sales calls and product literature are the usual training methods. But a few companies make more effort. Black & Decker, for example, brings new reps to its Towson, Md., headquarters for two to three days of formal sales training.

When it comes to training a new incentive salesman, however, the methods used depend mainly on the size of the company. Major suppliers have formal programs. Smaller ones use an on-the-job approach. Both, however, agree that it takes the average man about two years to get established and really start producing. "Time and experience are the only factors that will really train a man," says Al Stein, president, Promotions With Results, Cincinnati, who echoes a familiar industry refrain. But, Stein adds, "a man can accelerate his growth by really learning the product and doing other homework, such as reading industry trade magazines."

EFFICIENT SALES TERRITORY COVERAGE HIGHLY IMPORTANT

"Coverage is the important thing in our business," says G. W. "Joe" Manuel, vice president, Robert F. Sanford Co., Mountain Lakes, N.J., who sold Nestlé buyers the program that won NPSE's award for 1973's best dealer incentive. Says Manuel, "Every company is different in what it wants. Some just want product. Others want the salesman involved up to his teeth. You never know where sales are going to come from. But if you're out there talking to enough of your accounts, you'll sell."

In the future, Manuel and his colleagues in industry companies big and small may be selling a lot more than sales and dealer incentives. Alarmed by the setback in traditional incentive programs earlier this year, the industry is accelerating its effort to tap new markets. Opportunities lie in areas such as promoting plant safety, increasing productivity, cutting absenteeism, getting people to work overtime, recruiting, training, and speeding order processing.

As S&H's vice president Johnson puts it, "The incentive business has just scratched the surface of its applications to American industry." And it's certainly worth sharpening sales tactics to get at the potential sales underneath.

SM, September 23, 1974, pp. 35-41.

The "chauvinistic" and "liberated" letters illustrate the following article, "Liberate Your Sales Letters."

CHAUVINISTIC

Dear Mrs. Hepner:

Pleasing your husband is no doubt your main goal in life.

Let's face it. It just makes you feel tremendous when you win praise for your cooking. A "gourmet" dinner makes that man in your life sit up and take notice—of YOU.

To help you in your battle for praise, I'm enclosing a Discount Certificate. It entitles you to 10% off on today's really new and different cookbook, Cooking to Please Your Man, by Amy Edwards, a wife and mother of five children.

Do order your copy today—it'll take only a minute between your household chores. (Just fill out the handy order form enclosed.) You'll soon be winning more praise from your man than you can handle.

And that's a promise!

Sincerely,

Al Hemp

LIBERATED

Dear Ms. Hepner:

Everybody loves to eat!

And that includes Mom, Dad, Junior, Sis, single people, young people—everybody! Although you, no doubt, enjoy receiving praise for your "gourmet specials," what's more important to you is becoming the kind of cook YOU want to be.

This is why I'm particularly happy to enclose a Discount Certificate. It entitles you to 10% off on today's new and different cookbook, Cooking to Please YOU, by Amy Edwards.

Do order your copy today—it'll take only a minute. (Just fill out the handy order form enclosed.) You'll soon be pleasing—really pleasing—yourself, and winning praise, too, for your kitchen creations.

Sincerely,

Al Hemp

Liberate Your Sales Letters

by Dr. Luther A. Brock, Professor of Business Communications, North Texas State University

The sales director of a large mail order firm that specializes in selling architectural products complains that his latest sales letter didn't go over very well in certain quarters. What was so different about the letter that earned it such a poor showing? *"Nothing* was different about it," he says. "We've been sending out letters like it for years."

Indeed he has—and that's his problem. In his letter were such time-honored sentences as these:

"Surveys show these 'how to' manuals are invaluable to any man in the field of architecture."

"You're busy. Not only are you a man who's a professional but you're also a busy man. One who simply doesn't have time to. . . ."

You have spotted the sales director's problem. Matter of fact, so has he. At last count, he's had 11 letters of complaint from women architects who received his mailing, every one of whom agrees with the architect in Indiana who wrote saying she would *never* buy from a firm that is "so blatantly and obviously chauvinistic."

The sales director never intended to be chauvinistic, of course. Keelhaul him instead for writing a sales letter that was badly out of joint with the times. No matter if you're pro or con about today's feminist movement, your sales letters are being directly affected by that revolution.

Times they are a-changin'. The old stereotypes no longer hold true. Today's men sew, crochet, embroider, do all sorts of things once reserved for women. Rosey Grier, a man's man if ever there was one, has a new book out, *Needlepoint for Men.* I doubt that there's a man alive who has the courage to tangle with Rosey about his choice of pastimes.

According to Shirley Wilkins, a vice president at the Roper Organization, nearly half of the 3,000 women who participated in the just-completed Virginia Slims American Women's Opinion Poll, conducted by Roper, prefer a marriage where husband and wife share work, homemaking, and child-rearing responsibilities, to the traditional marriage in which the husband wins the wages and the wife manages the home.

Indeed, women today can be purchasing agents who buy lathes as well as homemakers who buy fix-it kits. They take karate lessons. They drive trucks. They are leaders in virtually every profession. Men and women are becoming persons first, male or female second. The point is that letters that take it for granted that men will make the buying decision are dead letters.

Here are ways you can liberate your sales letters:

Unless you know for certain that your next sales letter will be read by men only or by women only, you must watch out for all gender references. Many firms are finding that it's wiser and safer to avoid any reference to sex (gender, that is) when their letters mention such things as occupations, hobbies, or lifestyles.

Some sales managers are being tricky—they use "he or she" or "him and her" each time they need to refer to gender. But such letters have a tendency to sound awkward. Consider these:

"Your customer will really take to these raised-letter business cards. Hand one to him or her and notice how he or she reacts."

Sometimes you can get away with using a plural form, such as "they" or "them."

"Your customers will really take to these raised-letter business cards. Hand one to them and notice how they react."

Of course, the problem with that solution is that you cannot hand *one card* to a "them." You hand one card to one person, a him or a her. Probably the best way to escape here is to make the entire reference plural:

"Your customers will really take to these raised-letter business cards. Let them take one glance—and notice how they react."

Take the traditional salutation *Gentlemen.* This is usually used when you're writing to a firm as a whole. Because a firm is now usually made up of both men and women, should the salutation be changed to *Ladies and Gentlemen?* Probably not, because it tends to make you sound like a master of ceremonies.

The traditional *Dear Sir* may have to give way to *Dear Sir or Madam,* or strange as it sounds, *Dear Person.* If the latter sounds laughable, it is only because we are not used to it. Use it as a salutation for, say, six months and it will sound just as natural as any other word combination. Your customers, too, will get used to it. Remember how strange *chairperson* once sounded?

Actually, attaching the suffix *person* to most any word now using *man* could work *(nurseryman* to *nurseryperson, garbageman* to *garbageperson).* All it takes is some getting used to.

Now about the term *Ms.* Use it whenever you're in doubt about the marital status of a woman. Be certain to use it when your customer prefers that title—many, both married and single, do. A good rule here is that if your letters are to be directed at higher-income, better-educated, younger women, *Ms.* can't miss.

"American women," consumer pollster Burns W. Roper says, "are decidedly not a generation of swingers. Yet there are distinct signs of change—an erosion of traditional restraints." He notes that 9 out of 10 women in the Virginia Slims survey want schools to have cooking classes for boys and 8 out of 10 favor woodworking and shop classes for girls. Also, one in four women thinks playing with tea sets and doll houses is all right for boys, and half of the women are in favor of model kits and construction sets for both girls and boys.

Clearly, we are in the midst of changing times. Just as clearly, your sales letters must change, too.

In the final analysis, the feminist movement will be more than women's liberation. It will be people's liberation. Could you ask for anything better than that?

SM, November 11, 1974, pp. 46–48.

96

Section 13 / The Preapproach: Getting in to See the Decision-Maker

A Buyer's Guide to Salesmen

Meet End-Run Ed, Talk-Down Tom, and some other "salesmen" who purchasing director Bill Perry, MFA Insurance Co., only wishes were fictitious.

Remember those marvelous slow burns comedian Edgar Kennedy entertained us with in the days of the two-reel comedies? I have a theory: Kennedy was once a buyer and the kinds of salesmen I describe below were his inspiration. To be sure, such salesmen are the exception, but every buyer buying today will recognize each and every one. A terrible thought: Are any of these men trying to sell for you?

Hard-Sell Harry—This salesman never takes no for an answer, even if it jeopardizes his other business.

Demanding Dan—Enters the reception area demanding to see the buyer. If he gets in, he tells the buyer he expects his share of the business.

Talk-Down Tom—Lets the buyer know immediately that no other company can come close to competing with his (after all, it hired him). The buyer may have been in the business 20 years, whereas Tom has been selling for just one, but that doesn't stop Tom from dispensing his opinions, especially about the buyer.

Overpowering Orville—Enters the buyer's office with a briefcase in each hand and one under each arm. This makes the buyer wonder if Orville and he will finish the presentation together.

Sitting Sam—Gets into the buyer's office and sits. He *really* risks trouble, however, when he sits through the buyer's lunch hour.

Fiddling Fred—Starts rearranging the furniture as soon as he gets into the office. To ensure that he gets attention, he may also rearrange the items on the buyer's desk.

Meek Mel—Sits in the buyer's office and doesn't say a word. This gets the buyer to talk about almost anything in sheer desperation.

Nervous Ned—Paces back and forth in the lobby to get the receptionist to notice him. For the same reason, he'll tap a pencil on the buyer's desk.

Awkward Art—Takes 15 minutes trying to make a graceful exit.

End-Run Ed—Tries to get to the top man if he can't sell the buyer or user.

Scheduling Sid—Calls on the customer every week, regardless of the buyer's needs, or sends a stream of post cards. Sid makes his biggest impression, however, when he notifies you countless times of the hour when he'll come calling, then arrives 30 minutes late.

Rabbit Ron—Promises the customer anything but never looks back after he gets the order (the customer might need service).

Bad-Time Bart—Blames the competition and the buyer if he loses an order.

Promising Pete—Tells the customer what he wants to hear (he can always give him an excuse later).

Repeater Ralph—Makes sure the customer understands by explaining everything three different ways. Unless stopped, he is also certain to throw in 15 minutes of irrelevant information about the order.

These people are all for real, and all call themselves salesmen. Fortunately, they are the minority. But they should make you worry about what impression your salesmen are making on customers, especially potential ones.

The following tips can help both you and your salesmen make a good impression on buyers. Some are basic, but you'd be surprised how often the salesman may abuse them—to his company's disadvantage.

1. Be well groomed and neatly—not flashily—dressed. Drive a nice, but not flashy, car. Flashiness makes the buyer question your lifestyle and the profits you and your company are making.

2. Make a good impression on the receptionist and the buyer's secretary. Either can put in a good word for you with the buyer.

3. Find out who is doing the purchasing in a company and call on only that person. He may refer you to someone else in the company, or you can request that he let you call on the user and others who have a say in the purchasing decision.

4. If you are calling on a buyer for the first time, introduce yourself, explain briefly the company and products you represent, and then leave. (First impressions are very important: if the buyer reads you as someone who is going to waste his time, expect trouble seeing him again.) Wait until at least the second call before you ask for an order.

5. Shake hands firmly—but without crushing any bones.

6. When you enter a buyer's office for the first time, look at the walls. This will give you immediate insight into his interests. That, in turn, can give you a good conversation opener.

7. Do not *demand* to see the buyer. If he is a professional, he will see you as soon as possible. If you start pushing him, he will find reasons why he cannot see you.

8. Approach the buyer with the attitude that "I am here to serve you, and I want to serve you." Don't come in with the attitude that "We have the best product available, and you are a fool if you don't buy it."

9. Keep canned presentations and visuals to a minimum. These may tend to bore the buyer and may indicate to him that you need to lean on sales tools.

10. Be sure you organize your call beforehand. Do your homework to determine which of your products will most interest the particular buyer you are seeing.

Anticipate his objections and have ready answers. Really know your product—the buyer could ask questions that you have not anticipated.

11. If possible, get the buyer talking. You will find out a lot more about him and his needs. It pays to be a good listener.

12. The day of the hard sell is gone. You have to convince the buyer that you have a product that he needs and that you can be depended on to supply it. Remember: Even if he needs your product, you still have to sell him.

13. Most purchasing agents buy on a combination of price, service, and quality. Also, they have contracts with and loyalties to present suppliers. Don't walk in and expect to take over immediately. The best you can hope for in most instances is a trial order.

14. Don't run down your competition. If the buyer is buying from someone else, criticizing that competitor reflects on his judgment.

15. Don't waste a buyer's time. Learn to read how busy he is at the time you call and adjust the length of your call accordingly. Learn the buyer's habits to find the best time of the day or week to call on him.

16. The clue to a good salesman is how well he services the account after he's gotten an order. Anyone can write the order; the successful salesman is the man who follows up with service.

17. Don't be a problem ignorer. Problems don't go away; they get worse. If you don't have the solution, be honest. Telling the buyer the truth is infinitely better than making him look bad in the eyes of his own management because he "bought" a solution from you that later failed.

18. Don't change the customer's order. If you think it is to his advantage to do so, notify him before proceeding. You may find out that he doesn't share your enthusiasm.

19. Set up surefire ways for the customer to reach you. Nothing turns a buyer off faster than to hear an answering service announce that you can't be reached for several days if he has a problem requiring attention.

20. Without being arrogant, show confidence in your product and yourself.

Also, never tell the buyer how bad your business has been. He'll start wondering why.

SM, November 3, 1975, pp. 42–43.

How to Use Advertising to Make Cold Calls

by **John M. Trytten**, Contributing Editor

Ideally, few salesmen should have to make cold calls.

First, salesmen don't like to make cold calls and for that reason don't do well at them.

John Trytten, who has had wide experience creating advertising to help sales, is with Management & Marketing Services, Inc., in Royal Oak, Mich.

Second, salesmen have more important tasks to do and their time should be free for those tasks.

And third, advertising can be used to make cold calls and can usually do so more effectively and at lower cost.

Just so we're all talking about the same thing, let's define the "cold call" as a call on a prospect without introduction, without previous contact between the prospect and the salesman or company, and with no indication that the prospect has a need for or interest in what we are selling.

Those are the calls the average salesman hates to make. Even when training and discipline cause salesmen to make cold calls, few do well at them. At least subconsciously, the salesman realizes that his cold call sets up a new and strange situation for the prospect to cope with. Indeed, he collides head on with the buyer's resistance on the first call by making the buyer see that the *benefits* of the change greatly outweigh the *trauma* of the change.

But faced with the necessity for cold calls, the salesman goes ahead and makes them anyhow. He may not make as many as his sales manager would like; he's not likely to accomplish as much as either he or his manager might wish. But he makes them.

He makes them because he realizes that the cold call is the method closest at hand for him to develop *sales leads*. Before the cold first call, all he knows is that the buyer is a possibility. After the call he should know either that the buyer is a genuine prospect or that he can be forgotten. In other words, the initial cold call is a way of qualifying a prospect for further, more purposeful, calls.

A salesman has better things to do than qualify prospects, however. In most sales situations, he has the unique responsibility of fitting his product or service to the prospect's problems or objectives, answering specific questions, clearing away competition, and getting the signed order. He should be given as much of his time as possible for the performance of those tasks. And advertising—in one form or another—is a way of giving additional valuable time to the salesman for those purposes because advertising is a device for qualifying prospects and producing live sales leads. In fact, advertising, properly oriented, can do this job better than the sales force and at much less cost:

A few examples:

1. A vice president of sales for a small instrument company had only five salesmen to cover the entire U.S. These men had no time whatsoever in which to make cold calls, and even if they had, they wouldn't have known on whom to call because perhaps 1 out of 200 "smokestacks" represented a prospect for their equipment.

   So the advertising was aimed at producing *inquiries,* and each inquiry was followed up. Some by phone, some by mail, but most by personal calls.

   Thus when the salesman made his first call, he already knew that the prospect knew something about his product and had shown some interest. The salesman's job was to fan that interest, solve a problem, and recommend the correct equipment purchase.

2. Or, take the case of the creative printer in Milwaukee. Nearly every business uses printing. But most in this company's area didn't use much; not the costly high-volume color printing the firm produced. Because no one could tell a good prospect from a poor one, a regular monthly direct mail campaign was set up.

These direct mail pieces contained a sample of the printer's work, enclosed in an attractive file folder. Inside the folder was interesting information about the job, the buyer of the job, or occasionally the printing salesman who handled the job.

It was customary for a salesman to wait until a prospect had received four or five mailings before calling for an appointment. When he did call, he was often met with the comment "Oh! You're with the outfit that sends out those beautiful file folders. Yes, I can arrange to see you."

3. An electronic components manufacturer in Chicago used advertising to generate thousands more inquiries each year than the sales staff could follow up. Each one, of course, was answered by mail.

Each inquiry reply included a reply card. The inquirer was urged to return the card after checking off boxes that would give the nature and imminence of his application, indicate if he wanted a salesman to call, and give other pertinent qualifying information.

Although the original inquiry slips were forwarded to the salesmen, they were free to follow up or disregard them as they saw fit. But each returned *reply card* required personal follow-up by the salesmen and a written report on results of the call. Those cards constituted a principal source of leads to new prospects.

Magazine advertising and direct mail are two highly effective ways of developing leads and qualifying prospects. Either medium is far less costly than using salesmen's personal calls for the same purpose.

Further, the product literature sent in reply to the inquiry serves to educate the prospect about the product and its application, if any, to his problems and objectives. He can study the literature at his leisure, in the absence of the salesman, and thus be far more ready and informed when the salesman calls to discuss specifics. The result is that the salesman accomplishes more and does so with less waste of time.

These are just a few of the ways that advertising can help your salesmen generate new business. In your situation, there will be many others to be explored and tested. The end result of what you do can easily be measured: total the number of leads of qualified prospects developed by advertising and multiply by your dollar cost-per-call. I'll wager the total will be far greater than the actual cost of the advertising.

PART IV Working the Plan: Steps in the Selling Process

OVERVIEW

The following four logical, progressive steps are basic to any sales presentation:

Attention: Introduce yourself effectively in order to gain and hold the prospect's attention and interest so that he willingly gives you the information that will enable you to determine his needs, wants, or problems. It is around these factors that you will build your product or service appeal, in terms of benefits and value to him.

Interest: Hold the prospect's interest while you help him to discover and clarify these needs, wants, or problems, to admit them, and to indicate his willingness to consider your proposal as a solution.

Desire: Arouse his desire to enjoy the benefits that your products or service offers in fulfilling his needs and wants, secure his assurance that the benefits offered are of value to him, and handle any questions or objections that he might raise.

Action: Close the sale, which means that action of getting the order.

Do not underrate the simplicity of these four basic steps, since they can be expanded in countless and often sophisticated ways, depending on experience, type of product or service being sold, or company training or policy.

The attention-getting first part of the sales presentation is called *the approach* in sales terminology. It covers the first few (usually less than five minutes) of the presentation, and is divided into these two phases: (1) the first five seconds, and (2) the balance of approach time necessary to attain your objectives.

Following that, the presentation strategy is to (1) create and hold interest, (2) arouse desire and secure conviction, and (3) close the sale.

The two greatest problems faced by both new and experienced sales representatives and salespersons are (1) how to handle objections, and (2) how to close the sale. With only rare exceptions, a sale cannot be closed as long as the prospect has any major objection or objections. Thus it is essential to understand the principles and techniques of handling objections before attempting to master closing techniques.

Closing the sale or getting the order is the chief justification for the *real sales representative's existence* (contrasted to sales promotion representatives, route sales representatives, or many retail salespersons who are not asked or not expected to try and close sales during every sales interview); getting the signed order is what the real sales representative is paid to do!

Since mastery of these four basic steps is essential to success in personal selling, reviewing the Part III chapters in *Modern Applied Salesmanship*, 2d ed., will help you to understand some of the principles, practices, and techniques presented in not only the readings that follow Sections 14 to 16, but also in many of the other readings in this book.

Section 14 – The Approach: The Important First Few Minutes of the Sales Interview

Section 15 – The Sales Presentation

Section 16 – Principles and Techniques of Handling Objections and Closing the Sale

Section 14 / The Approach: The Important First Few Minutes of the Sales Interview

Negotiation: Your Meal Ticket to a Greater Share of Market

by **Mack Hanan**, Contributing Editor

When times are good, the key word in sales planning is *growth*. The Gross National Product grows, markets expand, and product lines proliferate. Sales plans are aimed at getting a larger piece of a growing pie. When times get tough, however, the scenario changes abruptly. Growth slows, stops altogether, or even becomes negative. The size of the pie shrinks. The key phrase becomes *market share*. Everyone wants a large piece of the smaller pie.

Selling intended to enlarge your share of market is a world apart from growth-type selling. It is competition at its toughest. Every supplier competes with every other for participation in a customer's business. Suppliers also find themselves competing against their customers, who often turn to self-manufacture during tough times. . . .

Without growth, a bigger slice for one company has to come out of someone else's share. That puts a premium on three sales strategies: (1) selling in a consultative manner, (2) selling in a way that improves customer profit, and (3) selling by means of negotiation so that both suppliers and customer feel they are winning added values not obtainable elsewhere. If a customer is in a materials-scarce industry, incidentally, he may have an equal stake in winning new values from his supplier relationships.

As negotiation becomes the basic sales medium in virtually all major customer relationships, it is obvious that improved market share will go to the supplier with superior negotiation skills. To prepare their salespeople for such assignments, managers will have to teach them three fundamentals of developing "win-win" relationships with their key customers: (1) Set and achieve a common objective. (2) Create partnerships. (3) Communicate as much as possible through cooperative negotiation strategies. This is the only way to supplant the "win-lose" syndrome, wherein a salesman feels it is his job to overcome the buyer.

THE COMMON OBJECTIVE

In traditional supplier-customer relationships, it is more the exception than the rule to share common goals. The supplier wants to win even if the customer loses, and vice versa. In a win-win relationship, however, it is not only possible but necessary to establish a common objective for major sales transactions. The best objective, of course, is mutual profit improvement.

When a salesman sells, he positions his products and services as agents for improving customer profit in one of two ways: reducing costs or improving the customer's revenues. Either way, the idea is to demonstrate that the value of his products exceeds their price. In return for receiving top value, the customer contributes to improving the salesman's profit by paying a premium price. Thus each party becomes the other's profit improver.

BECOMING PARTNERS

Negotiation is the language of partners. Each uses negotiation to make sure that the other wins at the same time he does. If only one partner wins consistently, the partnership ends. Now, let's look at how partners do business with each other.

Besides having a common objective, they must value the long-term rewards of working together in favor of limited advantages they might gain at each other's expense. Also, over a period of time, partners foster a special relationship with each other; and they avoid surprises. They teach each other new ways to solve problems together. They try to make each other rich.

Negotiation between partners seeks to improve the financial and emotional health of the partnership. In that way, the relationship itself takes on an added value that enhances a sale and can often justify a premium price.

COOPERATIVE NEGOTIATION

Cooperative negotiation is designed to avoid or heal the "pernicious contraries" that can separate partners by causing them to pursue exclusive, rather than common, objectives. Both salesman and customer try to accommodate each other's views about achieving their objectives. They seek to complement each other's needs rather than confront them antagonistically. Instead of manipulating each other for advantage, they try to make each other look good. That change in strategy not only allows buyer and seller to converse in the language of partners but demonstrates to them that the partnership is working, that its standards of performance are being met.

A THREE-PART COURSE

Sales managers who teach their salespeople how to negotiate with key decision-makers at customer companies will have to teach them how to

1. Analyze a customer's personal and professional needs, the types of influence he feels most comfortable with, and any constraints on his negotiating ti at are imposed by his own organization. Those factors constitute prenegotiation homework.
2. Sort out the issues that are negotiable. Salesmen must be taught how to separate essential issues from minor ones to make their negotiations as cost effective as possible.
3. Use specific cooperative negotiation strategies for each sales situation. The idea of becoming partners will mean something different to each of your customers, depending on their markets and their position in them.

With this three-way approach, salesmen stand the best chance of enlarging their key account business at the expense of competitors. They will improve their company's market share against rivals who continue to regard customers as adversaries rather than partners with mutual goals of improved profitability.

SM, June 2, 1975, pp. 63–66.

Gabriel's Shock Resistance

Back when there was an alarming gas shortage, one of the prime candidates for a sales disaster seemed to be the shock absorber industry. People would drive less, the reasoning went, and at slower speeds, which would make shocks last longer and hence cut replacement sales.

"We were affected in January and February," admits Jim Hamling, sales vice president for Maremont's Gabriel brand of shock absorbers. "But March was stronger and by now we're definitely seeing a pickup." Prospects are so encouraging, in fact, that Gabriel is going ahead with a market test next month for its SL shocks, touted as the "first self-contained, completely automatic, self-levelling" shocks on the market.

Hamling credits Gabriel's upsurge to a reorganized sales force committed to a consumer goods selling approach.

SL shocks, Hamling hopes, will be another step in Gabriel's rise to industry leadership. "We've increased sales more than 700% since 1969," he claims, "going from a weak No. 4 to a strong No. 2." GM's Delco line and Questor's AP are the ones that have been passed; Monroe remains the branded shock king. (Maremont, which makes private label shocks for a variety of oil companies and mass merchandisers, is probably the over-all leader in the $250 million market.) "When I came here, salesmen tended to be judged on mechanical aptitude. We began hiring salesmen from pharmaceutical companies, oil companies, and food companies [including Carnation, Hamling's alma mater] who might not be able to do their own tune-ups, but who could sell." The 30 salesmen who were with the company five years ago have virtually all departed, replaced by "over 100" new ones.

Gabriel's consumer goods approach is visible in other ways. The company spends more than $7 million a year on consumer advertising, with emphasis on "buff books"—auto enthusiast magazines—and TV sports shows. New products have been introduced with snappy names—Red Ryder, Strider, Hi-Jacker—and colorful packages. . . .

SL shocks, Hamling feels, are so unusual that he'll use demonstrations to show what they can do. Hamling is considering invading the ultimate province of the consumer goods marketer—the suburban shopping mall—for some Saturday afternoon show-and-tell sessions.
SM, June 10, 1974, p. 3.

Want to Be the Leader in Your Market? Follow These Easy-to-Read Directions

by Mack Hanan, Contributing Editor

"Leadership," the sales manager said. "That's what we're known for in our industry. We get the business because people know we're the best."

"The best in what?" I asked.

"That's a good question," he answered. "It depends. Last year we led the industry in sales, but we paid such a high price for them that our profits fell out of bed. Up to a few years ago, we were the acknowledged price leader. Now we wheel and deal with the best of them.

"We still lead in quality, though. But unfortunately, we put so much into our products that there's no way we can claim leadership as the low-cost producer. I guess leadership is a complicated business. How do you define it?"

"I generally use a single standard. I say that the leader in an industry is the company that helps its customers the most."

"Oh," said the manager, "a customer-oriented definition of leadership. So what do you do, run around and ask all the customers in an industry who helps them the most before you can identify the leader?"

"That's one way. But there's another. A leadership company sells in a distinctive style that's based on five characteristics. If you look for those characteristics, you can generally pick out the leader even without knowing very much about his markets." . . .

To pursue the matter, I asked the man what his company sells.

"We sell product performance at a price," he said.

"Well, that's not what a leader sells. The prime benefit a leader sells is his ability to improve his customer's profit or reduce his costs. In one way or another, he promises to have a favorable effect on his customer's financial process."

"O.K. The leading supplier sells the best benefit. But improving a customer's profit is a service; what if you're a product company?"

A MATTER OF SERVICE

"Whether it's a product or a service supplier, a leadership company defines its business in terms of delivering a service that affects a customer's bottom line. Leaders always promote themselves as service organizations."

"What about their products?" the manager asked.

"They position their products as the *means,* not the *end.* Merchandise becomes simply a vehicle for profit improvement, which, as you say, is a service."   .

"If you push not the products, but their ability to deliver a service benefit, how do you talk to customers?"

TALKING LIKE A LEADER

"You talk to them about *their* business," I said, "not yours. Don't go around proclaiming how well you know your own processes or how good your own products are. Make it clear to the customer that you know his business and that's why you can help him improve its profit."

"But doesn't that suggest that you know a customer's business better than he does? In the first place, how can that be possible? And secondly, even if it's true, isn't it heresy to say it?"

"This takes a little tact, to be sure. But, realistically, if you're the leader, you know more than your customer about the areas of his business that you affect because you work with many companies. You bring him experience he can get only through you."

"I still don't see," the sales manager interrupted, "how you can dare say that."

"I don't see how you can dare *not* say it if it's accurate," I said. "Remember our definition of leadership: helping your customers the most. How can you help them unless you share your experience and expertise with them? That doesn't mean you tell a customer how to run his business. All you're saying is that he can run it more profitably with your help than without it."

"If talking about your knowledge of a customer's business is the third characteristic of a leader, what does that do to your advertising and your sales promotion?"

"Ideally, promotion is used to prove your claims of being able to deliver improved profit. You promote case histories of how your customers succeeded as a result of your help. Your whole approach is, Look what *they* did."

The sales manager reflected for a moment. "So if I want to be the leader, I have to throw away everything our sales force uses that says we are the best in the business in this or that, or we were the first to discover or invent such and such. Is that what you're suggesting?"

"Unless you want someone else to take the ball away from you by saying, Our *customers* are the best in *their* businesses, with our help."

"All right. So what's the fourth characteristic of a market leader?

CONSULTATIVE SELLING

"The salesman for a leading company teaches his customers a 'how to' approach. He consults with them on how they can obtain the benefits he is uniquely qualified to provide. When he does that teaching job well, he creates a strong partnership with his customers. They learn that together they can accomplish what neither of them can do alone: improve profits for both their companies. In that sense, the leader converts his customer into a client. All leaders have consultant-client relationships with their customers."

"So what's the fifth characteristic?" the manager asked. "I suppose it's something like, The leader is always loved."

"Just the opposite. Leaders are respected, needed, envied, and imitated, yes. But loved? I don't think so. In fact, you could say that the fifth characteristic of leadership is that *the leader's customers are often defensive about doing business with him.*

"That's not because he isn't good for them; it's because he's generally the high-priced supplier. Customers may have to justify doing business with the most expensive source when other options are available."

"If that's true, when I ask a customer who does business with a leader why he pays a premium price to do so, what answer should I get—'Because I want the best'?"

"No. A very defensive answer: Because I *had to.* The leader's customer should feel he really has no choice. Only the leader knows enough about improving the profit in his kind of business. If he can deliver on that promise, price is secondary."

"Your characteristics of leadership sound simple enough. Why can't salesmen for any company claim them?"

"They can."

"What if they deliver?"

"Then they've made *their company* the leader."

SM, June 24, 1974, pp. 34–37.

Section 15 / The Sales Presentation

What Makes a Good Presentation? It Depends on Where You Sit

Sales executives and their men often look at the same issues from opposite sides of the table, and their approach to sales presentations is no exception. To explore this controversy, *SM* sent identical questionnaires to its Leadership and Salesmen's panels and came up with a number of new facts about the art. Among the revelations:

Managers make formal presentations more often than salesmen do.

The use of such "canned" materials as flip charts and videotape by the leadership group is nearly double that of the salesmen.

Sales executives seem more inclined to take on the challenge of making a presentation to a group.

Although salesmen are apt to be concerned with the role of their personality and appearance in making a successful presentation, leaders are more inclined to emphasize the importance of such things as strategy and planning.

Among the 120 executives and salesmen responding to the survey, there is general agreement on many points, however. One is the question of what the key elements of a presentation are. A typical answer from one leader: "The most important elements in a good presentation are (1) knowing the customer's needs, (2) presenting facts about your product that are tailored to his needs, and (3) limiting the time to one hour." Advises another: "Be sure your message is simple, your presentation direct and uncluttered, and that you give the customer a chance to ask questions or participate in other ways." One manager sums up: "Homework, homework, homework! Know your customers' needs and fill them."

Salesmen echo these sentiments: "Knowing your product line and showing how it fits into a particular customer's business" and "relating the product to the prospect's problems" are typical answers. But significantly, salesmen have a great deal more to say than their bosses about how to gauge their personal effectiveness.

Although managers are more concerned about strategies and monthly volumes, their men dwell on tactics to use on a specific sales call. "The ability to speak clearly, interestingly, and with knowledge of the product" is at the top of one salesman's list. "I have been an active member of Toastmasters for 12 years in order to accomplish this," he goes on. Such things as confidence, enthusiasm, and "getting immediate interest or customer feedback" are also frequently mentioned by the men.

Asked how presentations to groups differ from those made to individuals, a number of respondents say it's all the same ball game. Many think the presence of more

Do you make formal sales presentations?

	Leadership	Salesmen
Yes	82%	73%
No	18	25
No answer	–	2

Approximately how many presentations do you make each month?

Presentations	Leadership	Salesmen
None	2%	3%
1-2	28	30
3-4	23	25
5-6	8	15
7-8	15	3
9-10	6	13
Over 10	9	8
No answer	9	5

How long does your average presentation last?

Presentation Itself	Leadership	Salesmen
Under 10 min.	6%	13%
10-20 min.	36	35
21-30 min.	19	25
31-40 min.	9	8
41-50 min.	6	8
51-60 min.	9	8
Over 60 min.	6	3
No answer	9	3

Dialogue Following	Leadership	Salesmen
Under 10 min.	6%	10%
10-20 min.	25	50
21-30 min.	26	18
31-40 min.	9	3
41-50 min.	6	10
51-60 min.	9	5
Over 60 min.	2	–
No answer	17	5

Do you use "canned" presentations?

	Leadership	Salesmen
Yes	49%	25%
No	49	75
No answer	2	–

If yes, what kind of "canned" materials are involved?

	Leadership	Salesmen
Flip charts	69%	50%
Videotape	15	10
Recordings	12	20
Color slides	85	60
Film	31	10
Exhibits	31	80
Chalkboard	23	60
Other	4	30

(Totals exceed 100% because of multiple answers.)

Approximately what percent of the material you use in your formal sales presentation is prepared by you personally, as opposed to being sent from, say, the home office?

Percent	Leadership	Salesmen
10%	9%	5%
20	4	3
30	2	15
40	2	3
50	8	10
60	2	8
70	15	15
80	15	18
90	15	15
100	19	18
No answer	4	3
None	6	–

Do you get help in preparing your sales presentation from your advertising department?

	Leadership	Salesmen
Yes	66%	55%
No	34	43
No answer	–	2

than one buyer is desirable, however. "Groups often sell each other," observes a salesman. "There's more pizzazz and hullabaloo!" Comments a sales manager: "Three or four people in a buying group will always ask more questions than an individual and, as a rule, will make possible a better demonstration of your product."

But one salesman points out that it is easier to keep the attention of individuals, whereas a group's concentration is likely to flag if the words aren't pertinent and interesting. *SM* also found exhortations not to let group discussions degenerate into internal problem-solving sessions or competitions in which group members seek one another's recognition.

The size of the groups to which presentations are made varies extraordinarily. Answers to the question "How many people are usually asked to sit in on your formal sales presentation?" ranged from "1 plus" and "1-2" all the way up to "100." There was a concentration of answers in the 2-5 range, however.

What things do sales and marketing men look for in gauging the effectiveness of a presentation? "Orders" is the most common response, but for many, the issue is not that simple. "Questions asked following the presentation, followed by *the* order, or an increase in orders," answers one Leadership Panel member. "Questions and objections determine if you're getting through," explains another. "Did we get the account? Did we sell a new product? Did we at least get a foot in the door?"

It's a salesman, though, who puts the matter most succinctly: "You must maintain the attention of your listeners and be aware of the quality and degree of their responses, and of the questions that follow. Do they understand what you're saying? Does it result in an order?"

SM, January 22, 1973, pp. 44–46.

Words That Count—Part I: Information Strategy Helps Snag New Accounts

by **Mack Hanan,** Contributing Editor

More and more companies are coming to accept the premise that information is the salesman's stock-in-trade. There is nothing revolutionary in this belief. Every old-time salesman enjoyed having his accounts ask him, "What's new?" Today's salesmen are being taught to manage their information resources as a prime selling tool. Not only are they learning how to tell people what's new, but they are receiving an education in how to use information as a means to penetrate new accounts and to create new opportunities with existing customers.

On a day-in, day-out basis, an account requires a salesman's information even more than his products or services. For many organizations, the salesman's knowledge of what is going on in the marketplace is the major input that enables the decision makers he calls on to keep up on the market. Without it, their knowledge would be far less realistic and their marketing activities correspondingly risky.

THE INFORMATION TRADEOFF

Sophisticated sales managers regard selling as partly a tradeoff between information their salesmen give and information they receive in return. They know that their sales forces cannot function without knowledge of customer businesses. They also know that the only way to get a customer to share such information is for the salesman to offer information in areas where the salesman's knowledge is superior. This is the salesman's essential leverage with his accounts: he knows things that can help them improve their profitability. The well-managed sales function of the 1970s provides marketing information systems that reach salesmen in the field so they can maximize this leverage.

An experienced salesman usually marvels at all the things his customers do *not* know "in spite of the fact that they've been in business for years." But all businesses, even a salesman's own company, are provincial. They tend to know their internal affairs far better than they know what goes on outside. This is because all companies are process- and product-centered at heart. Some fight to achieve a market sensitivity as well, but it is always a conscious struggle that goes against the natural tendencies of an enterprise. Thus, their suppliers' salesmen become important-even vital—to them when they can contribute new information about the external "uncontrollables" that always hold the ultimate threat over an account's planning and operating success.

THE FIVE UNCONTROLLABLES

Every buyer looks at what he calls "the real world" with limited and impaired vision, and must interpret what he sees. This is especially true of the "Five Uncontrollables" that every account must come to terms with. Helping an account understand and take advantage of these factors should become part of every salesman's expertise. The uncontrollables are:

1. The market and its needs. In spite of what sales managers are fond of telling their men every year at annual conventions, no salesman can ever know a customer's business as well as the customer himself. A superb salesman who has been a long-time supplier to an account can perhaps hope to know two-thirds of the account's business. But the same salesman can, and should, know 100% about the account's market. These same figures are probably reversed for most accounts. They know 100% of their own business but are fortunate to know as much as two-thirds of the market data they should. It is in this unknown third that the salesman must be the more knowledgeable of the two if he is to make the most effective use of information strategy.

2. Competition and its threats. No matter how closely customer companies watch their direct competitors, they can never rid themselves of the uneasy feeling that they don't know enough about what's going on "out there." Salesmen have been taking advantage of this information gap since time began and it is still an area worth concentrating on. There is also another aspect of competitive threat that can be significantly more important today because it is not generally under such scrutiny and far less is known about it. This is the new world of indirect competitors, companies whose processes or materials are different from yours but which nonetheless compete in the same markets.

   It is exceedingly difficult for a business to defend itself against an indirect competitor when it surfaces. It frequently brings about an account's most dreaded eventuality: finding himself preempted in his own market by a truly innovative rival who has made existing benefits, or the means of achieving them, obsolete. A salesman's task is to provide his account with maximum lead time and defensive or retaliatory insights.

3. Supplier technology and its benefits. From a customer's point of view, a supplier's investment in technology exists for only one purpose: to help him to improve the profitability of his own operations. The salesman's role is to validate the worth of his company's technology. The best way he can do this is to present a quantitative statement of its value in terms a customer understands best—not the jargon of supplier technology but the fiscal terms of customer cost-reduction and incremental profits. When a salesman becomes an interpreter of technology, therefore, he must speak in the language of dollars and cents, because these are the symbols of the benefits of any technology.

4. Legislation and its requirements. Once upon a time, only a few industries were regulated. Now, many are. In the near future, most types of business will probably operate under compliance with either federal, state, or local legislation. This progressive control opens up a whole new aspect of information strategy for a salesman. It is an area in which he will have to be knowledgeable about both the letter of the law and its interpretation. He will also be required to keep his customers abreast of trends in legislated compliance codes as well as to present his product and service systems as guaranteed responses to them. In underwriting a customer's continued ability to stay in business by helping him comply with legislation that affects his vital operations, a salesman is providing him with important protection for his profit.

5. Socioeconomics and its implications. Someone once said that if all the economic analysts and forecasters were placed end to end, they would never reach a conclusion. Adding salesmen to that group would not necessarily change the punch line. But salesmen do not have to be forecasters of socioeconomic influences on business in order to be a valuable source of information. Primarily, they must learn to act as guides who can take their customers safely through bread-and-butter changes that can alter their operations. Now that the economy is picking up, the salesman must be able to say, "Here are three strategies you should consider to convert the upturn into new profits," or, "Now that you have just about decided to penetrate a new life-style market, let me show you how I can help you pay for it by maintaining good cash flow from older markets you might otherwise abandon too swiftly." In taking an advisory but aggressive stance with his customers, a salesman can help them address change without destroying existing values they may both depend on.

THE NOSE CONE CONCEPT

Information strategy should make facts about the five uncontrollables the nose cone of the salesman's penetration plan for a new account. It is designed to do two things: get the salesman in the door, and get the buyer to listen to him. But arousing interest, as every salesman knows, is only a first step. Sales forces make their living by persuading accounts to act on interesting information. So the explosive package that follows the nose cone must open up new profit-making opportunities for a customer if penetration is to enjoy a favorable cost/value relationship.

This is where the salesman's expertise comes in. Only by applying it to his knowledge resources can he make the definitive selling statement to an account which his information strategy sets up for him: "I can help you take advantage of the positive implications—of the uncontrollables—so that your profit can be improved by reduced costs or additional income."

In Part Two of this article, we will explore ways of using information strategy for selling to new accounts.

SM, January 22, 1973, pp. 38–39.

This is the second of two articles by Mack Hanan on how sales managers can improve the performance of their men by helping them use information as an effective marketing tool.

Words That Count—Part II: Information Strategy for Selling to New Accounts

by **Mack Hanan,** Contributing Editor

In Part I of this article (*SM,* Jan. 22), we showed how information strategy is being used by field sales forces as a "nose cone" to crack new accounts. When information is used in this way, it is typically concerned with one or more of a customer's "five uncontrollables": (1) the market and its needs, (2) competition and its threats, (3) supplier technology and its benefits, (4) legislation and its requirements, and (5) socioeconomics and its implications.

These are areas of doubt and perplexity that haunt most customer operations. Information strategy allows a salesman to become a supplier of added knowledge in these uncontrollable areas so that he can improve his performance in penetrating new accounts.

Now, in Part II, we will outline how some companies are teaching their salesmen to follow up penetration of a new account with information strategy designed to help make the sale.

The most likely targets for a salesman's information strategy are an account's two major processes—manufacturing and marketing. Each of these processes is vital. Manufacturing adds value by converting raw materials into finished goods. The value added by marketing is found by measuring the difference between manufacturing costs and selling price. As value is added, however, costs are incurred.

Manufacturing and marketing are therefore principal magnets for costs and the most attractive targets for cost reduction. They are also fertile ground in most companies for introducing strategies that can add even more to the values they create.

Salesmen put information strategy to work with their customers' manufacturing and marketing processes in two ways. First, they can help in designing cost-reduction programs based on the salesmen's products and attendant services. They can simplify a manufacturing operation, for example, or eliminate it altogether. Sometimes they help improve quality control by more closely approaching a condition of zero defects. At other times, they help reduce a product's size or weight or otherwise scale down its composition and cost. In marketing, they offer for the customer's customer new values that can be communicated through more cost-effective advertising or sales promotion.

At the same time, salesmen also put their information strategy to work in order to add marketable improvements to their customer's products. They thus help their accounts improve volume by adding to their existing market shares. Or they deliver sufficient new values to enable their accounts to command a higher per-unit price. All these beneficial acts stem from the salesman's information about his customers' two target processes, to which he applies his own expertise—and his company's products.

THE BEST NEWS: "I CAN HELP"

The salesman who wants to apply information strategy to his accounts must become *process-smart*. He must get inside the key cost points of his accounts' manufacturing processes to find ways to relieve burdens or add to product value. In marketing, the salesman has a dual job: not only must he penetrate his accounts' marketing processes to seek out their principal cost points and opportunities for adding new values, but he must get involved with the marketing processes of his customers' customers when these costs and values make important differences in their own selling operations.

To a new account's traditional question, "What's new?" the salesman who employs information strategy has an answer that carries the best news of all. It begins with three of the sweetest words in the English language: "I can help." The rest of the answer specifies *how*. "Working from my knowledge base, and relating my own applications expertise to the products of my company, I can help you improve your profit," is the salesman's selling promise to his customer. It is not, of course, the salesman's information that is being sold; it is the salesman. He is using his process information to make a sale by emphasizing the end-benefit of improved profitability for the customer. This can provide him with the economic justifications a new account may require to consider doing business with a third or fourth source of supply.

THE PROFIT-IMPROVEMENT PORTFOLIO

An information strategist can be thought of as a salesman who works out of two portfolios. One is his information resource. It remains internal, seen by him alone. The second portfolio is external. It is his collection of selling projects which have been inspired by his information resource. Each selling project is designed to help increase a customer's profit.

With the latter portfolio under his arm, the salesman who practices information strategy can sit down with his accounts' decision-makers and influencers and present his long-term sales plan for the coming year or two. "Based on your needs," he will say, "these are the profit improvement projects I would like to pursue with you." Each project will be presented in order of priority in terms of meeting two requirements: (1) it must contribute importantly to customer profit improvements, and (2) it must do the same for the profit of the salesman's own company. On this basis of mutual profitability, long lasting and successful supplier-customer relationships can be established and maintained.

Let's consider some concrete situations for salesmen charged with applying a profit-improvement portfolio to accounts:

A salesman for the Plastics Container Div. of Continental Can would position himself as the man who can help reduce packaging materials, trim manufacturing and shipping costs for household products manufacturers, or help improve brand identity and consumer acceptance that will add incremental new revenues.

A salesman for the Materials Cleaning Systems Div. of Wheelabrator-Frye would position himself as the man who can help reduce the cost of removing rust, corrosion, or burns from metals and plastics during their manufacturing process—or help improve appearance and performance benefits of the finished products so that added profit can come from increased market share or the ability to sell at a higher price.

A salesman for the Kaydon Bearing Div. of Keene Corp. would position himself as the man who can help mobile equipment manufacturers lower their manufacturing costs or help improve the marketability of their finished products by endowing the manufacturers with benefits that can attract new sources of income.

The new role for the information-based salesman therefore becomes one where his product is de-emphasized and his ability to influence costs and income is stressed. Salesmen who work this way have one characteristic in common, regardless of the industry their companies are in: *they are all in the profit improvement business.* Not accidentally, this is also the same business their customers are in.

With this new harmony, it is the hope of information strategists that sellers and customers may come closer together and work more productively than ever before.
SM, February 5, 1973, pp. 40–46.

Your Salesmen's Best Tool
Is a Well-Planned Catalogue

by **John M. Trytten,** Contributing Editor

Which catalogue does a prospective buyer reach for first? Yours? Or one of your competitors'?

For any given product line, buyers come to prefer one catalogue over another and to keep this one at their fingertips for ready reference. The lucky manufacturer who puts out the preferred catalogue obviously has a leg up on his competition—he is the first to have his product considered. There is no reason why you should not be this "lucky" manufacturer. All it requires is your recognition that one catalogue can be preferred over another; you and your ad manager must then put into your catalogue those ingredients that will keep it at the buyer's fingertips.

Luck—let's make it clear at the outset—has nothing to do with it. It's a matter of forethought, planning, and close cooperation between sales manager and ad manager to insure that your catalogue will be more helpful to the customer than anyone else's.

INGREDIENTS OF A HELPFUL CATALOGUE

The main elements of a catalogue are: format, design, words, illustrations, and where required, charts and tables. The essential ingredient, however, is planning—the one ingredient that enables you to combine the others in a catalogue that is informative, complete, accurate, and easy to use.

Let's take another look at the adjectives at the end of the preceding paragraph.

Informative: Be specific rather than general in what you say about your product. Don't say, "It's a tool of 1,001 uses," but actually list specific applications or areas of use. Don't say it's "fast," but that its rated production is 5,600 pieces per hour.

Complete: You know from your own experience the information a prospect needs and the kinds of questions the majority of them ask you. These questions should be answered in the catalogue, even if it takes a few more pages.

Accurate: Inaccurate data, specifications, drawings, charts, and tables will come home to haunt you. One manufacturer we know feels so strongly about accuracy that he guarantees that the dimension drawings in his catalogue *may be used* for installation layout purposes. On occasion he has picked up the tab for costs that infrequent errors have caused his customers.

Easy to use: No matter how much accurate information it contains, your catalogue's usefulness is impaired if the reader has a hard time finding his way around in it. Material should be presented in an organized and uniform way; related products should be grouped; frequently consulted data should be similarly located on the pages for each product.

THE SALES MANAGER'S CONTRIBUTION

You are, of course, grateful that the time-consuming work of producing your catalogue falls to the advertising manager. To give you the most effective catalogue in your business, however, the ad manager needs your help in many ways. `

Feedback: While the ad manager may have given you an excellent catalogue, he knows it isn't perfect. To make the next edition even better, he needs feedback from you and your sales force regarding errors, omissions, and suggestions for improvement. Your salesmen constantly use the catalogue as a selling tool and come face-to-face with buyers who also use it. Your ad manager will welcome their suggestions.

Information: Again, you and your salesmen are likely to know more than anyone else about what information your customers require. You also know which information may be enchanting to your own people but of no concern to your customers and should therefore be omitted. You can also help the ad manager check the accuracy and completeness of data given to him from engineering and manufacturing; these are data you work with daily, whereas the ad manager uses them perhaps once or twice a year.

Format: You should be able to advise the ad manager on whether permanent or loose-leaf binding is preferable in the field, and whether a number of separate product bulletins would be better than one large catalogue. There are many other ways in which you can work with your ad manager to develop the leading catalogue in your industry. Between the two of you, find out what they are and work on them.

CATALOGUE DISTRIBUTION AND MAINTENANCE

Production of the catalogue is not an end in itself. It will help neither you nor your customers to have the supply sitting on a shelf in your warehouse. Your ad manager must rely heavily on you for guidance and participation in their distribution.

The cost of your catalogue is a factor to be reckoned with in its distribution. While strictly controlled distribution does you no good, neither does uncontrolled distribution to people who can in no way influence buying. Nevertheless, you will frequently get requests from such people that must be satisfied in some way.

This even includes certain salesmen who are wont to ask for two or three times as many catalogues as they can place in proper hands. The trick here is to give a salesman few enough catalogues so that he will hand them out judiciously, while at the same time giving him enough copies to prevent his hoarding them. It is often a good practice to require each salesman to give you the name, title, company, and address of each person he gives a catalogue to; naturally, these names should also become part of your mailing list.

When you have a loose-leaf catalogue, you and your salesmen undertake the job of keeping your customers' catalogues up to date. You cannot rely on your customers to do this as you'd like it done. It is even hard to rely on salesmen to do the job, but it's worth the effort. If you encounter excessive difficulty in updating looseleaf catalogues, give serious thought to a permanent-bound format.

If your total catalogue is unusually expensive, you should consider breaking it into separate catalogue sections, either by product line or by market. This will enable you to give an interested buyer a smaller catalogue covering only those products in which he is interested.

Remember: The catalogue you give your salesman is almost always directly related to the sales he makes for himself—and you.

SM, February 5, 1973, p. 46.

To Get Volume Up, Sell Down

by John Vollbrecht

Let's say you're selling billiard tables at prices ranging from $329 to $3,000.

If you were a billiard table dealer, which would you advertise—the $329 model or the $3,000 model? The chances are you would promote the low-priced item and hope to trade the customer up when he comes to buy. But G. Warren Kelley, new business promotion manager at Brunswick, says you could be wrong. After years of teaching salesmen to sell *up,* he has deduced that there is more profit in teaching them to sell *down.*

Well, not exactly down. Kelley means "sell from the top, not from the bottom." He recently dramatized his idea in a series of coast-to-coast meetings of franchised Brunswick billiard dealers.

"Every customer for a billiard table has his personal buying range," Kelley says. "There is a price point below which he absolutely will not buy, and also a price point above which he cannot buy, for equally absolute reasons."

"It makes no difference," Kelley says, "whether you're selling billiard tables, cars, couches, or Caribbean cruises. When a customer comes in looking for a buy, the habit of showing him the lowest-priced item and trading him up will not pay off as well as the method in which the customer is first shown the very best the company has to offer, and then is led through a series of more modest choices in an attempt to determine not what he will buy, but what he can buy."

Regardless of what advertised item attracts the customer to a billiard salesman, Kelley's advice is to show that customer a $3,000 table first and to point out its quality features, such as genuine-cowhide-covered rails, imported playing cloth, and inch-thick, imported, matched and registered slate. "It's no trick," he says, "to get that customer to agree that the best *is* the best. Perhaps he can't afford a $3,000

John Vollbrecht has written on a variety of subjects for SM. *He spends the rest of his time on creative assignments for his Chicago ad agency, Vollbrecht/Carver.*

table, but when you show him something slightly less expensive, he has the ultimate table with which to compare the less costly item."

Kelley notes that the customer knows he has to give up something, such as the cowhide-covered rails or the 100% wool playing cloth, in order to enjoy the lower price, but he still gets the full 1" slate and the lifetime guarantee. "If he can't afford that, of course, there's always the 3/4" slate table and a hand-rubbed wood rail. But eventually, as you go down the line, the customer will reach a point below which he will not wish to go. He will be compelled to buy the best piece of merchandise he can afford."

Kelley compares that with the situations in which the customer is always shown the lowest-priced item. "In such cases, you're bringing a customer in at the bottom of his range and trying to move him up to the *most* he'll accept. My approach is to bring that same customer in at the top and let him work down through the line until he reaches the point representing the *least* he will accept. The result is that instead of selling him at the lower end, you gain a chance to sell him at the top. But only if you start at the top."

To prove his point, Kelley has actual sales figures from a representative store in which both the traditional selling up approach and the selling down method were used during alternate weeks. During the first week, customers asking to see lower-priced tables were shown the low end of the line (just over $300) and then encouraged to consider more expensive models—the traditional trading-up approach. It worked. Indeed, because trading up *does* work, many salesmen never think beyond the method. The average table sale that week was $550, considered a not-bad showing.

However, during the second week, customers in that same store were led instantly to a $3,000 table, regardless of what they asked to see. They were given the full demonstration of the top-priced table and then allowed to shop the rest of the line, in declining order of price and quality. The result of selling down was an average sale of over $1,000.

All of which has led Kelley to formulate Kelley's Law: "To get volume up, sell down."

SM, July 22, 1974, p. 29.

Section 16 / Principles and Techniques of Handling Objections and Closing the Sale

Pricing the Profitable Sale Has a Lot to Do with Perception

by **Daniel A. Nimer**, President, The DNA Group

Pricing would be so simple if people would only remember the rules. For example, it is axiomatic that (a) the most profitable sale begins with the best price and (b) the best price is determined in the marketplace and *not* by production costs.

Yet once controls were removed in 1974, most companies in the U.S. announced price increases based almost solely on escalating costs "to protect or improve profit margins." The role of the sales force during that period was to contact customers and justify price rises on the basis of "increased costs of raw materials and labor."

Little attention was paid to the value of the product or service in the mind of the buyer. No wonder customers stayed away in droves. Never before has the marketplace been so chaotic and unpredictable. And never have traditional price *setting* and price *selling* techniques been so inappropriate.

It is time to take a new look at the role of pricing objectives, strategies, and tactics in determining the profitability of the firm, and at the role of the sales force in the market. Perhaps more significantly, many concerns, large and small, should realize that they actually do not have any pricing objectives at all. A discerning glance at their policies would reveal that they have confused a means of *measuring* performance with an *objective*. Apparently, many have come to regard such yardsticks as return-on-sales and return-on-investment as objectives in their own right. This is an outright fallacy, as the auto industry demonstrated recently with its attempts to lure reluctant customers with cash rebates.

The only valid pricing objective in today's uncertain environment is to ask the customer to pay for the "perceived value" of what he is buying. That holds for products or services, consumer or industrial goods.

What is perceived value? It is what the customer is willing to pay for the "bundle" of benefits offered by the supplier. To the industrial buyer, it includes not

---

An internationally recognized authority on pricing, Dan Nimer is president of The DNA Group, a Skokie, Ill., firm that specializes in pricing, marketing, and planning strategies.

only the physical product, but such features as availability, quality, service, breadth of the line offered by a single supplier, technological and design service, and even the personal relationship with the sales representative. The buyer of consumer goods considers such factors as social status implied by the label or the place of purchase, price/value relationships, appearance, quality, and, once again, personal relationships with the seller.

You can affect the perceived value of your products by manipulating the *nonprice* variables in the marketing mix—such things as advertising, sales promotion, distribution, and the nature of the product itself. Price is then used as the variable to recover those costs from the buyer. That may be done by such steps as improving the product, increasing advertising and sales promotion, or—and this is often overlooked—using the sales force to carry the value message to customers more effectively.

After prices have been set on the basis of perceived value, the next step is to sell the price to the customer. That, naturally, is the job of the sales organization, but it requires a special understanding of the marketplace. Thus the salesperson must be well grounded in

1. The customer's business.
2. Strengths and weaknesses of the competition.
3. His own company's position in the marketplace.
4. The competitive "perceived value ratio."
5. Using the professional skills needed to sell the price.

Unfortunately, corporate management often fails to provide the sales force with the required ammunition. Instead, when confronted with a crisis, it prefers to cut marketing research, advertising, promotion, and all the other functions that aid in selling a price to customers.

Now is an ideal time for top management to get some corporate priorities straight by letting each department perform its proper function. The Marketing Dept. should set and sell prices. Then it's up to the Financial Dept. to *measure* the impact of those prices on the company's profit performance. Until those roles are clearly understood, there is bound to be conflict between the two departments, and pricing the profitable sale will be an impossible task.

SM, May 19, 1975, pp. 13–14.

Unfreezing Your Prospects

by Dr. Dillard B. Tinsley and Dr. Vinay Kothari

What do the following incidents have in common?

A salesman calls upon the head buyer of men's clothing for a large, independent

Drs. Tinsley and Kothari are on the teaching staff of the Stephen F. Austin State Univ., Nacogdoches, Texas.

department store. Knowing the characteristics of the store and its community, the salesman has selected samples of merchandise that should move rapidly for the store. The salesman makes his pitch and shows the merchandise, only to be met with this refusal: "I'm sorry, but we have had poor delivery service on rush orders previously placed with your company."

Another salesman calls upon a manufacturer's purchasing agent, offering pocket calculators at bargain prices. Although the pocket calculator is a well-known brand, the purchasing agent refuses it, saying, "Our present brand has served us well in the past, and we don't want to take a chance on a new one."

Both salesmen have encountered "frozen" prospects. Each prospect is "frozen" into a thought pattern that does not include the salesman's products. In the first incident, the buyer has previously had a bad experience with the supplier. In the second case, the buyer may be afraid to change brands because he really does not understand the possible mathematical calculations or technical specifications of the pocket calculators. Neither prospect has really listened to the sales presentations because his mind is already frozen into a rejection of the products.

For the sales presentation to be effective, a salesman must first "unfreeze" the prospect's mind. Unfreezing in the first case might be accomplished by asserting, We have completely changed our approach to product delivery and now feature a new quick-reaction service. In the second case, the refusal should lead to a presentation of product simplicity, reliability, and guarantee. In each case, the product benefits should be quickly reviewed. Another attempt to close the sale should be made because the prospect's mind may now be unfrozen.

The responses to refusals may be ovious, but the causes of freezing and the ways to unfreeze are not always obvious. One of the most popular ways of understanding the process is through the sequence of unfreeze, change, and refreeze. Training salesmen to understand that sequence facilitates the unfreezing of prospects. Salesmen can then make their sales presentations to prospects who are open for change, rather than wasting their presentations on closed minds.

Salesmen already know about the basis for unfreezing: creating a motivation to change. It is often used in the attention-gaining part of a sales presentation or in the transition from the attention part to the interest part. The important point is that salesmen must recognize th need to unfreeze their prospects.

Unfreezing can be accomplished in several different ways, depending on the reasons why a prospect is frozen. The following list includes the most common ways to unfreeze prospects; others will become apparent when the causes of freezing are considered:

1. *Promise rewards greater than those now received.* This includes both economic benefits and psychological benefits, such as satisfaction from buying the most modern product available.

2. *Reduce a threat.* For example, promises of assured quality or of adequate supply could be used.

3. *Reduce a barrier.* Lowered prices, increased service, or quicker deliveries may remove a barrier previously erected.

4. *Induce inadequacy feelings.* This is directed at self-image in such questions as, Are you aware that the trend in your industry is to use the particular materials that our product offers in its key parts? It also suggests possible failure to please others in statements such as, Your production people are depending on you to select the supplier who can provide product service without delay.

5. *Introduce a situation that calls for new action.* Refer to changes in technologies, customer needs, economic trends, or competitors' activities that might require the prospect to change.

To select the best approach for unfreezing, salesmen should be alert to the reasons why a prospect might be frozen. Some common ones:

1. *Previous economic rewards as a result of present behavior.* Emphasize the effects of changing technology in making processes, products, modes of operation, and people obsolete.

2. *Perception of change as not needed or unworkable.* Establish that system changes should always be considered because no system is perfect. Refer to successful product implementation or use by other organizations.

3. *Uncertainty of results, of ability to understand or to perform new role.* Use charts, pictures, and simple examples. Illustrate the flow of product to the prospect's organization, and carefully explain the exact role that he will play.

4. *Threats to interpersonal relationships, relationships to other groups, and personal status.* Refer to the enhanced status and better relationships that should result from the prospect's giving personnel in his company a product that fits their needs better than previous products. Other prestige factors may be furnishing a product with the latest technology, dealing with the supplier that leads its industry, better service, or faster delivery.

5. *Past violation of expectations.* If your company or its products have disappointed the prospect in the past, you must convince the prospect that appropriate changes have been made to correct past problems and to prevent further problems.

6. *Inconvenience to present habits.* The power of habit should never be underestimated. Make the point that changes must occur to meet the changing business environment. Psychological appeals can also be made, such as, You cannot afford to get into a rut.

Once a prospect's thought patterns are unfrozen, the sales presentation can do its job. However, a successful sales presentation should be followed by efforts to refreeze your customer's thought patterns—to *include* your product automatically. A one-time sale is not enough; return customers and continuing sales are the goal. Refreezing can aid in making repeat sales to your customers.

THINKING OF YOU

A continuing relationship between salesman and customer is necessary for refreezing. This gets the customer into the *habit* of thinking of your company and its products when needs arise. The salesman must ascertain that the customer's expectations are met; that the buyer is fitting into any necessary role changes (including the techniques for submitting orders); and that the product is meeting the customer's needs. This is especially necessary for new customers when the refreezing process is underway, but it is also required to keep old customers frozen onto your products.

Ultimately, freezing is not workable if the product is unsatisfactory. Unsatisfactory products unfreeze customers, making them prospects for competitors. However, finding a competitor with product weaknesses may result in finding a string of his customers who are already unfrozen. Unfrozen prospects are prime prospects. If nothing else has unfrozen prospects, your salesmen must be prepared to do it.

SM, June 2, 1975, pp. 51–52.

A Salesman's Dream Come True

"The cost of a sales call has increased so much that buyers should do their part to make the salesman's call as productive as possible." Practicing what he preaches, William H. Brady, Jr., chairman of W.H. Brady, Milwaukee, which makes industrial and consumer labels, signs, nameplates, and such, sees to it that every salesman trying to sell his company something gets at least a royal welcome.

It starts outside, where the company's 25 most convenient parking spots are reserved for salesmen. Inside, the lobby is comfortable, the receptionist friendly, and the magazines up-to-date. There is also a phone for salesmen to use.

Most important, if a salesman has been kept waiting 10 minutes, the receptionist has instructions to find out what's causing the delay. Notes purchasing manager Eldon A. Meier, "We try to get the 40 to 50 salesmen we see each week to schedule their appointments. But we'll see them promptly even when they're making a cold call."

Says chairman Brady, "You won't find a sign here saying, Salesmen interviewed Tuesday and Thursday, 1:00 to 3:00 p.m. only. That sort of thing is abominable— it shows an incomprehensible ignorance of the role of the salesman. He's the conduit between the supplier and his customers, the source of information about products and services the customer needs to stay in business."

What makes Brady so solicitous? Before he became chairman, he was a company salesman. "In fact," he says, "I still am a salesman."

SM, November 3, 1975, p. 22.

PART V After-Sale Follow-Through and Special Applications

OVERVIEW

Having considered in Part IV how a sales representative goes about selling to a customer or prospect face-to-face, we will now consider what he or she should do once the sales presentation has ended, either unsuccessfully (failed to close a sale) or successfully (closed the sale).

Failure to get the sale imposes some professional obligations. The prospect should be thanked for his time and courtesy, left with some valuable ideas, if possible, and left with a favorable image of you, the sales representative, your company, and sales representatives in general. Loss of the sale may also be turned to your advantage. You can lay the groundwork for a future callback if it appears that such a callback may lead to future sales, and you can ask the prospect for the names of any friends or business acquaintances who might be interested in your proposal. Perhaps, if asked, he will write an introduction for you or even call them on the spot. If asked honestly to voice his real reasons for not buying, the prospect may give you insights that will help you sell more successfully at your future sales presentations.

After successfully closing the sale, even more professional obligations are involved, since your aim is to have a satisfied customer (or user). This may involve callbacks to see whether or not your product or service is being used properly, or if there are any problems which you or your company's customer service technicians can solve. Efficient follow-up and follow-through service represents good selling at its best. And it's good business, since it is normally easier to sell more to a current satisfied customer than to sell to an entirely new prospect. The readings in Section 17 will touch upon some of these points.

Some special applications of selling principles as applied to in-store retail selling, and to telephone, industrial, groups, and exhibition selling will be pinpointed in Sections 18 to 19.

Section 17 – The Follow-up and Follow-through
Section 18 – Some Special Applications to Retail Selling
Section 19 – Some Special Applications to Telephone, Industrial, Group, and Exhibition Selling

Section 17 / The Follow-up and Follow-through

12 Tips No Salesman Wants to Hear (or Can Afford to Live Without)

It hurts, but it's true: unless your salespeople have a working knowledge of customer service, they may wind up giving away the store.

by **Warren Blanding**, Contributing Editor

You are a salesman and you want to lock in your customers by giving them better service than they can get from anybody else. Good. The battle is half won because you recognize that customer service can be a persuasive selling tool. Satisfied customers are loyal customers, repeat customers. As they grow, so do you. Especially if you sell generic-type products, you know that in many cases customers service is *the main thing* you have to sell.

But before you nod too vigorously in agreement, read these rules of the game. They'll help you capitalize on some of the strengths of your firm's customer service activity and offset its weaknesses.

1. Learn what customer service is (and what it isn't). There's a tendency in many firms to equate customer service with "customer satisfaction." Sure, providing satisfaction is *one* objective of customer service, but it's a goal also of design, production, quality control, and of the sales effort that you tailor for each of your customers.

Customer service has a more specific goal of its own: getting product to customers at service levels that are equal to or better than the competition's, and doing so at costs that permit competitive pricing and adequate profit contribution. This means that the customer service manager can select one of two possible missions for his department: (1) Provide improved levels of customer service without increasing cost. (2) Provide the same levels but at reduced cost.

If you have to beat the competition's service, the first is the obvious choice. But if you're already offering better service, there's no point in improving it because it probably won't get you any more business. In this situation, cutting costs improves the profit contribution.

Customer service relates to "customer satisfaction" only insofar as the degree of satisfaction that it produces is sufficient for your company's needs. To keep things in perspective, think of the goal of customer service as insuring that customers are *less dissatisfied* with your service than with the competition's. Improving customer service beyond the levels needed to get and keep an account may make your customers like you better, but would you want the added cost to come out of *your* paycheck? The customer service manager loves humanity just as you do (though you may sometimes find that hard to believe). However, he gets a paycheck, too, and he wants to keep on getting it.

2. Do your part to speed up the order cycle.   The customer service cycle really begins when the buyer *decides* to place an order. If he happens to make that decision while fishing in the middle of Lake Mooselookmeguntic, there isn't much you can do to get it into the order mill before he gets back to the office.

But this illustrates an important point: It's up to you to get orders in as soon as possible after the buyer makes his decision and to show him how he can get better service by planning in accordance with your standard order cycle. If you walk around with his order in your pocket and mail it in with some others over the weekend, you may delay order processing by as much as a week. Don't expect your customer service to make up *that* time. They can't, and they shouldn't.

Don't forget, either, that it's your job to make the customer aware of the benefits of improved ordering practices. This is true whether the customer orders direct or through you. There may already be built-in delays within his own company if a formal purchase order must be requisitioned and approved.

Show your customer how he can get better service by bringing his purchasing patterns into phase with your company's order cycle. He'll thus avoid paying premium transportation charges and quite possibly avert a major crisis. What's more, you'll be spared the bother of expediting his order—and the fireworks when it doesn't come through on time anyway.

3. Improve the accuracy of your orders.   You're in the best position to see that orders are accurate, complete, and processable. Be sure your customers are equipped with the latest product data and specifications. They must also understand the importance of providing all the information that is required, of course. But if you're writing the orders, the final responsibility is yours.

A sloppy order can wreak havoc with the order cycle and with customer service. If it can't be interpreted by your customer service people, it will probably be set aside, and it may be a week or more before a query reaches you or your customer. If the order is processed but specifies the wrong items or quantities, you probably won't hear about it until the customer receives shipment—at which point you will hear about it loud and clear.

Then, besides having to lean on customer service to get out a replacement shipment (assuming the product is still available), you have to go through the tedious business of authorizing return of the original one. Even if the customer isn't mad at you, you surely aren't making any money on that account.

4. Let customer service set lead times and shipping points. Some companies have a flat rule that salesmen cannot specify either shipping dates or locations. There is good logic to that policy. Most customer service organizations operate on standard lead times that permit efficient use of the work force and economical

transportation arrangements. Decisions on shipping locations are usually governed by economics as well, and occasionally by product availability.

When you try to override standard practices, you add to costs without necessarily improving service. If you know Joe, the shipping dock foreman at a particular warehouse or distribution center, you may get improved customer service in a given situation—at someone else's expense. But remember that there are Joes in other warehouses who are friends of other salesmen. If you flout the standards on behalf of your customers, you can be sure your fellow salesmen will try exactly the same thing—at your expense.

Obviously, there are times when overriding the rules is justified. Ideally, the criteria and authority are spelled out in advance and agreed to by both the sales department and customer service. If it cramps your style to tell a customer you can't break the rules on your own, explain that you're helping ensure that, over the long term, he will get his orders within the lead times you quote.

If that doesn't satisfy him, buck the matter up to your boss. That's one reason he's there. But before you do, see if the customer really needs the service he says he does.

5. Take a hard look at customer requirements. Customer service people are conditioned to believe that salesmen are the worst authorities on what customers really need. You may not like that idea, but it does contain some truth. After all, you can hardly be blamed for wanting the best for your customer!

By the same token, if you ask a customer to choose good, average, or inferior service, he's not likely to choose either of the last two. Ask him whether he would like short lead times or long, and you know what the answer will be. Yet your primary interest should not be in what he would *like* but in making him like what you know he can *live with*—and still give you his business.

If you know his minimum requirements (as opposed to his maximum wants), you can give your customer service people something tangible to work with. That can be improved as the occasion warrants. If you set unrealistic goals, however, you're compromising your profit potential. What's more, you may be getting customers into the habit of expecting service that may one day become too expensive to maintain.

6. Don't depend on complaints as a measure of customer service. Although noise from customers is almost always a sign that service is in bad shape, the *absence* of static doesn't necessarily mean that all is well. Your customers probably articulate only about 1 complaint in 20.

Beware, too, of looking upon complaints as an accurate indicator of all your customer service problems. The griping may be little more than a cross-section of your more vocal accounts. A small company that doesn't have the resources to accommodate your mistakes (stock to cover short shipment, personnel to handle accounting errors, etc.) is likely to make more noise than a larger one. The buyer in a big corporation may not even be aware of what's happening—until his operations manager blows his stack.

Remember, too, that even in a face-to-face situation, some customers won't, or can't, tell you how bad your customer service is. To find out what's happening, you need objective measures, such as length of total order cycle, arrival on or before wanted date, condition of shipment on arrival, accuracy of billing, and so forth. These facts are usually best unearthed by somebody who doesn't have your type of personal relationship with the customer.

7. Encourage customer contacts with your service personnel.   This may rub you the wrong way. In some companies, the salesman expects to be the sole contact with his customers. He tells customer service people to keep *their* hands off *his* customers. In certain situations, that hands-off rule may be warranted, but from the customer's point of view it can lead to an unsatisfactory relationship. If the buyer's only contact is with you, whom does he contact when he can't reach you? What's more, if he calls you and you have to call customer service, what have you gained?

If your customer service function is properly organized, the buyer will get the attention he deserves when he calls. If you call customer service *after* he does, it will be at least as effective as if you had called first.

Many customer service departments are set up to give quick answers on order status, thanks to computers and CRT (cathode ray tube) screens, which display information on orders. It would be pointless to deny customers the advantages of this technology.

8. When customer service goofs, start yelling.   If customer service people really and truly mess up your accounts, you've got a problem. In some companies, personnel are poorly trained, poorly paid, poorly supervised, poorly motivated—did we miss anything?—and their managers earn about half what you earn. They have something like 10 times as many accounts to supervise as you do and they probably don't have enough authority to do anything about customer problems.

If those things are true in your company, raise hell about it. The sooner you make it known that an effective customer service organization will let you concentrate on the job you do best—selling—the sooner management will do what it should have done years ago.

9. Keep the economics of customer service in mind when making a sale.   Customer service standards are usually based on the requirements of the marketplace. Just as pricing reflects economies of scale, so shipping units, lead times, and delivery schedules should be integrated to achieve the most cost-effective customer service mix for a particular company.

In general it is more economical to have a long lead time if competitive conditions permit. That way, order processing and order assembly work loads can be balanced to avoid peaks and valleys of activity in the warehouse. Month-end and quarter-end periods often cause trouble because salesmen are trying to get their orders shipped so they can get credit for that sales period. Beating the deadline often means overtime in the warehouse. With one warehouseman and a forklift truck costing between $15 and $20 an hour, you can figure what the overtime looks like, especially when he is likely to be sitting on his hands half the time in the weeks to come.

Similar economics apply to shipping. It costs something like $30 an hour to run a delivery truck, whether it's standing still or moving, empty or loaded. If the truck takes one hour to handle one shipment, it costs $30, but if it can handle 30, the cost drops to $1 per shipment.

When you don't sell in terms of customer service economics you not only eat into profits, you probably won't get better service for the customer. A shipment sent by itself today costs more and very often doesn't arrive any sooner than one that moves in a consolidated load three days from now. Why? Because the small shipment goes through up to 16 intermediate handlings at origin and destination, whereas the consolidated orders move directly to the destination city for distribution. That means less cost and less time.

10. Program for exceptions before they happen.   In customer service jargon, an "exception" is an order that can't be handled with the normal procedure. The most common exception probably is not having enough stock to fill the orders. Because that is a fairly frequent occurrence, most companies develop routines for handling it. They either back-order the item or cancel the order altogether and instruct the customer to reorder. There are variations on this when some items are available and some are not. One customer may accept partial shipments or substitutions, and another may not.

You will help your customers and yourself by finding out their requirements beforehand. That way, special instructions for handling exceptions can be programmed into their file. There is a limit to the number of exceptions per customer, but you can always program the file for "call customer." That avoids the problems created when customer service personnel have to make decisions with no guidelines at all.

11. Know your firm's customer service policy and see that customers know it, too.   Some aspects of policy overlap with the terms of sale, such as the procedure for returning merchandise. Others may be unique to customer service, such as order cutoffs and shipment dates. Units of shipment, shipping locations, mode of transport, rules governing pickup of merchandise by customers—all fall under customer service. So do such things as change orders, made-to-order products, and allocation practices for materials in short supply. Each company and each industry has different rules, and the degree of latitude may depend on whether it's a buyers' or a sellers' market.

Should customer service policies be printed up and given to customers? Some companies do that, and some don't. A printed document gives you something to point to, authority to back you up. The buyer knows the rules of the game and can reasonably assume they apply equally to all customers. The disadvantage is that policies change, and you suddenly discover there are a lot of customers still going by the old rules because somehow they haven't gotten copies of the new ones.

12. Learn your logistics.   How many facecloths in a truckload? How many cases of peas on a standard GMA pallet, and what do they weigh? Can the cartons be stacked five-high without toppling? What about pallet exchange and backhaul allowances? These are some of the logistical questions customers are likely to ask

you. They all relate to customer service, and knowing the answers is an important part of your customer service.

If yours is a large concern selling to smaller companies, bear in mind that they may be considerably less sophisticated in logistical matters and may not be able to cope with the volume shipments you've sold them on. Some companies with unit load shipment programs have devastated their customer relations because they failed to realize that a number of their accounts buying in carload lots didn't have adequate storage facilities or capital to tie up in large inventories.

One final word. Customer service works to everybody's advantages when the rules are intelligently drawn, known to all, and observed by all, especially salesmen.

SM, February 17, 1975, pp. 26–30.

Paper Mate Flourishes by Making Sure Customers Do, Too

Sales Vice President Kiernan's advice to profit-minded sales representatives who work with retail accounts: "Be a sales promotion rep."

When Art Kiernan plans for profitability, he doesn't think only of how many ball point pens, refills, porous point pens, and broad-tip markers his salespeople will sell. He's equally concerned with *where* they will sell those products, and what happens afterward. Kiernan, 41, who is sales vice president of Boston-based Gillette's Paper Mate Div., believes that to strengthen profits you must "exploit your distribution outlets and maximize them." Moreover, "Just selling to those outlets is not profitable; you must sell *to* and sell *through.*"

He seems to have found the right answers to his particular problems of profitability. Writing instruments is a highly competitive market. Yet despite the costs— mainly advertising and new product development—of meeting the competition, Paper Mate sales and profits have been moving quietly but steadily upward for the past several years. In 1974, sales rose 12%. Profits, Kiernan says, "kept pace, and we established a new record."

At the same time, Paper Mate has been strengthening its market position. It is now the leader in porous point pens, with 45% of that $100 million market. In the ball point pen category, Kiernan explains, "Bic is primarily in the 50¢-and-under line, and Cross made its reputation in high-priced items. We sell everything from a 25¢ stick pen to a $15 gold pen and pencil set, and we compete well all along the line."

How has Paper Mate managed to show a profit despite the costs of meeting competition on so many fronts? One way has been by looking for more profitable distribution outlets, a move in which Kiernan has played a large part. He joined Paper Mate in 1970 and soon became aware of a gap in its sales coverage. "Commercial and wholesale stationers and the stationery trade represent a massive business," he says. "I couldn't believe that Paper Mate wasn't in that potentially lucrative area. We developed a commercial sales force to capitalize on that opportunity and have made dramatic inroads in the last few years. It's now our fastest-growing segment."

The main reason that Paper Mate was not in the profitable commercial area was that it lacked the right products. It needed low-cost items to compete with such manufacturers as Bic, which had about 70% of that market. However, the development in 1972 of the Write Bros. line gave it the products it needed. The commercial force—a national sales manager, his assistant, four district managers, and 20 salesmen—now emphasizes such items as the 59¢ Flair porous point pen and the Write Bros. stick pens (25¢) and porous point pens (39¢).

Although the commercial sales force added an important dimension to Paper Mate's marketing, Kiernan points out that Paper Mate is "basically a consumer products company that has gone into the commercial business. In terms of sales dollar value, the general [retail] force does more business today." The general sales force includes three regional managers and 65 salespeople who call on pen wholesalers, tobacco and drug wholesalers, toiletry merchandisers, and retail, drug, food, and discount outlets. Headquarters calls on major chains are handled by a national accounts manager, a "highly sophisticated, highly professional" individual who makes detailed presentations to key accounts and sets up complete promotion programs for them, sometimes for as much as a year in advance.

PROFIT-CONSCIOUS SALES FORCES

"Our salesmen are not really responsible for the profit of a product," Kiernan stresses; "that's my responsibility." Nevertheless, he tries to make both sales forces profit conscious by explaining to them the importance of selling to and through their accounts. As a result, salesmen know full well that no product makes a profit for the division simply because it has been sold to a distributor or wholesaler; something must happen to it after that.

Helping to make profits happen for the commercial sales force are its four "end-user specialists." Those missionaries, trained by the commercial managers and also by local commercial salesmen, work full time calling on large businesses in major markets—the Fortune 500, airline offices, government offices—giving product samples to purchasing agents and key buying influences.

"In the commercial business," Kiernan explains, "if you can get the purchasing agent to test a product, you make him more receptive to buying it." Thus the end-user specialists try to pull product through the pipeline by getting the purchasing agent to buy Paper Mate pens from the wholesaler. It's an important function, and Kiernan plans to expand the end-user force this summer.

In the general sales force, on the other hand, there is more emphasis on pushing product through the pipeline. (Pull is supplied mainly by consumer advertising.) To do that, salesmen become merchandising specialists versed in retail promotion and co-op advertising. "We train our people to be conscious of all aspects of selling," Kiernan says proudly. "I think the trade will tell you that the Paper Mate guy is probably the most professional in the writing instrument business."

A salesman on the general force takes his first step toward profitability by selling merchandise to an account during one of Paper Mate's seven yearly promotions. Frequent promotions help Paper Mate meet the competition and also give the retailer more opportunities to increase his own profits. The salesman might, for example, sell a customer merchandise in January for shipment the following month. February and March are the sell-through period, during which the pens move through to retail counters and distributor inventories are depleted.

The salesman must use his merchandising skills to see that goods do move through the pipeline. A drug chain may have counter-top tub displays of Flair pens and want a program to help sell the pens. "We tell the salesman how much profit the chain will make on a certain sales volume," Kiernan says.

"Then I say to the salesman, 'Be a sales promotion man. Maybe set up a contest. Get the buyer to sit down with you and agree on a promotion.' The salesman helps set up an ad, then sends memos to individual store managers telling them how to use their displays in line with the ad." All along, the salesman is stressing the profit that the retailer will make in the promotion. He knows that's also the way Paper Mate will make a profit.

INCENTIVE PROGRAMS ENCOURAGE PROFITABLE SELL-TO AND SELL-THROUGH

Profitable sell-through is the focal point of incentive programs, too. For the annual back-to-school promotion, the division's major effort, which begins in March and runs right through August, the sales force is given targets in all four product categories: ball point pens, refills, porous point pens, and broad-tip markers (the El Marko brand).

But, cautions Kiernan, "If a guy sells 200% of target, and the merchandise stays in the distributor's warehouse, what have we accomplished?" Thus the incentive awards—which range from a $250 gift certificate from a local department store to a $1,000 trip for two—are based on the highest percentage of sell-to and sell-through. Equally important, top awards go only to those who have been successful in moving the entire product line, not just one or two fast-selling items.

Though Kiernan relies on incentives to encourage profitable selling, he does not try to use commissions for that purpose. In fact, he doesn't use them at all, mainly because he feels commissions can actually be a *deterrent* to profits. "If you pay commission, an overzealous guy can load up an account with merchandise, and we won't make any money," he says. "It doesn't do any good to sell a lot of stuff to the wrong account."

Because of his confidence in the ability of his general sales force to move goods through the distribution network, Kiernan says he doesn't have to worry too much about the profit prospects for new products. Thus by the time Paper Mate's new 79¢ Hardhead ("writes like a ball pen but has the vividness of a porous pen") comes on the market next month, much of the groundwork will have been laid.

For the past two months, Paper Mate salespeople have been showing customers a promotional film that bills Hardhead as "the one pen nobody will be able to imitate." Kiernan himself appears briefly, urging the trade to "give the consumer a chance to purchase" the new pens. It looks like another hardheaded approach to selling through that's likely to produce more of those Paper Mate profits.

SM, May 19, 1975, pp. 15–17.

To Reach Survival, Change Here

Vince Hammil, sales vice president at Western Union Data Services, offers some never-more-timely tips on how you can make your selling approach crisis proof.

[Note: Most of the excellent suggestions in this article, which is addressed to sales managers, applies equally well to sales representatives in any type of selling who have the opportunity to work as local market or territory managers.]

National economies are fractured regularly. The causes change, but the results are nearly always the same for sales and marketing. Sales come hard, supplies get tight, collections slow up.

Here are some specific ways sales managers can cope with the problems of a recession, a downturn, and, especially, a shortage economy.

1. Use your influence.   Keep your company in its principal and profitable business. When a market is tough, marketers—and management—naturally look around for greener alternatives. But a shortage crunch works against diversification, and, in fact, diversification may make the basic business still more vulnerable to a slump. The best use of scarce capital is in sound, rather than speculative, businesses.

2. Service your profitable customers.   If accounts are to be lost because you cannot supply products, the last to go should be your proven money-makers.

3. Sell if you can profitably service.   Two prospects for a similar purchase may be equally easy to sell but not equally serviceable and therefore not equally profitable.

The cost of servicing potential accounts can be estimated. A good estimate can help avoid unpleasant surprises—like learning that a prospect could lead to excessive support costs and also drain the service given to established profitable accounts.

From a sales point of view, the three most important costs are marketing cost, product cost, and service cost. Service costs are the easiest to overlook because they are spread out in time and are the most difficult to figure.

4. Concentrate your selling.   Prospects come in clusters. If your sales team concentrates on clusters, your marketing and service costs will be low—if the pros-

pects are eventually converted to customers. In tight times, salesmen must get to know their territories and must find the prospect clusters.

Besides fixed concentrations, there are also temporary clusters, such as conventions and shows. Salesmen can be encouraged to exploit convention opportunities in their regions. An alternative to natural clusters is groups created for marketing purposes, such as company-sponsored seminars.

5. Be creative.   If unforeseen developments force a departure from plans, respond creatively and consider more options than usual in your planning. One area of opportunity is in making deals. The following example is an illustration of what can be done.

A company in the communications industry was trying to sell its products to a computer services firm. Driving a hard bargain, the customer wanted a number of free systems from the vendor and wanted the free systems in its headquarters. The vendor went along with the horse trading, developing a counter offer. It proposed that instead of free systems for headquarters, it would provide the freebies for the customer's own customers, but only for the initial new customers in initial new cities. The vendor's deal was to provide an incentive to open new demand for his product in conjunction with assisting the customer's marketing effort.

The plan was accepted, with good results. It gave the computer firm's salesmen extra reason to open new territory and a good selling point to offer the first new customer. The deal also opened new markets for the communications company at relatively low cost.

6. Develop standard marketing.   Opportunities for creative selling should be sought, but an effort should be made to do nearly the opposite at the same time: standardize the selling approach. The goal is to lower the costs of marketing by minimizing special materials and training and by using proven techniques in all areas. Part of the standardization program should be a conscious attempt to avoid offering extra features, customer options, and design changes that lead to higher product and service costs.

7. Position yourself for the future.   When product is short and selling patterns are upset, fill in by doing market research, looking ahead to new products with development efforts, and catching up on training.

SM, August 5, 1974, pp. 28–29.

Profit Improvement Doesn't Mean Service with a Strained Smile

by **Mack Hanan**, Contributing Editor

"We got the department's profit objectives the other day," the regional manager said. "They told us what we're trying to accomplish and where we're trying to go—at least in terms of the economics of the department. But they never talked about how we can grow 10% a year in profit and still move closer to the marketplace."

"Do you see a problem coordinating the two—profit growth and market closeness?" he was asked.

"If you tell me I must grow by 10% per year and that I have to get that 10% regardless of how I do it, you immediately make me volume oriented rather than concerned with needs. I'm going to get out and push, not serve."

Now that many companies have been emphasizing market orientation among their first-line managers for several years, and have lately begun to stress profit, sales managers are encountering problems correlating the two ideas. Top management would like to think simply that A equals B: that market orientation produces profit, and that the company that is able to get closest to its customers will naturally pull down the most profitable sales volume. In a reassuring number of cases, that has been shown to work.

But is the reverse true? Regional and district managers say, in effect, We're being presented with objectives and we're told to manage by objectives. That's not a sales strategy. It's an answer to a program without the program. From a market-orientation standpoint, what sort of role does that mean we should select for ourselves?

Regional and district managers who have been operating on a customer-orientation basis have learned that it has three characteristics that can work against short-term profit.

The first is that getting close to a customer takes time.   In the words of one first-line manager, "Getting to know what an account's needs really are—and not what you think they are or what you'd like them to be just because you have the product on hand—is a long-term operation. You have to go through a lot of people. You have to be patient in putting together their answers to your need-seeking questions. How can you do a good job in searching out needs and still produce short-term profit growth?"

A second characteristic of getting close to customers is that it is expensive. "Back in the old days, which I can still remember well because they really aren't that old, selling was relatively inexpensive," a district manager says. "Take the order, ship, and collect.

"Now, because our charter commits us to serve our customers and not just sell them, we're loaded with front-end and rear-end costs. 'Penetrate a customer in depth,' we're told. 'Ask questions. Verify needs. Anticipate needs you can't yet verify. Don't just sell a single product, sell a system. Don't just sell it, install it.' All the while, our costs are eating up our profit."

The cost of customer closeness can perhaps be summed up this way: The advantages of getting close are obvious. The costs of getting close are less obvious but just as real. It's a lot like a relationship between the sexes. The closer the relationship, the greater the benefits—but the bigger the bill.

A third characteristic of getting close to a market is that it fosters interdependence.   "If you invest a lot of time and money and the talent of your best salesmen in developing a close relationship with a piece of business, a certain amount of inter-twining takes place between your two companies," observes one manager. "When times are good, that pays off for us. We're the preferred supplier.

"But what happens when a customer gets into trouble? Once you've grown close, you don't walk away from him and say, 'Thanks for your business when things were going well for you. Call me when they get better.' No, you roll up your sleeves and go to work to help him even when it costs you. And there goes your short-term profit."

THE KEY TO PROFITABLE TOGETHERNESS

Profit-improvement selling is being taught to first-line managers by companies whose managements are sensitive to the confusion between customer orientation and profit and who want to ease their conflict. As those companies see it, the ability of their sales forces to improve the profit of their customers is the best way to recover the time and dollar costs of market orientation and to reduce the possibility of having a key piece of business get into trouble. This is the way it works:

1. First-line managers are taught how profits are made by their key accounts. They then pass that knowledge along to their field forces.
2. Because customers regard profit making as the chief benefit, first line managers position their sales forces as profit improvers. Their mission is to help customers improve profits by using the salesman's products, services, and personal profit-improvement expertise. In some cases, salesmen can help customers add revenues that improve profit. More often, salesmen can help customers reduce costs. Either strategy can improve profit.
3. As customers find their profit improving as a direct, measurable result of doing business with a particular salesman, they are encouraged to do more business. They also have an incentive to let the salesman become more deeply involved with their problems and their plans. In this way, profit-improvement selling can lead to intense customer closeness.

Profit-improvement selling allows a sales force to push hard for profit and still be market oriented because it supplies the otherwise missing link in the situation: it enables the customer to improve his profit at the same time the supplier is improving his own. With mutual profit improvement now linking their objectives, both companies can grow close and, moreover, expect short-term profit.

They can also put a long-term base under their profit making as the two companies move from a similarity of objectives to a business style that emphasizes similar strategies for achieving them and similar control procedures to monitor their achievement.

SM, March 4, 1974, pp. 40-44.

Section 18 / Some Special Applications to Retail Selling

Upstairs and Downstairs— Retailing Discovers Services

by **Arthur Bragg**, Senior Editor

Buying a dishwasher or any other major appliance at Montgomery Ward stores is apt to be an anticlimax. Customers swear that the really hard sell involves the company's service contract, which guarantees that the machine will chug happily until the $26.95 (in metropolitan New York City) contract expires. Montgomery Ward says that "a majority" of appliance customers can't resist the salesman's in-store sell and take the contract.

Those who don't can expect to hear from Roy Brown, Montgomery Ward's service sales manager, whose job it is to contact the reluctant via direct mail or telephone solicitation. The company won't reveal how often Brown and his staff score, but it is often indeed, especially among customers whose original contracts are about to expire and who need to be resold.

As a result, "Service contracts have become a very important part of our total business," says Dean Lewis, Montgomery Ward's national customer service manager. Two other customer service ideas that are also adding to profits are the company's life and casualty insurance programs (Montgomery Ward will even insure customers' credit account balances) and its new Auto Club, a nationwide program whereby, for $12.50 a year, a member can call any repairman he wishes when his auto breaks down. In its first 12 months, the Auto Club signed up 165,000 car owners.

To find service sales, Montgomery Ward taps its hordes of credit account holders, estimated at somewhere between 6 and 10 million. Judging by its success so far, Montgomery Ward will return to that source again, just as soon as it can find another customer service idea to sell.

Many retailers' appetites for service sales are now sharper than ever because today's higher quality products need fewer repairs, and service contracts are thus more profitable. Solid-state TV sets, for example, require so little repair work that servicing dealers and independent service organizations are busily looking elsewhere for opportunities, often in auto repair.

ZERO HOUR

At Sears, national service manager William P. Zabler is pushing a development he predicts will ensure that Sears's service contracts continue to grow in profitability. Increasingly, the company's service centers across the nation are pressing for appointments for service calls. "Many wives work now and their time is too important to waste waiting for a repairman to call," Zabler says. "And, naturally, calls made when nobody is at home drive our costs up considerably. We're hoping that appointments will solve that problem for us." Sears has not yet begun to talk about its program in its ads, but it could do so soon. Sears also sells driver training courses in selected stores.

Other retailers who see gold in customer services include
Steinbeck's stores, Asbury, N.J. It sells its customers "M.D." cards—imprinted with their name, blood type, and any physical disorder (heart disease, diabetes, etc.)—which they carry in case of accident.
Rich's, Atlanta. Shoppers can leave their children, aged six months to six years, in a special nursery while they shop.
J. C. Penney. Sewing instruction is sold in a number of its outlets, with classes most often set up in an area of the stores near pattern catalogues, sewing machines, and supplies.
Harrod's, London. Customers can buy a "complete and first-class" funeral.

Other customer services that retailers expect one day to sell in their stores include housecleaning, nursing, tutoring, a full range of beauty treatment beyond anything now offered, weddings, catered parties of all kinds, investment counselling, and retirement advice. This "new retailing" is as inevitable, they say, as electronic data processing machines in stores. Says Philip M. Hawley, president of Carter Hawley Hale, the sixth largest department store chain, "We see big opportunities in the service area—travel, auto, and financial services, to mention a few."

Dayton's, the Minneapolis-based department store, is reaping sales through a new customer service idea it calls Masterplan. "This is a service that appeals to the customer who would not ordinarily consider using interior decorating services," says Ken Lever, general merchandise manager for home products. "Masterplan means that, without obligation, the potential customer is encouraged to call one of our room designers to his home," he says. "The Masterplanner will draw up a plan with suggestions for fabrics, textures, colors, and accessorizing, using the customer's ideas, taste, and budget, and all at no charge." Lever says the program pays off for Dayton's: "We find that customers usually come back to our store for their furnishings."

A number of retailers are already launched in the "new retailing" and can either credit or blame consumerism for it. Cleveland's Higbee Co. has initiated an in-store program of consumer services under three general headings: Consumer Redress (consisting of a generous return policy, customer service bureau, a special attorney

for consumer affairs, and an Officer-for-a-Day program); Consumer Protection
(labelling sleepwear, monitoring toys, drugs, and cosmetics); and Consumer Information (how-to-do-it courses, distribution of permanent-care label charts, letters to
explain labels).

Once a month, customers can even find a top management officer—Higbee's
Officer for the Day—readily available to hear complaints and, hopefully, solve them
himself. The program, store management says, also helps its executives keep in personal touch with problem departments, new types of consumer problems, and re-
curring merchandise difficulties. Another new idea in retailing is creating customer
advisory boards, composed of store customers who meet regularly with management
to suggest how selling can be improved and complaints avoided, what new services
and products might be tested, and the like.

At its recent national convention in New York, the National Retail Merchants
Assn. heard predictions that stores will one day assign "sales counsellors"—professional salespersons, some with degrees in consumerism—to their counters in place of
mere sales clerks. The theory: It will take a sophisticated salesperson to sell to
tomorrow's highly sophisticated customer.

Retailers' new eagerness to provide better service is already causing waves for
marketers who sell to them. The National Retail Merchants Assn. has just voted a
much stiffer policy on vendor relations "to help the vendors improve the quality
and efficiency of their services" to retailers and "bring the consumer the best product or service at the lowest price." Henceforth, the association has ruled, marketers
will be graded on a long list of functions, but especially on how they handle purchase orders and returns and how often they ship only partial orders. Records of
their performance will be kept on file.

Stores that participate in the scheme are supplied with forms for requesting information about specific vendors' performances and forms for reporting any difficulties they have with their vendors. "We intend to make it easier for our members
in their relationships with their suppliers," says association president James R.
Williams. "They can now recognize the good manufacturers by the absence of
complaints."

J.C. Penney merchandising chief Walter Neppl takes a fundamentalist view of
customer service, which he defines as customers receiving from sales personnel the
benefits of sound product knowledge and sound selling skills. Accordingly, Neppl
has audiovisual units placed literally at salespersons' elbows during the day, teaching them to sell the way he wants them to sell. One of Neppl's biggest goals is to
wipe out friction between salespersons and Penney customers. "It is very dismay-
ing indeed," a spokesman says, "to come across a salesperson refusing to take back
a purchase, and thinking she is right in doing it, when we have a guaranteed-return
policy we are proud of."

Some marketers are stepping in to help retailers, thereby making impressive gains
for themselves. Macy's and Uniroyal have long had a salesperson training liaison;
the marketer supplies a whole range of training aides that the retailer features in

off-the-selling-floor instruction. Revlon's three product divisions all believe in getting closer to the point-of-purchase by sending their people into stores to show clerks how to use Revlon products and how best to sell them.

THE MORE THEY KNOW

Sales of Bonne Bell cosmetics skyrocketed at Illinois Thrifty Drug outlets soon after Bonne Belle's national training and sales promotion director, Ray Clarke, instituted all-day sessions for the drug chain's clerks to stress product training. Clarke also offers the drug chain, as well as other accounts that sign up for his program, a free, extended in-home study course for clerks. "The more they know, the more they sell," he says. Indeed, Clarke's program is credited with a successful repositioning of Bonne Belle as a line for all age groups, not just teen-agers.

When it recently brought out a line of consumer calculators, Rockwell International's Microelectronics Div. decided that its best hope for success in that seriously overcrowded market was to teach dealers' clerks how to sell its machines and also make a strong selling point of its service centers. Says Rockwell vice president Harold L. Edge, "Our merchandising emphasis is on realiability and service as well as product features. In addition, we see to it that retail sales personnel in each of our market areas are trained by us." Result: Rockwell's calculators now have one of the highest "awareness" ratings among clerks, and dealers—long bitter over "being ignored except at order writing time"—ask Edge's competitors, "Why can't you be more like Rockwell?"

SM, February 17, 1975, pp. 39–42.

DAC Stores' David A. Collins

David Collins was still in college when he decided to open a retail clothing store, David's of Arkansas, in Little Rock. "I had saved about $4,000 working as a part-time salesman," Collins says, "and I borrowed everything I could. I had a friend in the retail business who gave me enough clothes—on credit—to stock the store. The opportunity presented itself; so I just went ahead and did it."

After that, he just went ahead and opened three more David's stores, and purchased John Gerber department stores and the Gus Mayer chain of women's specialty stores. Thus Memphis-based DAC Stores, of which the 29-year-old Collins is chairman and president, now includes 27 stores in eight states in the South and Southwest. Sales for fiscal 1973 were $45 million, and Collins is shooting for $50 million in 1974.

When DAC Stores purchased John Gerber in April 1973, the family-owned stores, Collins says, "lacked aggressive management. We created great profitability." He tells how: "If I've got X amount in sales, I don't gamble that I can increase those sales to meet expenses. Instead, I'll try to get expenses in line with sales.

"In this type of business, there's a great deal of fat. We reorganized people and combined selling areas. For example, if you have a camera department and a stationery department with a wall between them, you can knock down the wall and have one salesperson cover both departments."

Even with the emphasis on cost cutting, Collins does not downgrade the need to increase sales. He explains a procedure that's successful at Gerber's and that he plans to establish at Mayer's: "If a customer buys over $10 in merchandise, the salesperson who made the sale sends a postcard thanking the customer for the business. And 60 days later, if the customer hasn't been back to the store, there's a follow-up note."

Although Collins is clearly an aggressive man who knows how to make things happen, he remains unassuming. He says quietly, "I just want you to realize that it hasn't been all David Collins. There are a lot of people with me—a good group of very professional people."

SM, August 19, 1974, p. 10.

Section 19 / Some Special Applications to Telephone, Industrial, Group, and Exhibition Selling

Purchasing Men: More Aggressive On and Off the Job

The man your salesman calls on has changed—and is still changing. He's younger, better educated, more highly paid, and has more influence in his company than ever before. So reports *Purchasing World* magazine, which has just surveyed about 1,000 of its readers, who are industrial buyers and purchasing executives. Here's what the survey shows about today's buying pro:

Age—The typical buying professional is 35 to 40 years old. Only 1% are under 25. Some 22% are between 25 and 34 years old. The largest contingent (43%) fits into the 35- to 49-year-old bracket.

Education—The typical respondent to the *Purchasing World* survey is a college graduate with a degree in Business Administration. A full 83% of the respondents have at least some college, 33% hold undergraduate degrees, 7% attended graduate school, and 3% have advanced degrees.

Pay and Background—Although many buying pros think they're underpaid (and some of them are), the majority aren't doing that badly. About 37% earn between $15,000 and $25,000; 7% make more than $25,000. Some 45% have previous purchasing experience: 35% worked in production or inventory control; 26% of them tried their hands at selling.

The survey shows also how the purchasing function is changing. Today's buying pros spend less time buying and more time making sure they're getting the best buy. Close to 90% participate in make-or-buy decisions; 70% are interested in lease vs. buy possibilities; and 93% are responsible for evaluating supplier capabilities. More than half the purchasing executives queried use computers or computer time. In the larger companies, the percentage climbs to over 80%. Eighteen percent of the smaller firms represented in the survey have their purchasing departments using computer time regularly.

Purchasing executives are also adding new responsibilities. "Take traffic, for instance," *Purchasing World* researchers say. "About 12% of the respondents claim prior traffic department experience. That training is being put to good use. Proof:

Four of five respondents are now involved in transportation buying decisions. A full 80% say they specify the mode of transit for incoming shipments, and 61% actually name the carrier." Outgoing shipments, the researchers report, also are controlled by purchasing, although not to the same degree. About 25% route out-going shipments by mode, and 21% name the carrier. Similarly, the researchers say, half of the buying personnel contacted in the survey manage inventories of products and materials, 65% evaluate and select subcontractors, and 70% help establish or modify specifications.

Seven out of ten buyers now use company-wide blanket orders or national agree-ments; one out of four has formal value analysis programs, two out of four work from approved vendor lists, and four out of ten use vendor performance ratings as normal purchasing procedure.

All that would indicate that purchasing is doing a better job than ever before; indeed 80% of the respondents report that their companies have policies requiring all vendors to clear through the purchasing department before making contact with other company personnel. *Purchasing World*'s survey also touches on how the buy-ing professional spends his free time. More than 52% play golf or tennis or partici-pate in some other active sport. Travel runs a close second. Those responses stand in sharp contrast to answers supplied only a few years ago when gardening, wood-working, and church work were listed as the main outside activities.

Purchasing World agrees that it's a tougher sell today. "But not if you work it right," it adds. "Today's buying pro is more receptive to facts. If you've got them, he'll listen and, more important, understand them and act on them." Also, the magazine notes, he should be able to give salesmen answers and decisions faster, more knowledgeably, and more decisively than ever. It's a brisker as well as a tougher sell.

SM, July 9, 1973, p. 36.

Stranger, Thy Name Is Salesman

Are industrial salesmen making enough sales calls on customers? A just-released study by Chilton, major publisher of business magazines and books, concludes that for the most part they are not. Chilton's researchers personally asked 4,420 buyers in a wide spectrum of industrial products companies across the nation how many times in a two-month period a salesman had called to discuss a product they nor-mally purchase. Sixty-one percent said that no salesman had appeared at all.

Even when salesmen make frequent calls, they may end up practicing "tunnel sell," the researchers say. "Companies that do make the most direct sales calls on known buying influences are able to contact only a small percent of the known buying influences for any given product or service. This ranges from 13.3% for the average highest number of calls made to an average low of only 2.1%," the study notes. Buying influences identified as most likely to be missed by salesmen are the higher corporate and functional titles, especially in production, engineering, and design.

The physical distribution, natural gas, and trucking industries earned the highest grades for frequency of sales calls; companies selling electronics and instruments and controls, despite the fast-changing nature of those industries, made the fewest sales calls.

The researchers also raise doubts about how effective a selling job had been done on the buyers they talked to. Almost 50% of all the salesmen's companies "do not have a strong corporate or brand loyalty image and consequently do not rate with any consistent show of strength as a primary source of supply" in buyers' eyes, the study concludes. Buyers also complained about salesmen "underselling" them on the quality of products they are asked to purchase. Other problems buyers mentioned include difficulties with salesmen about pricing and inadequate service.

Chilton offers its survey findings to prove a point: that advertising in business publications is "an important source of information" for buyers. Indeed, nearly 90% of the buyers said they rely on ads to teach them things about products that salesmen selling the goods never brought up.

A point the researchers *do not* make is that salesmen's call frequency is now probably worse than ever—Chilton carried out its probe in 1972, long before the energy crisis and inflation pressured many a sales manager to cut back on sales calls.

SM, October 14, 1974, p. 14.

Industrial Selling Costs: Now It's $60 a Call

New programs designed to hold back the rising cost of making industrial sales calls are making their presence felt (*SM*, June 26, 1972) but there is no doubt that inflation, and assorted selling missteps, will boost the average call cost to $60 this year (consumer goods sales calls will also climb—to about $36). Among those that will be hardest hit—assuming that industry trends continue [see table, p. 148] — will be companies selling nonelectrical machinery, primary metals, and rubber and plastic products. Also, calls will continue to cost proportionately more at companies using fewer salesmen. A *Sales Management* survey, carried out last spring, showed that the average cost in 1971 was $63.90 at industrial companies with less than 10 salesmen, $60.69 for those with 11 to 25 salesmen. In contrast, companies employing between 26 and 50 salesmen spent $46.18 per call; those with more than 50 men averaged $45.18.

ATTACKING THE BASE SALARY

The strategies industrial sales managements are using to battle mounting sales costs range from reducing salesmen's entertainment allowances anywhere from 10% to 50% to banning first-class air tickets or curbing all travel, no matter how frugal. Other approaches include rewriting compensation programs (a favorite goal: reduce the base salary), reviewing expense accounts for excesses, encouraging greater use of telephone selling, and halting reimbursement of travel costs for calls on customers located close to field offices.

Rising call costs this year can be blamed, in no small way, on the fact that many sales managers manage salesmen almost as if time did not equal money. In "Time and Territorial Management for the Salesmen," a recent research report of the Sales Executive Club of New York, author Dr. Robert F. Vizza notes that 54% of 257 industrial and consumer goods companies surveyed had not conducted an organized study of salesmen's use of time. Twenty-five percent had no system of classifying accounts according to their potential, he found, and 51% had yet to determine the number of calls it is economical to make on their accounts.

Something akin to that was the situation at Kysor Industrial's Anchorpac Div. when Jack Brune, general sales manager, arrived. The division, he says, had no sales budget, no system for reporting salesmen's expenses, and few sales records of any kind. Now salesmen must submit weekly expense accounts, which are totalled monthly and compared with individual budgets the men must follow. Tighter salesmen control also helps trim call costs at Borden Chemical Co., where management insists that salesmen provide specifics about the number of daily calls they make, time spent on each call, distance traveled, and all related expenses. Celanese Plastics Co. aims for economy by having salesmen identify the decision-makers at their account-companies and develop detailed information—before making their calls.

Another stratagem likely to become popular is printing salesmen's expense account forms on the reverse side of call report forms; until the men include essential data about their calls, their expense accounts are not cleared for payment. Also, industrial firms are realizing that underpaying low-level salesmen . . . is false economy. Rather than trying to reach the carrot you dangle before them, a Conference

Ups and Downs of Industrial Salesmen's Call Costs

	Average Call Costs			% Change	
Industry	1971	1969	1967	1969 – 1971	1967 – 1969
Transportation Equipment	$89.94	$78.27	$106.42	+14.9%	−26.5%*
Nonelectrical Machinery	66.82	53.21	46.25	+25.6	+15.0
Primary Metal	61.17	46.37	39.92	+31.9	+16.2
Electrical Machinery, Equipment, & Supplies	59.97	51.90	41.70	+15.5	+24.5
Rubber, Miscellaneous Plastics	51.21	36.14	44.20	+41.7	−18.2
Chemicals	49.00	45.27	34.66	+ 8.2	+30.6
Instruments, Photographic & Optical Goods, Watches & Clocks	48.90	58.68	41.24	− 16.7	+42.3*
Fabricated Metals	45.19	48.46	39.97	− 6.7	+21.2

*Fluctuation is due to inclusion of very large companies with unusually high call costs.
Sources: *Sales Management*, McGraw-Hill.

Board report shows that most such salesmen soon quit for a better-paying spot somewhere else.*

Instead of parsimony, industrial companies need to develop "creative" selling practices, says McKinsey & Co.'s B. Charles Ames. "The sales force in many companies functions more as a collection of independent sales and distribution agents than as the integrated marketing arm it should be," he argues in *Harvard Business Review.* In his opinion, an excellent way to make salesmen cost-conscious is—like it or not—by showing them your actual cost and profit data.

SM, January 8, 1973, pp. 14–23.

The Rising Cost of an Industrial Sales Call

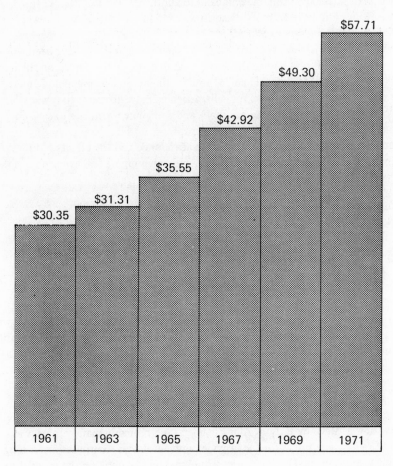

| 1961 | 1963 | 1965 | 1967 | 1969 | 1971 |

$30.35 $31.31 $35.55 $42.92 $49.30 $57.71

*Conference Board Report No. 545, "Salesmen's Turnover in Early Employment."

150

Industrial Selling Costs: $66.68 Per Call and Rising

The average cost of making an industrial sales call in 1973 was $66.68. A *Sales Management* survey of calls for 1971 put the average cost at $57.71. This means that sales managers spent $8.97 more per call last year.

The $66.68 figure emerges from a survey of 450 industrial companies carried out by McGraw-Hill Research and announced late last month. The survey notes that over the last 10 years, the cost of an industrial call has more than doubled.

Allen J. Cobb Jr., director of McGraw-Hill Research, says, "There is a wide range in the cost of sales calls from one company to another." The average expense last year for firms with more than 50 salesmen was $45.29. For those with fewer than 10 salesmen, the average was $80.55.

Bad as the news is, few are surprised by it. And it might easily have been worse. Sales managers who took part in the survey said that the tactics forced on them by the shortages crisis *(SM,* Jan. 21) helped to curb their costs. These include more selectivity in choosing customers for calls, assigning more accounts to fewer salesmen, calling less often on smaller accounts, and realigning territories to save on salesmen's travelling time as well as their expenses.

Many predict that when those tactics are abandoned and the effects of inflation hit home, sales call costs will zoom upward, with a whopping $80 average possible by year's end.

SM, July 22, 1974, p. 9.

The Price of Inflation: No One Likes to Sell It Twice

A very unfunny thing has happened to electrical equipment companies on their way to supply the nation's utilities this year, and Jack Oliver is right in the middle of it. "No one likes to sell an order twice," says the national field sales manager of Westinghouse's Power Systems Co. "It goes against the grain."

Yet that's what Oliver's 300-man sales force has been doing—or trying to do— since early spring. Despite a company announcement at that time, no one paid much attention until early this month. Then it became known that Westinghouse, along with GE, McGraw-Edison, Allis-Chalmers, and probably many others, was trying to renegotiate prices for the heavy equipment it sells to utilities under long lead-times. . . . Collectively, the stories would make a textbook on the miseries of selling in double-digit inflation.

Oliver's chapter is painfully simple. Prior to last January, his men sold such things as transformers, switch gears, and generators, with the price spelled out in the contract. Westinghouse had no such protection from its own suppliers, however. During the past eight months, prices on steel, copper, aluminum, and other key materials shot up as much as 56%, putting a severe squeeze on costs. When it came to heavy castings and forgings, the company did have contracts with suppliers, but they didn't do much good. Officials claim they were told they could not be assured of future supplies unless they agreed to pay higher prices, which meant swallowing increases of up to 75%.

"There is no such thing as a firm contract in today's economy," says Oliver calmly. So how do you tell that to a utility that buys millions of dollars of equipment from you? Oliver's men try to explain the situation tactfully to customers, emphasizing that cooperation will help insure the continued supply of quality equipment. "We haven't exactly been overwhelmed with acceptances," says the veteran manager, "but enough utilities have agreed to share some of our costs to make the effort worthwhile."

In an operation the size of Power Systems, every little bit helps. Oliver's sales force accounts for 70% of the unit's $2 billion volume. Many salesmen service a single customer and spend up to 40% of their time on the premises. A large utility may have four salesmen from the same company working on its account. "We're in a continual state of negotiation with the customer, even in normal times," says Oliver.

To protect itself in the future, Power Systems has put escalator clauses based on government indexes in all its contracts, but Oliver obviously regrets having to sell under those conditions. Even though he doesn't think it will happen soon, he says, "We want to get back to a firm price policy as soon as possible."

SM, September 23, 1974, p. 7.

Ansul Blazes New Sales Patterns

The company that is referred to as the Cadillac of fire protection proves that a flexible sales organization pays off handsomely in industrial selling.

by **Sally Scanlon**, Associate Editor

Selling for Ansul's Fire Protection Group wouldn't be every salesman's dream job. For one thing, its 30-odd salesmen and managers must be expert fire fighters. For another, the Marinette, Wis., company is pretty casual about sales force organization and titles. "If the selling environment changes a lot in six months, our sales organization changes to meet it," says David N. Francis.

Francis, one of the few men in the company whose title is relatively stable, is vice president and general manager of the Fire Protection Group. This year, his organization will account for about 51% of Ansul's projected $120 million sales volume and 73% of its pretax profits.

SALES FORCE FLEXIBILITY

In the past six years, half a dozen or more special sales forces have been created to help Ansul penetrate specific new market segments, such as the restaurant equipment industry. . . . Mission accomplished, these forces have been disbanded and their salesmen assigned to other duties. Salesmen and managers who don't like living with flux have left the organization. "Most of the people who remain," general manager Francis says, "understand that we'll stop changing only when the market does." The reason is simple: flexibility is paying off handsomely for Ansul and its 250 independent distributors.

Fire Protection Group sales have more than doubled in the past five years, rising from $27.4 million in 1970 to an estimated $61 million this year; profits have nearly doubled. Even more important in this time of economic uncertainty, there's no sign of a slowdown in the immediate future.

The company's major customers are the booming energy-related industries, which, at the moment, have no shortage of investment capital. Safety industry observers, who refer to Ansul as the Cadillac of the fire protection industry, estimate that it has 70% to 80% of the market for fire extinguishing equipment used in high-hazard, high-risk industrial areas, such as oil refineries, off-shore drilling rigs, chemical processing plants, and steel mills.

SATISFIED CUSTOMERS

Comments from industrial plant safety directors back observers' estimates. "Our refinery men swear by Ansul. They wouldn't think of using anything else," says Emil Gazeik, a Marathon Oil safety engineer. Adds Shell Oil's J. F. Byrne, "I'd venture to say that if you walked into any chemical or petroleum plant today, you'd find Ansul equipment. Its quality control is superb. Equally important, it offers good service and excellent manpower training."

SALESMEN PROMOTED TO KEY MANAGEMENT POSITIONS

Ansul sales, however, are no longer limited to the high-hazard, high-risk user. In the late 1960s, Ansul sales managers began moving into the top group management spots that formerly had been filled from outside the company. The newly promoted managers' first concern was to strengthen Ansul's relations with its distributors and customers by introducing a lower-priced line of extinguishers for use in commercial and light-industrial areas where its premium-priced, heavy-duty Red Line isn't needed.

NEW PRODUCT AND NEW SALES/MARKETING OPPORTUNITY

The new line, called Sentry, was introduced in 1970—just in time to put Ansul in the running (with some 15 fire equipment competitors) for a share of the vast new market for safety equipment that was legislated into existence by the federal Occupational Safety and Health Act (OSHA) of 1970. Ansul now has a 10% to 12% share of the still-growing light-industrial market. But the primary effect of OSHA on Ansul sales has been its function as a door opener to the OEM business.

"Prior to OSHA," Francis says, "there was no comprehensive national fire standards. So original equipment manufacturers didn't build fire protection equipment into their products because end users were not legally obligated to meet the same set of standards. Extra equipment would have added to the product's price without increasing its appeal." Now that end users have to meet OSHA standards, however, they want to buy a complete package. Ansul's sales story is that its equipment can satisfy the OEM's customer better than any of its competitors.

SALES FORCE ORGANIZATION

To make the most of its multiple market opportunities, Ansul currently has four sales groups: (1) a field sales force, divided into four zones in the U.S. and one in Canada; (2) a national accounts group, with a sales manager and four field managers; (3) an OEM group, with two salespeople and (4) a government group, also with two salespeople.

The first group works primarily with the distributor network, the others with potential end users. But don't let the distinction lead to false conclusions: Ansul does 98% of its North American fire protection business through distributors, and the distributors say that the company tries to cut them in even on national and OEM accounts. When it does have to bypass them, it explains the situation in advance to its 13-member Distributor Advisory Council.

Council member Richard P. Eisenmann, president, Interstate of Milwaukee, says, "We say fine, go ahead because Ansul sells direct only in limited areas that the distributor can't sell on his own. If every manufacturer handled us this way, it would be great for our business."

Keith Kellenberger, partner, Fox Valley Fire Equipment, Elgin, Ill., concurs. "We appreciate Ansul's selling policies," the distributor says. "We've gotten slapped in the face a lot by fire equipment manufacturers whose sales forces compete with us."

Ansul distributors weren't always so understanding. Roger Maire, distributor development manager, recalls that three years ago, when Ansul first went the national accounts route, some of its distributors lost local business. Says Maire, who was Chicago regional manager at the time, "We had to do a lot of convincing to show them that if we had not gone direct they would have lost the business anyway because the competition would have taken it all. By going direct, we're selling the distributor's services. The aftermarket in our business is fantastic."

Distributors now accept that. For example, Bob Colvin, vice president, Maryland Fire Equipment, Rockville, Md., says that in most cases, Ansul's OEM and national accounts selling is a door opener for him. "It gives my salesmen an opportunity to talk service and additional equipment sales with companies with which we'd probably never have become associated," says Colvin. The reason: their main buying offices are located in other parts of the country.

CHANGING NATURE OF THE ANSUL SALESMAN'S JOB

Distributors aren't the only ones whose relationship with Ansul is changing. The Ansul salesman's own job has changed tremendously in the past 20 years. When the company entered the fire protection business in 1939, via an acquisition, its salesmen sold direct. At the time, the men were actually missionaries because Ansul was pioneering the use of dry chemical fire protection extinguishers. Such extinguishers use a mixture of dry chemical powders, rather than water, to put out flames. The salesmen's job was to convince a skeptical market that dry chemicals were more effective than water in extinguishing certain types of fires.

To help its salesmen get the word across, Ansul established a school in 1940 to train users in fire fighting techniques. The school, now the largest of its kind in the world, was a first step in Ansul's meticulous attention to customer service. A second was its switch from direct selling to distributors.

As dry chemicals gained acceptance, Ansul had to assure customers of the availability of local service. The switch to a selected group of distributors accomplished that, and Ansul's own salesman's job became one of building the distributor organization and working with distributor sales and service men to sell and train end users.

The salesman still covers those areas. But his main assignment now is to develop the business skills of his distributors. "We're managers of our own territories," says 22-year sales veteran David W. Metzler, who, as a district manager headquartered in Frazer, Pa., calls on 13 distributors in five eastern states. He spends most of his time making joint calls with distributor salesmen, training them and distributor servicemen on new products, riding service trucks to see how Ansul customers and equipment are being cared for, and becoming deeply involved in training end users on the proper use of fire fighting equipment. For example, last month, Metzler spent two days with 72 Exxon men. Working with them in groups, he first showed slides, then led them outside for live fire fighting demonstrations.

"Salesmen in each zone work as a team," Metzler says. "We each have an individual quota [Metzler's is over $2 million; no salesman's is under $1 million], but our main goal is to make the objective for our zone. If any man has a problem, he can call on anyone else in the zone for help." And, he adds with pride, "Our zone has been No. 1 for the past three years."

SALES FORCE COMPENSATION

Ansul pays salesmen a salary plus bonus based on a percentage of sales after they hit 91% of quota. To keep them motivated, the company publishes a list of each man's standings once a month. It also uses spot incentives from time to time.

ANSUL AND THEIR DISTRIBUTOR'S SALESMEN AS PART OF THE OVERALL MARKETING MANAGEMENT TEAM

More important, perhaps, top management really listens to the field force. Says Metzler, "We meet occasionally with top managers. They understand our problems and needs, and they do something about them."

"They" also work constantly to upgrade communications between salesmen and distributors. Eighteen months ago, Ansul formed the first Distributor Advisory Council in the fire protection industry. DAC members say that Ansul's top management sits in on every meeting and really listens to their opinions about the market, proposed new products, and such. "I can remember one time when we had a complaint about something," says Interstate's Eisenmann, a DAC member. "The company president happened to be at the meeting. He ground our complaint down to specifics, then went out and did something about it."

CONTINUED EDUCATION AND TRAINING PROGRAMS

This year, Ansul began offering distributors a 10-month self-study course called Profitable Distributor Management . . . , or PDM for short. First graduates say the course has been an eye-opener for them in terms of analyzing and upgrading their operations, particularly in the critical financial area. Ansul salesmen also took the course, and the result, says distributor development manager Maire, is a big improvement in communication with distributors. "Prior to PDM training," Maire says, "a salesman might have chewed out a distributor who wasn't producing. Now he really understands the distributor's business so he can help him analyze the situation and come up with a solution that's profitable for both of us."

In working with distributor principals, however, Ansul hasn't forgotten the distributor's sales and service personnel. The company is experimenting with a modular training program to help distributor salesmen make the most of its OEM effort. It also has a new course in the works to upgrade sales and service training for distributor employees.

With new technologies creating new fire hazards—and new marketing opportunities for fire protection system and equipment—Ansul's present sales policies will continue to evolve to meet changing market needs, say its top management—built around its flexible sales force.

SM, December 9, 1974, pp. 25–28.

156

Trade Shows:
1876: The Way We Were

Americans greeted the new year in a dour mood. Several presidential confidants had been exposed as influence peddlers, and impeachment rumors ricocheted through the Capitol. In Philadelphia, local luminaries prepared to host the nation's Centennial, with one eye on newspaper editorials that wondered whether the birthday was worth celebrating in a country that might not survive another century.

But the 1876 Centennial put smiles on people's faces. The May 10th opening parade led by President Grant down Broad St. and through the Centennial Grand Triumph Arch had been followed into Fairmount Park by no fewer than 9,910,966 visitors by the time the Great Exhibition closed in November. Within the three-square-mile fence that ringed the Fairmount Park grounds were 190 special buildings housing 31,000 exhibits from 50 countries. Ranging from the ornate Horticultural Hall . . . —it cost $367,073.47, Philadelphians boasted—to the wickedly popular Turkish Pavilion Café and Bar, they accounted for what one historian called "the most overwhelming, absorbing, entertaining public exhibitions ever seen in the United States."

In contrast with the 1976 Bicentennial, business played a prominent role in Philadelphia. American Fusee Co. (safety matches) had its own building. So did Gillinder & Sons, a local company. It paid an unprecedented $3,000 for the fair's glassware concession, then recouped its ante manyfold by producing souvenir statuettes and paperweights on the spot. Corliss Steam Engine Co. lacked a building only because its 680-ton, 1,500-horsepower model engine was too large to fit inside one.

The fair was also ideal for introducing new products and marketing techniques. The Franklin Institute celebrated its 50th anniversary by introducing Americans to the ice cream soda. Visitors also got their first taste of Vienna bread, which they downed with coffee at little marble tables manned by Goff, Fleishman & Co. Another big attraction was a pavilion by Cook, Son & Jenkins Co. featuring such exotic oddities as a 3,000-year-old Egyptian mummy and a desert campsite recreated as it would supposedly look in Palestine. The purpose: to interest America's growing middle class in the new idea of popular-priced group travel. The company, now Thomas Cook World Travel Service, obviously had the right idea.

Elisha Otis also had a good idea, even though it scared most folks at the time. Although he had already patented his elevator—and a safety system to prevent it from plunging down a shaft—only the heartiest fair visitors dared ride the up-and-down exhibit sponsored by his young Otis Elevator Co. That's why his descendants are especially pleased that when Penn Mutual Insurance opens its new headquarters in Philadelphia later this year, its most striking feature will be the outdoor observation elevators (Otis, of course) that overlook Independence Hall.

SM, February 18, 1974, p. 32.

Trade Shows:
Print 74 Makes an Impression

There may still be some traces of a paper shortage, but they were certainly not evident at Chicago's McCormick Place last month during Print 74's 10-day run. Literally hundreds of machines hummed away, showing prospective buyers what they could do to the stacks of paper on hand, whether it be printing, folding, cutting, binding, wrapping, or copying.

Nor was there a shortage of exhibitors or buyers at the show aimed at the graphic arts industry. Held only once every six years, it is one of the nation's biggest machinery exhibitions. A record crowd of over 17,000 turned out the first day, and total attendance topped 60,000. Buyers could visit more than 400 exhibitors, including such familiar names as Xerox, Kodak, 3M, Du Pont, Rockwell International, Singer, and GAF, and a good selection of overseas companies.

Most exhibitors agreed that Print 74 met or exceeded expectations. "We've had five times the traffic we thought we would," said Bob Cranston, Chicago branch manager for Xerox's Cheshire Div. Dave Ruane, a power equipment specialist who sells for Signode, concurred: "We're introducing a $40,000 strapping machine," he remarked on the show's third day, "and I think we're going to sell a dozen of them before it's over."

Many of the companies introduced new products. Rockwell alone had six, marketing services manager Kent Martin said. "We think new product introductions help create excitement for the whole show," he explained. Rockwell was one of several companies (others included Harris and Mergenthaler) showing electronic editing and layout terminals, which proved to be among the show's top traffic-stoppers.

Other new products included Cyrel plastic printing plates, which eliminate engraving, from Du Pont; room-light-handling contact films, which need no darkrooms, from Kodak; and a plain paper copier with a lifetime-guaranteed "imaging material," from A. B. Dick. Xerox Cheshire, basically a labelling equipment company, introduced a binder that rents for $40 a month. "It can handle reports as thin as one thirty-second of an inch or as thick as an inch and a half," Cranston said. "We tested it this summer in New York City, and now we're taking it to Chicago and the West Coast. Cheshire's salesmen will be the ones handling it, but in many cases they're going around with Xerox copier salesmen, who introduce them to their customers."

This flurry of new products is a sign that the inflation economy has not hit the graphic arts equipment industry very hard. "I'm having my best year ever," reports Charlie Carpenter, a Kansas City-based salesman for Bell & Howell's Baumfolder Div., a maker of folding machines. "Our equipment saves labor, and as printing industry wages keep going up, that's a good selling point." Signode's Ruane also stresses the wage-saving sell—his company's new $40,000 strapping machine does the work of two men. At today's wage rates, it practically pays for itself after one year.

That seemed to be the kind of economics that buyers at Print 74 could appreciate.

SM, December 9, 1974, pp. 3–5.

Sarah Coventry's David L. Gibson

What's bad for the economy is in many ways good for Sarah Coventry, which claims to be the country's leading seller of costume jewelry. "It's the nature of the business," says Dave Gibson, 50, who last month was promoted from executive vice president to president of the direct-selling company. "When times are tight, people in in-home selling work harder to increase their commissions. It's easier to recruit, too, because people are working less overtime and inflation has diminished their income." He adds, "The direct selling business grew by 15% last year, and sales are expected to increase 18% this year. We will outshine the industry by far."

But Gibson is hardly going to let the recession take full credit for the 26-year-old company's continued increases in sales and profits. What's really responsible, he says, is its personalized approach to selling. Customers—whom Gibson calls "guests"—see Sarah Coventry jewelry at an in-home gathering run by a fashion show coordinator, the company's basic salesperson.

"It beats the indifference of in-store sales," Gibson says. "We offer product knowledge, and we can say where the items are made and what the guarantee is. A store clerk couldn't learn all that about a product. We even teach guests how to wear jewelry and how to use it better. Also, we offer a nonsales atmosphere. Our show doesn't sell the merchandise; the guests sell each other."

There's a personal approach to sales force management, too. Branch managers, the first-level managers, hold weekly meetings that Gibson says are "a combination of motivation, inspiration, instruction, and recognition. We point out to a person— in front of the others—the progress she is making, even if she increased her sales by only $5 last week."

There are 35,000 salespersons in the "Sarah family," and Gibson estimates that between 12 and 15 million people will attend the company's fashion shows in 1975. He's proud of those numbers, but says that they're the merest beginning. "We've saturated only one-fifth of the country; there's still lots of room for us to grow."

SM, May 5, 1975, pp. 15–16.

Telephone Selling: Dial "G" for Gypsum

Inside salesmen aren't the hottest new idea in selling, but lingering effects of the energy crisis and, especially, inflation's added burden on selling costs are prompting more companies to try selling via the telephone. One of the latest converts is U.S. Gypsum, which now has 23 inside salesmen.

"We have the same incentive program for them as we do for our outside salesmen," marketing vice president Bob Day says. "And we measure their performance in the same way—on the sales dollars they bring in." The big difference, Day says, is the kind of account they handle. Gypsum sales executives believe that telephone selling works best with those customers who have fairly regular buying patterns or who don't need much personal follow-up.

In addition to permitting U.S. Gypsum to realize significant savings on salesmen's over-all travel expenses and allowing it to service customers whose purchases no longer merit personal sales calls, its inside sales program gives the company a chance to move more women into sales. "Women sometimes can build better telephone relationships than men can," Day says. Accordingly, of his 23-person inside sales staff, 13 are better-relationship-building women.

SM, October 14, 1974, pp. 12–14.

PART VI How to Reach your Personal Sales or Management Objectives

OVERVIEW

This concluding series of readings offers helpful factual and motivational guidelines to readers who feel that selling might be a career they will follow, and who wish to know how to land a sales job of their choice, how to most rapidly progress to higher sales and earnings through personal selling, and how to win promotion to managerial ranks. Most of this material applies equally well to those younger men or women already embarked upon a sales career, who wish to advance themselves most rapidly. Sections 20 to 23 indicate the topics that will be covered.

Sales/marketing, a term used to integrate marketing and personal selling, is a growth area offering unlimited career opportunities for ambitious men and women of all ages. Provided that one selects a growth industry or organization in a field of interest, the sales road to marketing management offers one of the quickest paths to career success. Opportunities for higher earnings or promotion to top management through selling have reached, and will continue to reach, new highs in the United States and Canada, and indeed in most countries of the world, for most individuals regardless of age, sex, race, educational level, or social origin.

If you (the reader) wish to take advantage of these opportunities, however, you will have to develop your knowledge and skills through study and practical application, and become managerially oriented. A major purpose of both the text *Modern Applied Salesmanship,* 2d ed., and this accompanying *Readings in Modern Applied Salesmanship* is to help you accomplish this.

Section 20 – How to Sell Yourself for the Sales Position of Your Choice
Section 21 – Plan Your Work – Work Your Plan: The Self-Management of Selling
Section 22 – Programming Your Career Toward Higher Earnings and Management
Section 23 – Your Personal Audit: That Magic 10 Percent Plus

Section 20 / How to Sell Yourself for the Sales Position of Your Choice

How Rapistan Ltda. Hired a Salesman

HELP WANTED

Technical Salesman Needed. International company, expanding its market, seeks a dynamic individual with sales experience in medium and heavy machinery. He should have secondary education, good health and appearance, a proven interest in mechanical problems, and facility in communication. Salary open, plus car and other fringe benefits.

Responding to the above advertisement in a São Paulo, Brazil, newspaper, 10 job candidates find themselves in the office of Dr. A. H. Fuerstenthal, a management psychologist, at 5:30 one Thursday afternoon. They are there to participate in a unique experiment in salesman selection. Henry Hanelt, director of Rapistan Ind. e Com. Ltda. (the local licensee of Rapistan, Inc., Grand Rapids, Mich.), is present. His company needs a salesman for its materials handling equipment and he will decide which candidate gets the job.

The candidates have been told only to appear at 5:30. When they arrive, Dr. Fuerstenthal explains that each one will have five minutes in which to stand up and sell himself; then the others, seated around the table with him, will have five minutes in which to question him and try to punch holes in his arguments. Meanwhile Fuerstenthal and Hanelt will observe the presentations, the questioning, and the emerging personalities of the candidates, and decide which ones they want to interview further.

Dr. Fuerstenthal worked out his system for selecting salesmen because "nobody has succeeded thus far in devising a reliable test for salesmen." He notes: "Sales is a communication job, while other jobs are a mixture of communication and operation, and for operation it is easy to devise tests. What I have tried to do is create a communication situation in which the pressure is similar to that of an actual sales call. I expose a man to his own competitors in the act of selling himself. When a man can define his own position, he can define a product to a customer."

Rapistan, which entered Brazil last January, is introducing a varied line of equipment for materials handling. Management is looking for a man who can explain and describe the new products and convince prospective customers that they are not only useful but necessary to their operations. As Fuerstenthal explains, "Some salesmen hunt rabbits, others hunt tigers." Rapistan's equipment is a "tiger"—it may take a whole year of patient work to sell a full line of equipment to a factory; so the company needs a man whose sales philosophy is adapted to that kind of strategy.

Before the "testing" session starts, two candidates beg off and leave, not being sufficiently interested in the job to expose themselves to the pressure of the meeting. A third eliminates himself by refusing to speak first.

Finally, after a few words of explanation from Fuerstenthal, the session gets under way. The candidates are surprisingly poised, and talk easily and well. But as the meeting progresses, some begin to stand out—they are more convincing, convey more authority.

Candidate M leads off. He is 24 years old and has been selling throughout Brazil since he was 17. Although he talks well, he seems immature.

Candidate J is a graduate mechanical engineer with several years' experience selling various types of medium equipment. He is impressive, and the others react to the scent of competition with some probing questions in an effort to throw him off balance. Some typical questions: "What was the most expensive piece of equipment you ever sold?" "How did you convince people that your automatic welding process was more economic than manual welding in a cheap labor market?" J answers all the questions agreeably and with assurance, giving sound technical explanations. There is a general feeling in the room that here is a formidable contender.

Candidate A has years of excellent experience but is a poor communicator. He talks fluently, but he is colorless and without warmth; it is obvious that he isn't coming across.

But F makes people sit up and take notice. He is attractive, smooth, almost overconfident as he describes a bewildering series of jobs in which he has sold everything from shoes to sewing machines. He arouses a variety of reactions. Fuerstenthal, in order to provoke him, asks: "You are obviously a born salesman and could probably sell anything, but can you also play the part of a technical salesman, as opposed to a jack-of-all-trades?" Others feel that his superslick manner inspires distrust.

The questions now come thick and fast. "What arguments did you use to sell your elevators over those of your competitors?" "What real technical sales have you handled?" "Did you ever take any courses in mechanics or sales?" "How would you handle a completely new product?"

It gradually becomes apparent that most of the loaded questions are being asked by candidate L. At first that seems to indicate interest and a keen mind, but gradually it degenerates into sheer antagonism and meanness. L is asking questions framed to trip up the other candidates and to show off his own knowledge. In the end that tells against him and annuls his qualifications. Says Fuerstenthal: "A sales-man should be aggressive, but not nasty."

Fuerstenthal is especially interested in knowing what outside courses the candi-dates have taken. He explains that that indicates not only interest and ambition but a certain dedication to one type of sales and a knowledge of the direction in which a man wants to progress.

The remaining candidates are negligible, with poor personalities and inadequate experience. The choice boils down to J, the mechanical engineer, N, or H, the two widely experienced middle-aged men.

Rapistan chooses J. As director Hanelt explains: "He was so eager for the job that he lowered his salary requirements considerably to meet what his competitors were asking. Frankly, I couldn't afford to turn down such a bargain." Especially, he adds, if he can sell machinery as well as he sold himself to a jury of his peers.

SM, September 8, 1975, pp. 69–70.

Section 21 / Plan Your Work— Work Your Plan: The Self-Management of Selling

Selling by Measurable Objectives

by **Robert A. Else,** Sales Manager for General Electric's Apparatus Service Division

Sales planning by the individual field salesman is cursed, caressed, enshrined, rejected, and studied by just about everyone. The purpose and meaning of sales planning usually depend entirely on who's doing the viewing. The first and most important viewer—the field salesman himself—sees sales planning as something that is forced on him from above, as "filling out forms to satisfy headquarters." Only after completing the forms can he "get back to work."

The marketing or product manager at headquarters has an entirely different view of sales planning. He is inclined to be nervous about the daily activities of the field sales force. It's easy for him to see how much it costs to keep salesmen in the field; it is not easy for him to see what they are doing to earn that money. This same manager usually receives weekly or monthly reports from persons on his own staff documenting their past month's activities and their next month's plans. Consequently, it is completely logical for the manager to request sales plans from his field salesmen so that he can feel equally comfortable about their activities. This is particularly true for salesmen who are responsible for selling large ticket items to a few large customers.

DINING ROOM EFFORT

So, classically, the request goes out to field sales management to draw up sales plans and have them at headquarters by a certain date. After resisting his part in all this for as long as possible, the salesman finally sits down at his dining room table and

---

Robert A. Else has been with GE since graduating from Southern Methodist Univ. in 1946. He was a district manager of Apparatus and Distribution Sales from 1961 to 1968 and a regional manager for the Information Service Dept. from 1968 to 1970, when he assumed his present title. GE's Apparatus Service Div. is in the industrial maintenance and repair business, with facilities in most major cities of the United States and in 12 foreign countries.

writes a summary of how he is going to perform his job over the coming months. If he has any dramatic flair at all, he will be quite elaborate in describing his "strategy" in manipulating his major accounts into making purchasing decisions.

If we could get each one of our salesmen to document his planning this way, we could feel assured that he has a strategy for obtaining his sales results. Or could we?

When we analyze sales plans that are prepared in this manner, we find that they are usually a "snapshot" of a selling situation at a particular time. The salesman has taken the history of sales, conversations, product complaints, etc., and has devised a strategy for the future. That strategy (1) sets dates for his future actions, (2) assumes the reactions of his customer, (3) states additional actions on his part, and (4) includes additional reactions on the part of the customer. The problem here is obvious: The salesman *cannot* predict the reaction of his customer to each situation in advance. This kind of sales plan deludes headquarters into believing that the salesman has a sales strategy worked out—but, in fact, he has no viable plan at all. Companies that encourage this kind of sales planning by salesmen have created the classic situation wherein the field is supporting headquarters rather than headquarters supporting the field.

STRATEGIES VS. TACTICS

By carefully dissecting the salesman's activities as outlined above, we can see that although he is trying to combine broad strategies and implementation tactics, he has set down nothing except vast, vague objectives. The solution to his dilemma, and yours, is simple, although it is often completely overlooked by sales managers.

Strategies for an account or for a whole territory can and should be identified. These could include a plan to emphasize engineering quality of a product or service, bringing company management from headquarters into the sales situation, a "group sell" presentation to all the key buying influences, or a heavy local advertising campaign.

Tactics, in selling, is the implementation of these strategies. It involves interacting with the customer, an activity that cannot be planned in advance because the *exact* reaction of the customer cannot be predicted. Implementation of tactics *is* professional selling, a fact good salesmen realize.

Effective planning of strategy and the implementation of tactics are only part of the job. A third element, the one that makes selling "go," is often overlooked in sales planning. I refer, of course, to setting objectives: territory objectives, market objectives, objectives by geography, objectives by account. After having set good, measurable objectives, it is necessary to identify the steps in attaining the objective.

To illustrate this, let me take an example from General Electric's own procedures:

Salesman's Objective:
Obtain $5,000 in mechanical repair work from the XYZ Co.

Such an objective meets the acid tests of (1) having economic value and (2) requiring an action or decision on the part of the customer. But is the sales planning job complete? Not if we consider what has to happen before this objective can be met. For example:

1. Identify the decision maker(s) in XYZ Co.
2. Identify the kind of repair work now being done.
3. Identify the competition.
4. Identify areas of customer dissatisfaction.
5. Make a sales presentation.
6. Ask for an order.

All these steps become subgoals. When an industrial salesman does this kind of planning with his major accounts *and* then goes two steps further, he is doing an effective sales planning job. What are the two additional steps? (1) Set dates to accomplish the goals/objectives and (2) commit the plan to his sales manager.

Until two years ago, sales planning in General Electric's Apparatus Service Div. was conducted much like that described in the beginning of this article. It is always harder for a new salesman in a service environment than for one in a product-oriented business. Our business is industrial maintenance and repair, a service environment that requires our salesmen to be quick to react *after* an equipment failure in a customer's plant. Our problem was to get them working ahead with new prospects *before* a failure occurred.

Sales Planning by Objectives at GE was implemented first with only a part of our facilities; they used a format similar to the two tables shown [pp. 167, 168]. The results have been excellent. The salesman is able to identify those product service lines that he has been obtaining from his major customers as well as those that have

Territory Sales Plan

Sales Engineer *Sam Doaks*

Account Name	Sales History ($000)			Est. Available ($000)	No. of Sales Calls Allocated Per Year	Planned Sales (or Available Sales) By Product Line ($000)				
	1969	1970	1971			Prod. A	Prod. B	Prod. C	Prod. D	Prod. E
XYZ Co.	100	110	90	250	48	10	25	25	75	25
ABC Co.	75	75	90	300	48	25	50	25	10	5
EEG Co.	40	50	60	175	24	10	10	40	20	10
GFF Co.	20	30	50	150	24	10	20	–	10	30
FFH Co.	10	10	25	100	18	30	–	25	–	–
HGG Co.	0	0	30	100	18	–	10	30	–	40
JKL Co.	0	0	0	80	18	25	–	–	10	40
KGG Co.	0	10	20	75	12	–	10	10	20	30
MNO Co.	0	5	12	60	12	20	20	20	–	–
QEC Co.	0	0	10	60	12	–	10	–	40	–
ZZZ Co.	10	8	9	50	12	2	5	5	20	5

Note: Since product line goals should have stretch, they should *not* be added either horizontally or vertically.

been going to competitors. With that data in front of him on a yearly or semi-annual basis (see Territory Sales Plan table), he is in a position to do his major account planning on a monthly or bimonthly basis (Major Account Sales Plan table). Most important, on each sales call he has clear-cut objectives aimed at his over-all account objectives. The results to date for us are marked improvement in sales dollars and in product-service mix for those facilities which have adopted the system. We intend to implement Sales Planning by Objectives for all our service shop locations.

Our salesmen are now finding that they aren't "filling out forms to satisfy headquarters." They are organizing themselves to be more effective and more professional at their jobs.

SM, May 14, 1973, pp. 22–24.

Major Account Sales Plan

XYZ Co.
_____
Firm Name

Center City
_____
City

Sales Engineer *Sam Doaks*

Major Objective(s)	Measurable Attainable Realistic	Date to Accomplish	Persons Affecting Decision(s)	Planned Steps to Accomplish Objective	Date to Accomplish
1. Assure continued purchase of product "B" by convincing purchasing agent of the superiority of our paint.		10/1	John Jones *Purchasing Agent*	1. Convince Jones to come to our plant for a visit—make appointment.	9/15
2. Obtain an initial order for product "C" of at least $5,000.		11/15	John Smith *Plant Engineer*	2. Conduct tour of plant and demonstrate paint finish.	10/1
			Jim Brown *Maintenance Superintendent*	1. Make appointment with John Smith to find current supplier and find out decision maker.	9/5
			John Jones *Purchasing Agent*	2. Determine whether moisture or aging is most important problem to Smith.	9/5
				3. Get appointment for demonstration of product "C" to Smith, Brown, & Jones.	9/15
				4. Hold presentation and ask for order.	10/1

Airbus: Selling on a Wing and a Prayer

by Dan Rosen, Contributing Editor

Considering the well-known woes of most U.S. airlines, this would seem to be the worst time to try to sell them costly airplanes. Nevertheless, the marketing timetable of the European consortium responsible for the new A300B Airbus calls for an all-out selling effort now; and marketing director Ken Gordon, a corps of salesmen, and a demonstration Airbus were recently off and selling in the western hemisphere.

Gordon's main goal: to get at least one U.S. airline on his order book—earlier customers include Air France, Lufthansa, and Iberia—in the hope that other American carriers would follow suit. His chief selling points: the short-to-medium-range, twin-engined Airbus is quieter, more economical to operate (a 17% cut in operating costs is claimed), and meets the future needs of U.S. lines better than any other wide-bodied jet.

SM sent contributing editor Dan Rosen to ride on Airbus's historic sales mission (a mission that is also vital to 40 U.S. firms, including General Electric, that have products built into the plane). Here is Rosen's report on Airbus's gutsy but frustrating sell.

DAY ONE

I'm standing on the airport ramp in the muggy sunlight of a Miami afternoon when the Airbus pulls up. The plane just starred at a week-long air show in São Paulo, Brazil. The flight crew is dog tired, the cargo hold is brimming over with test equipment and selling brochures, and the sample cabin is a tight-packed jumble of personal luggage, 40 selling executives, and 22 cases of French champagne. Nothing much scheduled today, except prepare to start selling.

This is a command performance. Late last summer, after months of selling effort, Michael Wall received a phone call from Fred Luhm. Wall is the top-ranking man for Airbus in the U.S.; Luhm is in charge of new-aircraft evaluation for National Airlines—and National is the seventh-largest commercial carrier in America.

Luhm told Wall that he wanted him to come down from New York for "serious talks," and Wall made the trip the following day. They talked about delivery dates, price concessions, and spare parts—proof that as far as they were concerned, selling was about to get really hot. At that summer meeting, Luhm asked to see the Airbus here in Miami. And so it's now out there on the apron, on schedule.

DAY TWO

9:30 A.M.　National has sent its chief pilot and a group of flight operations supervisors for the first demonstration flight. "Standard procedure," Wall tells me later. "Most airlines want to be sure about a plane before they put their key people aboard." I am talking with a local reporter as the crowd arrives. There is no special welcome, just a steady flow of visitors up the boarding stairs. I get in the line taking a press kit from a sweating public relations man.

Adam Brown, the Airbus general sales manager, joins me. Brown, a wiry, blond Englishman, is yet another reminder that the A300 project is crossing all sorts of national boundaries. Airbus Industrie, the manufacturer, is actually a consortium of all the best-known aircraft companies in Europe. The production models are being assembled in France, but the wings are constructed in Great Britain, the fuselage and tail sections in West Germany and Spain, the control surfaces in Holland, and the engine mounts in West Germany. The governments of France and West Germany are underwriting 70% of the $580 million development costs. The Netherlands, Spain, and Hawker-Siddeley Aircraft of Great Britain are backing the rest.

Brown and I talk as the plane taxis to the runway. The Muzak on the loudspeaker has been switched to one of those deep-voiced, gee-whiz, piped-in sales pitches, but it sounds like a 78 rpm recording played at 33-1/3. The pitch ends and a stewardess begins the usual oxygen-crash landing patter. We all settle back in our seats.

The plane is off the ground in an almost unbelievable burst of power! The engines, two behemoths with—Brown tells me matter-of-factly—51,000 lbs. of thrust apiece, are General Electric CF6-50C's. It's the same type of engine that powers the C5A Galaxy, the DC-10 Trijet, and a longer-ranged version of the Boeing 747 now being flight-tested in Seattle. Brown argues that having an engine in common with other airplanes will cut down on maintenance costs and spare-parts investments.

Whatever their economic advantages, they are certainly quiet. Quieter, as a matter of fact, than they are actually required to be under the FAA's new antinoise regulations. We level off at 25,000 feet and head out toward Bimini. I unhitch my seat belt and start to explore.

The area behind the flight deck—the first-class cabin area in a working airliner—is filled with dials and measuring devices. In this part of the plane, at least, selling is taking a second place to the prosaic task of making sure that everything is working.

The passenger cabin is divided into sample seating arrangements: a spacious, easy-chair design for well-heeled customers in the front, a nine-abreast pattern for charters in the back.

Brown's selling is low-key but determined: small talk and technical things over champagne and caviar. There seem, though, to be almost as many Airbus salesmen as visitors aboard.

Back on the ground now, the selling revs up.

12:30 P.M.　The place is a private dining room in the Marriott Hotel near the airport. Five Airbus salesmen and five National Airlines executives face each other across a long table. The menu: cracked crab, New York sirloin, salad, coffee, and ice cream. Arthur Howes doesn't get to eat his ice cream: he's the Airbus specialist on the National Airlines account, and he does most of the talking.

3 P.M.   A smaller group of men is gathered in Howard Dolansky's office. Dolansky is executive vice president of National, and with him is Fred Luhm, National's evaluator for new aircraft. Robert Blanchet is talking for Airbus. Blanchet, an amiable Frenchman with an excellent command of English vernacular, is worldwide sales and marketing chief. (He reports only to board chairman Henri Ziegler.)

Blanchet argues that National needs 22 A300s, at about $15 million each, to meet its market needs of 1980. Dolansky, knowing that any sale Airbus makes to him could lead to sales to other U.S. carriers, brings up price concessions. He presses hard on financing and spare parts. Blanchet isn't able to land the order, although he tells me later that he thinks there's a good chance that he'll do so in the next six months.

DAY THREE

9:30 A.M.   Another demonstration flight in Miami, this time for Eastern Airlines. The Airbus people don't expect much: Eastern is floundering in losses and it is still trying to cope with a disastrous overcommitment to the new Lockheed 1011s. "We're happy to let them see the airplane," North American sales manager Ken Gordon remarks. Eastern's people make the flight—and Gordon does his thing anyway.

3:30 P.M.   Off to Mexico City. The flight is a long one; so I have plenty of time for a talk with Bob Blanchet. "The important thing about a selling tour," he says, "is that it helps to establish your credibility. We proved that we could put together a trans-European airplane in the first place, but people still want to see it before they'll really believe it. I'm the top sales and marketing man for this outfit. The main offices are in Toulouse, France."

Like production aspects of Airbus, its selling is a multi-national effort. Dennis Little, a red-haired Englishman, is sales promotion manager; Maurice Lelong, who heads up sales engineering, is French; market research manager Russ Shanahan is an American who emigrated to West Germany; public relations manager Ray Paikine is a sharp-witted Frenchman. All are with us on the plane.

Englishman Adam Brown, the general sales manager, runs the field sales force. Tony Lawler, another Englishman, takes care of Africa and South America. Ken Gordon, an American who's an old Boeing hand, handles North American out of an office in Greenwich, Conn. There's another area manager for Europe, of course. But although each of the area managers has a great deal of autonomy, Blanchet watches the over-all selling strategy closely.

Blanchet says about the selling approach in America: "We're reaching the people we want to reach, of course—the small minority who actually buy airplanes—but we don't want to raise any nationalistic issues. We want to get our normal share of the market—but without scaring anybody."

DAY FOUR

9 A.M.   The action in Mexico City is with Mexicana Airlines, a privately owned local carrier with a growing network of tourist routes. "They're going to need new airplanes," Jim Beaumont confides, "and whoever sells them will probably sell them two airplanes to start with and one a year through 1980."

Beaumont, the Airbus specialist for Mexicana, is aware that his chances of selling Mexicana are pretty slim right now. "You get your information in all sorts of ways," he says. "Some things you learn in serious talks and some in drunken lunches that last until eleven at night. The key with Mexicana, I'm afraid, is to first sell the plane to a major American carrier. I don't think the Mexicana people will have enough confidence in the program if we don't."

After two demonstration flights for Mexicana and an extravagant cocktail party at the Hacienda de las Morelas, Beaumont admits no orders are signed.

DAY SIX

7 P.M.   We arrive in Chicago, headquarters of United Airlines. The visit has some sentimental significance—United was the only U.S. carrier to order the old French Caravelle. But that was years ago, and Blanchet tells me that he isn't hopeful of any repeat performances in the near future. This stands to reason. Most airline analysts are reporting that United's earnings are in a steady decline.

DAY SEVEN

2 P.M.   U.S. Customs has impounded the airplane. Here's a blow-by-blow account: Jim Beaumont was standing at the foot of the boarding ramp when an inspector came over. "I'd like to see your entry permit and customs declaration forms," he said. "No problem," Beaumont answered. "I'll take you to the right man." But the "right man" didn't have the papers. The plane sat on the ramp, fully loaded and ready to leave for another appearance in Cincinnati. The customs inspector demanded a $15 million bond, to ensure that neither the plane nor its contents would be sold in the U.S. A $15 million surety bond costs about $16,000. Board chairman Henri Ziegler, who was on the plane, got adamant. "We're staying here until we work it out. If we're going to be late getting to Cincinnati, we might as well be *very* late."

7 P.M.   A compromise has been reached: the plane is permitted to leave, pro-

vided that the necessary papers are filed before it departs the country. It's a minor incident, but it highlights yet another selling problem: the Airbus is vulnerable to U.S. government pressure, even when the pressure is completely justified. And should Douglas, Lockheed, and Boeing decide to gang up on the project, there's no telling where that pressure might lead. Airbus salesmen privately say they won't be surprised if new "problems" crop up in the future.

DAY EIGHT

9 A.M.   Cincinnati. The sky is squinty bright and there's excitement in the air. The Airbus is the chief performer at a seminar on aircraft engines sponsored by General Electric, and the ramp is thick with people from 40 airlines. This is a show for pros given by pros, and when Airbus chief pilot Fischl takes off, he lets it all hang out. The plane climbs to altitude, executes steep-banking turns, then screams earthward, levelling off at 300 feet for a strafing run over the airport. Connie Whiles, GE's "Best Buy Quality Queen," is aboard. It's her first airplane flight—a fact that's obvious. She's turned green.

12:30 P.M.   Bob Blanchet takes reporter Larry Surrant of the Cincinnati *Post & Times Star* to lunch. The questions are basic and Blanchet fields them easily. It's a jackets-off, cocktails-on-the-table, note-pad-in-hand replay of interviews in every other city the Airbus has visited, and I wonder how Blanchet avoids boredom.

7:30 P.M.   GE plays host to a cocktail party for the Airbus team. Blanchet admits that the selling in Cincinnati has been pretty soft. "It's GE's show, after all," he explains. "An event like this gives us a chance to talk practical business with potential customers, but we can't turn it into a full-blown selling exercise."

DAY NINE

10:30 A.M.   We arrive in St. Louis for a meeting of the Assn. of Local Transport Airline Operators. Top executives from Allegheny, Ozark, Trans-Texas, and the other regional carriers are in attendance, and there's another round of demonstration flights, receptions, speeches, and private meetings. I decide to go home. I've been with the airplane for a week and a half, and the 15-hour days are getting to me.

DAY FIFTEEN

I rejoin the Airbus team in New York. By now, the airplane has covered more than 20,000 miles on its current tour. It has logged 101.5 hours of flying time, made 61 takeoffs and landings, and taken aloft more than 2,000 people. It will be months before anyone can say how much all that has cost Airbus—but $1 million is a fair estimate.

What did it all accomplish? Bob Blanchet didn't sign a single order, but confesses that he didn't expect to. It takes years to sell a new airplane, years of route studies, market analyses, meetings, and sales presentations. When you've finally sold an airline on the idea that your plane is the best one for its needs, your efforts can fall apart for lack of financing, to name a single danger.

"Our experience is that the U.S. airline industry has never paved the way for general acceptance of an airplane from Europe," Blanchet told me today. Nevertheless, Airbus's entire program certainly looks as if it will stand or fall on its success in the U.S.

Airbus's U.S. sales chief, Michael Wall, says flatly, "The key in the U.S. is National Airlines. We have to sell a major trunk carrier, and National remains our most immediate prospect. Once we do that, the local carriers here are likely to fall into line."

He may be right. For the time being, at least, the Airbus has no direct competition. The narrow-bodied short-haul aircraft of today—the 727s, the DC-9s, the Caravelles—are certainly not the aircraft of the future. Boeing is thinking about a wide-bodied twin engine called the 7X7, but the project is still on the drawing boards—or maybe a little beyond that stage.

Then there's the fuel crisis. In the short run, its effects on Airbus are, admittedly, devastating. "I don't know when *any* of us will start selling airplanes again," one U.S. aviation industry spokesman tells me. With airlines cutting back flights and grounding flight crews, it's easy to see why. But when the crisis passes (yes, even the energy crunch will one day be a memory), Airbus management figures it can sell successfully. After all, "it's a great airplane that meets marketing's needs."

It takes about four years to get from the drawing boards to a working prototype of a new airliner. Add another couple of years of selling efforts to get one of the planes into actual service with an airline. But this April, a production model Airbus starts flying Air France routes, and that's as big a head start as anyone at Airbus could have hoped for.

SM, February 4, 1974, pp. 28–35.

Section 22 / Programming Your Career Toward Higher Earnings and Management

Computers Take Over Paper Work, Speed Customers Service Calls

Computer-based information systems are giving two powerful and vital assists to the marketer's service function: (1) boosting salesmen's productivity by taking over many of the manual chores that eat into critical selling time, and (2) strengthening all-important customer relations by triggering more effective responses to customer needs.

On the one hand, computers provide salesmen with more effective support by eliminating time-consuming paperwork, feeding them better information with which to control accounts, and elevating prospecting to a more scientific plane. On the other hand, they contribute to stronger, long-term customer relations by facilitating the efficient handling of customer requests, making sure that customer orders are delivered at the right time and place, and making it easier for marketers to answer customer inquiries. Here are some examples of how the computer can help [the sales force offer better service to customers.]

MANN MANUFACTURING

Terminals that are equipped with TV-like display screens help the salesmen of Mann Manufacturing, an El Paso, Texas, clothing concern (estimated sales: $33 million) give flash answers to customer inquiries. The company, which ships slacks and jeans to more than 7,000 stores around the country, stores complete records of styles, sizes, sales, customers, and inventory in its IBM System/370. Also filed in the computer's massive memory are detailed information on customer orders, including styles, colors, pairs shipped, freight lines, number of cartons, bill of lading numbers, and back order promise dates.

Salesmen can directly interrogate this bank of information, and can view the needed facts on display screens. "When a customer calls to check an order," says Harvey L. Falk, vice president, finance, "the salesman has all the facts he needs at his fingertips and can give an answer in 30 seconds. Before we had this system, it took him as long as two days."

Because slacks and jeans fads are mercurial, Falk is looking to the computer to give the sales department a faster response to shifting market trends. Future applications will include customer demand forecasting, order allocation, and customer bookings. "In the fashion industry, where product lines change constantly," he says, "the computer gives us flexibility."

XEROX

Another ambitious effort to harness the computer in the vital service area is Xerox's COIN (Customer Oriented Information Network), a six-year program that will put the Information Systems Group's sales branches into the computer age. Scheduled to be completed some time in 1978, COIN includes (1) a centralized information bank in Rochester, N.Y., (2) visual-display terminals in all 80 sales branches that will feed information directly into the central data base, and (3) a linking communications network.

Of special significance to the sales force is that the bulk of its paperwork will eventually be taken over by the terminals. Daily business transactions—orders, installations, billings, accounts receivable, price changes, machine service, and so on— are now entered into a small Xerox 530 computer at each branch. During the night, bigger computers will process the information, updating all the records that branch management relies on to run the business, and transmit finished reports back to the branches by the following morning.

As is the case with many computer systems, much of the repetitive information salesmen have to write when taking orders will be stored in the computer's memory. When the operator enters the customer code, all the supporting information will be generated automatically by the terminal, thus reducing the possibility of errors as well as saving time for the salesmen. In addition, the orders that salesmen now fill out in duplicate each time they sell a piece of add-on hardware will be taken over by COIN.

Salesmen will also be able to promise speedier service. It now takes up to 17 days to get new orders into the data files; COIN's terminals will post transactions immediately. Billing adjustments can take as long as 20 days currently; under COIN, it will be just one day if only branch approval is needed. Accounts receivable inquiries that take three to four days to answer will, under COIN, be handled the day they are received.

Service histories on each machine that's in the field will be stored in the branch computers. By consulting those histories when a service call comes in, a service manager can gain a better idea of whether a technical specialist is required to solve a problem. Xerox says branch managers have said that "this is the most essential piece of information you can give us."

SM, February 17, 1975, pp. 18–21.

Welcome to a New World Where Profits Come Harder

[A special *Sales Management* Report on what sales managers and sales representatives face in view of the economic realities of the marketplace in the late 1970s.]

by **Mack Hanan**, Contributing Editor

There's a song called "Make the World Go Away" that sales managers might well sing as they see their sales and profits threatened. Some managers choose to ride out the storm. Few, however, ask themselves the hard questions: What if the new world of higher costs, lower profits, and new constraints won't go away? What if that's the world in which most of us are going to do business from now on? How do we put a profitable handle on it?

If those negative views of the future turn out to be inaccurate, everyone will be relieved. But what if they don't? How many of us are prepared to run a profitable business in a world where many of the things we have taken for granted no longer hold? Are we rehearsing sales appeals that may not be able to include such old standbys as "new," "full line," "immediate delivery," "full range of colors," "free service," and "we will not be undersold?" We should be because from all indications, the economic realities in the second half of the 1970s will present us with the following facts:

Unemployment will remain high. At the average 7.8% rate for the next three years that President Ford predicts, the number of employable men and women out of work will be nearly double the 4.9% average that prevailed from 1960 to 1973. There will be more retired and pensioned people than ever before.

Inflation will slow but will still be high. The average annual rate of 7.1% that is forecast for 1975 through 1980 will be more than double the average annual increase in the 1960-73 period. That will continue to erode real spendable earnings severely.

The rise in the standard of living will slow. People addicted to the idea that "more is better" will find that more is also costlier. Their lifestyles will be altered accordingly.

Oil will remain in tight supply. It will continue to cost more than pre-1974 prices. That will affect productivity and growth and consumption rates for many products.

Many other raw materials will remain in short supply. Asbestos, tin, helium, and mercury are already endangered species. Other minerals may join the list.

The market for venture capital and growth financing will remain expensive to draw from and less rewarding to invest in. That will affect business expansion and new markets.

There are already a number of previews of how companies react to the new real world in which they must sell [see Check your Reaction to the Changing Sales Environment]. Look at the auto industry. Chrysler has begun a long-term restructuring of its business that will cut capital overhead by one third. That decision was based on industry sales projections in the range of 6 million cars a year, compared with the 8.8 million cars sold in 1974. General Motors has announced a four-year, $3 billion research program to make cars smaller and lighter so that they consume

CHECK YOUR REACTION TO THE
CHANGING SALES ENVIRONMENT

The Trend Will Be Toward . . .	*. . . And Away From*
1. Consolidation of company and division size.	1. Emphasis on being or becoming the biggest.
2. Short-term, cyclical ups and downs.	2. Reliance on long-range planning or commitments.
3. Emphasis on profits.	3. Emphasis on volume (unless it contributes directly to profit).
4. Insistence that each account make its maximum contribution to your profit.	4. Large numbers of customers solicited or served.
5. Insistence that each salesman make his maximum contribution to profit.	5. Large sales forces.
6. Insistence that each product and product line make its maximum contribution to profit.	6. Full product lines.
7. Insistence that each channel of distribution make its maximum contribution to profit.	7. Multiple distribution channels and large numbers of distributors and dealers.
8. Renovated products and acquired products.	8. Entirely new products.
9. Systems selling.	9. Interest in single-unit sales.
10. Emphasis on applying products and services to improve customer profit and promoting that effect as the prime benefit.	10. Product-benefit selling.

less material and use less gasoline. Ford is undertaking a similar product redesign. Following the trend in its cars, GM also wants to make its corporate organization structure "smaller and leaner."

Elsewhere, airlines are cutting back on their route structure and on services. Supermarkets are contracting their geographic marketing areas and closing many outlets. Most companies will take similar steps in the next few months if, indeed, they have not already done so. As a result:

1. Salesmen will have less to sell because product lines will be thinner across the board. Fewer models with fewer options will be the rule. If a product isn't a big winner or a potential winner, it won't be worth the materials and the labor and energy resources that go into it. It will be scrapped or divested.

2. Markets will become more concentrated by a similar thinning process. Emphasis on big-winner products will be paralleled by catering to heavy-user key accounts. Smaller customers may become too expensive to sell it. Unless they can use the big winners of their suppliers and afford to pay for them, they may be unable to buy what they need or prefer.

3. Product development will be significantly reduced. Product renovation and marginal line extensions will predominate over true innovations. Salesmen will have less that's "new" to sell.

4. Contribution to *customer* profit improvement will be the basis on which more products are sold. This will become the major justification for purchasing in many industries. Most customers, if not all, will need to improve profits by reducing costs and lowering their break-even points. So will their suppliers.

5. Sales staffs will be reduced. Top salesmen will be motivated more intensively than ever. They will also receive most of the training as programs for marginal producers are abandoned. Sales training will be far more results oriented. Before a program is approved, top management will require quantification on a return-on-investment basis. Some sales forces will be spun off by their parent organizations and set up as wholly owned subsidiaries that may also sell related products made by other manufacturers.

6. Sales plans will set smaller growth objectives. Targets will be well below the pre-1974 minimum rate of 8% that became popular because it was about twice the annual rise in the Gross National Product. With reduced GNP growth, sales increases will slow, too. The lower growth objectives will be expressed as *profit on sales* and *return on investment* rather than in terms of unit and dollar sales volume. Share of market and profit will be carefully correlated so that the profit per "market share point" can be maximized.

If these assumptions turn out to be true for your business, the "abnormal" will become the new norm. In case this happens in a hurry, you'd better start making contingency plans now. Rather than being a mere exercise, this should give you the kind of opportunity few managers ever get: the chance to recharter your business almost as if you were founding it today.

How would you set it up? Lean and hungry, of course.

How would you express your objectives? In terms of maximizing profit.

If you had a formula for sales success, what would it be? Concentrate on selling your big winners to your major accounts.

What would be your attitude toward costs? Low overhead.

One more question: Does that sound like a good way to run a business? You bet.

SM, May 19, 1975, pp. 3-4.

Use the 2-D Principle for Making the Most of Sales Time

by **Porter Henry**, President, Porter Henry & Co.

The fastest way to make sales calls more profitable is to allocate salespeople's calls and time so that they produce maximum profit per sales hour. That is done rather easily, though often not too accurately, if the company sells only one product to various types of customers. Allocating sales effort becomes more complicated, however, when the field force sells a *multiple* product line to different kinds of customers, such as wholesalers, large direct-buying dealers, government accounts, and original equipment manufacturers.

Take a person who is promoting various product lines to customer types A, B, and C. Each of those categories consists of a group of customers with similar characteristics, although the 2-D Principle we are about to describe can be applied to individual key accounts.

In planning sales calls to customer categories, most companies rely on dollar volume as a base, though it is sounder to use the customers' contribution to profit. That is obtained by taking the markup on products purchased by each customer category, and subtracting each category's portion of certain expenses. These should include the cost of such things as selling, inventory, receivables, and service. Whichever yardstick is used, the company or the individual salesman considers both present and future purchases, and tries to allocate his calls among customer categories to maximize the volume or profit contribution.

Setting aside the question of what percentage of his time the salesperson should invest in nonbuying prospect calls, let's say that he (or his company) decides that his sales calls on regular customers should be allocated like this (note that call allocation rarely matches the customer's volume because customers who buy in large quantities require less sales and service time per dollar than smaller customers):

A frequent contributor to Sales Management, *Porter Henry heads Porter Henry & Co., New York City, which specializes in sales management consulting and training sessions.*

Customer Type	% of Present Volume of Profit	% of Sales Calls
A	60.0%	40.0%
B	30.0%	35.0%
C	10.0%	25.0%

This salesman sells three different product lines. The profit contribution of each can be closely estimated by subtracting its sales, servicing, and distribution costs from its dollar markup. If the company allocates sales time by product volume or profitability, the result might look like this:

Product Line	% of Present Volume or Profit	% of Sales Calls Or Selling Time
1	20.0%	10.0%
2	50.0%	60.0%
3	30.0%	30.0%
	100.0%	100.0%

Instead of allocating sales effort either by customer type or by product line, the company should combine the two. Each salesperson is really confronted with a two-dimensional grid such as that shown in Table 1.

Table 1

	% of Sales Effort			
	Products			
Customers	1	2	3	TOTAL
A				40.0%
B				35.0%
C				25.0%
TOTAL	10.0%	60.0%	30.0%	100.0%

Most companies allocate sales time by one of the "Totals." Pharmaceutical concerns, for example, use the total across the bottom of the chart; salesmen are told what percentage of their total time to spend on assigned products. Many managers use the right-hand total, however. "Spend these percentages of your sales calls on these customers," they tell their salesmen. In both cases, the people in charge are assigning by totals, instead of wrestling with individual boxes in the grid as they should be.

As a result, salespeople tend to place the same relative emphasis on each product line when calling on all customers who use those products. Without being aware of it, they are filling in the boxes in the grid in proportion to their row and column totals; so the figures resemble those in Table 2.

That seat-of-the-pants procedure is really a case of working from the outside in—from totals to specifics. Salesmen will generate much more profit per unit of sales effort if they reverse the process and work from the inside out. To do that, they allocate a percentage of their effort to each of the individual boxes, and build

Table 2

| Customers | % of Sales Effort | | | |
| | Products | | | |
	1	2	3	TOTAL
A	4.0%	24.0%	12.0%	40.0%
B	3.5%	21.0%	10.5%	35.0%
C	2.5%	15.0%	7.5%	25.0%
TOTAL	10.0%	60.0%	30.0%	100.0%

up their totals from those.

Each box will then represent the sales effort expended on one product line with one type of customer. For each of those allocations we ask ourselves these questions:

1. What's the current volume and profit of this line with this customer?
2. What are the customer's total purchases of this type of product from us and our competitors?
3. What share of this potential business do we now have?
4. How profitable is the product itself?

Using the seat-of-the-pants method, our hypothetical salesman invested the biggest chunk of his time in Box A-2 just because it involved his largest customer group and his biggest-selling product. If he considers the individual pigeonhole, however, he might find that product 2 has a lower markup than the other two; furthermore, it may already have about 80% of the potential purchases by that customer category; so the opportunity for additional sales is limited.

The salesperson would do better to cut the time in this box from 24% down to 10%, which is all that would be required to hold the present share. Then he could invest the "saved" 14% in Product 1, which has a higher markup. Specifically, customer group C has the largest unrealized potential for Product 1, and so we add 10% to box C-1 and 2% each to boxes A-1 and B-1. If that were the only reallocation he made, the grid would now look like Table 3.

Table 3

| Customers | % of Sales Effort | | | |
| | Products | | | |
	1	2	3	TOTAL
A	6.0%	10.0%	12.0%	28.0%
B	5.5%	21.0%	10.5%	37.0%
C	12.5%	15.0%	7.5%	35.0%
TOTAL	24.0%	46.0%	30.0%	100.0%

To what extent might that approach increase a company's profit? We took the actual sales figures of one of our clients and fed them into our computerized simulation of a field sales force. The simulation juggles some 280 interacting variables that make up the operation of the sales force. Among them are time allocation; salesmen's salaries, commissions, and expenses; the markup, inventory cost, and receivables cost for each product line; present and potential purchases of each product line by customer category, and so on.

ON THE WAY TO HIGHER PROFITS

The actual company we used in this experiment manufactures five different product lines that it sells to totally different types of customers. Some customers have no application for some product lines, and so some of the pigeonholes in the real grid contain zeroes.

We first allocated salesmen's time in a simpleminded way: they called on all customers with equal frequency, and during their calls allocated their time to product lines in proportion to current dollar volume. With that method of time allocation, the sales force's contribution to profits (markup minus all costs, but without corporate overhead) was $10.7 million.

Ignoring the idea of allocating time by product line, we juggled the allocation for calls to customer groups to maximize the profit contribution. It increased to $10.9 million. Going back to the original allocation of customer time, we then changed the product effort so it encouraged maximum profitability; the result was $12.1 million.

After that we used the best possible allocation of total time to both customers and products (working from the outside in, using the row and column totals). That increased the profit contribution to $12.1 million. Next we carefully examined the potential profit and optimum sales effort for each individual pigeonhole and allocated time from the inside out. The result was a profit of $13.6 million.

The final 12.1% increase is a reasonably reliable projection of what the sales manager can accomplish by using the 2-D grid to allocate sales time for maximum profitability.

SM, May 19, 1975, pp. 25-26.

Why the Future of Your Company May Ride with Its Key Accounts

To explore the importance of key account selling to the marketing effort, *Sales Management* talked to four top executives from diverse industries.

by **Martin Everett**, Senior Editor

One of the first things a company has to do to assure its long-term profitability is to take a look at how well it serves its best customers: those 20% or so of the accounts that contribute something like 80% of any company's business. Not only are those companies the biggest source of sales and profits for a supplier but they are likely to be among the market leaders in *their* industries and thus provide valuable feedback on such things as market conditions and product innovation. That alone would justify assigning a special salesperson to minister to their needs.

Yet many sales and marketing executives seem to resist taking that step. Perhaps they have done so little sales analysis that they do not even know which accounts are most profitable. Or they may fear a political problem within the sales force. Who should become a key account salesman? Will that choice involve interfering with the relationships that other members of the sales force have built up with their accounts over the years? Will the added cost of such a plan eventually pay off?

GOOD CAUSE FOR KEY ACCOUNTS

Most obstacles are overcome, however, when managers see what is likely to happen if they *don't* adopt some sort of key account program. The risk of having their best customers stray into the grip of competitors is simply too great to ignore. Beyond that, there are several supporting reasons for a key account program. These include the following:

1. Profits. More companies are realizing that a "good customer" is one that makes a healthy contribution to your bottom line. Thus Richard W. Eddy, senior vice president, customer relations, with Union Carbide's Chemicals and Plastics Group, calls his plan the "Major Account Program for Profit."

2. Total interface between buyer and seller. This is as important to a grocery products operation such as that run by Dean F. Thomas, vice president, consumer companies, for Pillsbury, as it is to William W. Neal, sales vice president of Litton's Sweda International division, which sells a technical product.

As operations of both buyer and seller become more complex, and as the two companies become more dependent on each other, there are several reasons for assigning a salesman to monitor all aspects of a customer's business. There are two ways of looking at this:

From the seller's standpoint, there is an advantage in developing an in-depth relationship with his account to learn as much as possible about its processes. Over a period of time, this enables him to embed his products in the customer's operations, thus participating in its growth and keeping competitors at bay.

From the buyer's standpoint, a closer relationship with suppliers makes it possible to learn about their long-term capabilities for meeting the company's growing needs. This is especially vital in technical products, where a supplier's failure can seriously jeopardize the buyer's ability to achieve his own marketing objectives. Says one marketer: "They really want to get in your knickers to find out what you're doing these days."

3. Centralized buying. Whether at the national or regional level, major buying executives are a prime target for most marketers, including a growing number of industrial concerns. The sale may not be closed there, but it won't be closed anywhere else either without the approval of this key buying influence. That is a prime concern in a consumer electronics operation such as that run by Joseph A. Lagore, vice president of Sony's consumer sales division.

CLASSIFYING KEY ACCOUNTS

Deciding which customers merit special attention calls for doing some basic market research. The three main things to consider:
1. Your current business with the customer
2. His potential total business
3. Your chance of getting it

Once the potential for sales and profits from an account has been determined, other factors may be weighed. For example, Sony's Lagore takes a careful look at a major retailer's image in the marketplace. Does a department store have an effective advertising program? Are prices of the products it generally promotes in line with the quality image that Sony wants to project for its color TV sets and other items?

Ultimately, says Lagore, the selection of a key account has implications that go beyond the amount of business done with that particular customer. "Smaller dealers like to carry lines that the key account advertises," he says. "That way they can coattail their own advertising and perhaps promote a price discount. Because of this relationship, your choice of a key account determines how well you are likely to do in any given market."

Once a key account has been selected, there remains the problem of making sure that the sales effort is directed at the right place in the company. The cooperative buying offices of department store groups are important targets for companies like Sony, but the individual member stores maintain considerable buying autonomy at the local level. Thus Sony has sales personnel to cover buyers at both locations.

For similar reasons, Union Carbide makes sure that account executives who make headquarters calls also keep in touch with Carbide salesmen calling on the same company. . . . Pillsbury's Thomas notes that the trend toward regional buying in the grocery business has affected his key account program. "If you want to sell something to Safeway today, you can't just drop into the Oakland [Cal.] home office," he says. "You have to go to Dallas or one of the other regional centers."

GETTING ORGANIZED

The necessity for maintaining a two-pronged sales effort generally is the main factor that determines the structure of the key account operation. Major industrial companies are apt to have one top executive who is concerned with nothing but key accounts. Union Carbide's Eddy is an example. At Sweda, the man is Emilio Fontana, vice president, major account sales. Typically these individuals are veteran sales and marketing people who have a thorough knowledge of customer companies and the people who run them.

Because of the technical nature of Sweda's computerized point-of-sale equipment, Fontana maintains a staff of systems engineers to support some 30 major account salesmen, even to the point of flying out to assist on sales calls. Fontana is the eyes and ears of the program, monitoring key account progress to make sure that customers get the service they should.

For purposes of administration, most companies have a dual reporting system that requires major account men to be responsible to regional or area sales managers while they maintain a "dotted line" relationship with the headquarters staff. So intense is Sweda's concern for major accounts that the regional sales executive spends about 75% of *his* time on them.

Sony has a national accounts manager who concentrates on central buying offices, but it also stresses strong follow-through by key account salesmen in the field. Although they normally don't have any geographic territory, key account men may sell to small dealers in territories that can't support an additional salesperson.

AIMING AT THE UPPER ECHELONS

On average, Sony has two key account men per sales territory. In addition to being well versed in their own product line, they must be able to train retail salespeople, either in group sessions or in 15-minute spurts between customers on the selling floor. Another important qualification: thorough knowledge of cooperative advertising and how to use it for the mutual advantage of Sony and the retailer.

Because it is usually aimed at the upper echelons of the customer's executive ranks, key account selling incorporates procedures that sometimes border on pageantry. Sweda's Neal points out that most retail chains regard installation of a POS system as a major investment that must be approved by the chairman of the board. Often, that means that Sweda's own chief executive officer must enter the game to lend weight to the presentation. In such cases, the key account man acts as a kind of quarterback, calling in executives or technical people when he feels they are needed. Working for months on a project, he must be selfless enough to accept one fact of a key account man's life: his own president may wind up closing the sale.

Pillsbury likes to bring the top management of grocery chains such as Jewel, Kroger, and Food Fair into its Minneapolis headquarters at least once a year, if possible. There, they participate in "rap sessions" with Pillsbury executives to explore the present and future needs of their respective companies. Often, it falls to Pillsbury's chairman, William H. Spoor, to explain the full array of his company's resources, whether it be product development capabilities or the advantages of dealing with a company that has its hand in everything from Burger King to Souverain wines.

Regardless of the details, the objective remains the same: to translate Pillsbury product benefits into the food retailer's own marketing terms. This may mean describing the appeal a product has for certain psychographic or demographic groups so the buyer can compare the data with the market profile of his own customers. The final consideration, of course, is how much profit a product is likely to earn for stores in the chain.

KEY ACCOUNT SELLING IS NOT FOR EVERYONE

One advantage of introducing a key accounts program is that it is an ideal medium for talented salespeople who want to remain in selling rather than go into management. The job requires more than a firm handshake and a winning smile, however. In most companies, key account men are expected to be conversant with the profitability goals of their customers. But few concerns have progressed to the level of Pillsbury, which claims that all its account managers can talk profitability with a food retailer's most astute merchandising vice presidents.

Key account selling is not for everyone, though. "Some people can't live unless they sell something every day," says Sweda's Neal. "Selling one of our systems sometimes takes three years." Besides, there is another factor to consider: not everyone has the guts to ask someone for a $3 million order.

SM, May 19, 1975, pp. 29–30.

Salesman to Manager: Easy Doesn't Do It

If he's good, a Levi Strauss salesman can make district manager in five years—after going over the jumps.

by **Victor Horwitz**, National Sales Manager, Jeans Division, Levi Strauss & Co.

The transition from salesman to manager is a difficult one. At Levi Strauss we try to make it as orderly as possible. Men deemed by their supervisors to be ready for advancement to management positions are interviewed in depth by our training director and put through a battery of aptitude and attitude tests to pinpoint their strengths and weaknesses.

The final evaluation of a man's managerial potential depends on a variety of factors, however. The training director's report, test results, supervisors' recommendations, plus appraisal forms submitted throughout a man's career at Levi's are all taken into consideration. Thus, when a management position opens up, we are prepared with full reports on all the candidates for the job.

ORIENTATION PROGRAM FOR NEW SALES MANAGERS

Once a man has been promoted to manager, he undergoes a prescribed orientation program. New managers are brought to Levi's headquarters in San Francisco for a week-long seminar in which we try to cover all the bases connected with their new responsibilities. The men have sessions with representatives of the home office Personnel, Finance, Credit, Advertising, Sales, and Merchandising departments. The object is to inform the men of their new duties and the various services that the company provides for them.

Salesmen who reach high-level management positions at Levi Strauss are those who deal well with people, communicate easily, think analytically, and have those qualities we value most: honesty, integrity, imagination, and perseverance. They also must be able to accept a disagreeable assignment and convert it into a success.

We ask our managers to recommend salesmen for rapid or long-term advancement. An especially talented salesman can become a district manager in as little as five years. Those put forward as the best candidates for fast promotions are frequently described by their supervisors in such terms as: "He has discipline and self-control"; "He is self-confident, enthusiastic, and poised"; "He knows he has a lot to learn and is willing to be guided"; "He has a positive attitude toward selling"; "He is intensely loyal to Levi's."

Characteristics they most often list as negative, hindering a man's promotion to management, are impatience, impetuousness, and immaturity. One outstanding salesman who frequently worked as much as 20 hours in a day and turned in record sales was not considered management material because he demanded equal energy from everyone around him and was impatient with others who didn't compete as intensely and as well as he.

As a matter of policy, we look for management potential in every salesman we hire. Whether or not his ambition is to move into a management position, he *will be a better salesman* if he organizes his time and territory well to achieve his objectives. This also holds for adopting other "managerial" traits, such as communicating with people effectively and going after the greatest benefits for the company and the customer, not just financial gains for himself.

HOW OUR MANAGERS SELL

We recognize that a good salesman has to be a manager of many things and that our sales managers are in many ways still salesmen. They may no longer be traveling from city to city selling Levi's to department and specialty stores, but they have a selling job to do, and a tough one. In the long run, managing is selling ideas and responsibility and selling people on achievement. It's getting people to do what you want and getting them to enjoy doing it. So we want our salesmen to be good managers and our managers to be good salesmen.

HOW DOES LEVI'S PROMOTION FROM WITHIN PROGRAM WORK?

Levi's internal promotion program, which can carry a man from sales trainee right up the ladder to national sales manager, starts at the first interview, before a salesman is even hired. All our hiring and firing of salesmen is done by regional sales managers, not by the company's personnel department. Being salesmen themselves, our managers have a better idea of what characteristics and attitudes to look for in a man. They can sense a potential salesman's attitude and managerial aptitude.

At a recent sales managers' meeting we conducted a seminar on interviewing techniques and hiring considerations to give our managers some specific guidelines. As a final step in the hiring process, we in the home office review the paperwork on every man about to be hired. This gives us a chance to head off an occasional bad choice.

From the time a salesman is hired, his supervisors watch him and rate him for management potential and performance. On monthly appraisal forms managers grade each new salesman not only on the volume and distribution of his sales but on how well he resolves customer complaints and maintains call schedules, and how good his relations are with his accounts and with his regional office. The manager is asked, "Is he going to make it as a salesman?"

Mandatory forms force managers to watch their salesmen carefully; by posing specific questions they help supervisors to know what indicators to look for. Because the regional manager has to stay aware of how each new salesman is fitting into the job, we are better able to weed out the poor performers before they get locked into the company structure. It used to take too long to find out whether or not a new salesman would make it. The appraisal form functions as an early warning system.

We expect our regional managers to keep in close touch with their salesmen and to help them develop their management potential. If a salesman is having trouble organizing his territory or is running into other problems, we ask what his manager is doing to correct the situation. Our Field Visit Appraisal Form, filled out by a supervisor every time he has contact with a salesman, asks, "Have you developed a plan to make him a better salesman? What kind of plan?" And perhaps more important, it asks, "How much managerial potential does he have?"

Every so often we rotate the salesmen each supervisor works with. You can get too used to a man after working with him over an extended period, and pretty soon everything he does looks good, or everything he does looks bad. We prefer to have several different supervisors evaluate a salesman's performance. We get to know soon enough which of our managers are tough graders and which are halo-makers, and we take that into consideration.

SALES FORCE ORGANIZATION

Levi's currently employs about 500 salesmen in the U.S. Some 300 of these are in the Jeans Div., 125 in our Panatela Sportswear Div., 50 in Levi's for Gals, and about 20 in Boyswear. The line of advancement is the same in all divisions, and salesmen can and often do move from one division to another as they climb the promotion ladder.

Let's take the Jeans Div. as an example. The lowest position is stocktaker, usually a part-time job held by a college student. If he shows potential, a stocktaker is promoted to sales trainee, a position that pays $600-$700 a month. Trainees work with salesmen in the field learning the basics—how to pack a suitcase, how to write an order, and how to sell. Sometimes a salesman will give a trainee an account to handle on his own, under the salesman's supervision.

When a position becomes available, a good sales trainee is given a general territory with low annual sales volume, handling as many as 50 accounts and making our standard commission plus an incentive bonus of 25% over regular commission on sales above target level. (Target is developed by regional management with the agreement of the salesman.)

At the top of the salesman's promotion ladder is the account executive, who may handle a single large account or as many as six. Account executives receive a base salary augmented by commission on sales to target volume and double commission over target. In their daily dealings with difficult accounts they pick up a broad range of experience that prepares them for future management assignments. An account executive has to have the ability to conceive and carry out long-range plans, handle stocktakers and trainees, and deal with the complicated requirements of such multiple store groups as Macy's, May Co., Gimbel's, Abraham & Straus, and Marshall Field.

Most top salesmen are enthusiastic about coming into management. When a Levi's salesman moves from account executive into the first management level as a district sales manager, he takes on increased responsibility. There are two district managers in five of our regional offices and three in the New York regional office. Each district manager has from 12 to 25 salesmen under his supervision.

At the top of the field management progression is the regional sales manager, responsible for the smooth operation of the regional office and for the entire sales operation in his area. This year, for the first time, we have made each regional manager supervisor of from 6 to 10 salesmen as well. This is to ensure that regional managers do not become desk jockeys, out of touch with what salesmen encounter every day out in the field.

COMPENSATION FOR SALES MANAGERS

Compensation for regional and district managers includes a flat salary (higher for the regional manager), override commission for every percentage point of increased sales in the region over the previous year (also higher for the regional manager), and bonus payments distributed among managers according to their achievement of objectives established by us in sales administration with their agreement and acceptance.

Having a coherent company management philosophy helps smooth the transition from salesman to manager. At Levi's we strongly favor Management By Objectives, and we are working to carry the idea right down to the sales level within the sales department. Most of our managers are achievers. It is a desire for that *sense of achievement*, not the dollar, that makes Sammy Manager run today. We think that is as it should be. We give our sales managers a wide range of goals, such as increased sales; sales to target accounts; better control of transfers, returns and cancellations; elimination of unauthorized claims and deductions; careful management of controllable expenses; and compliance with company policies.

Then we divide a pool of funds, created by the volume of sales in the division for the fiscal year, among district and regional managers according to how well they have achieved the established goals. A man may receive nothing, or he may get as much as a $10,000-$12,000 bonus.

DOLLARS ARE MERE POKER CHIPS

New managers as well as old have reacted favorably to this program of objectives, introduced last year. They are proud of the targets they achieve and of the recognition their achievement brings; financial reward has become less important. I am convinced that achievement is the greatest motivation for success. Dollars become like poker chips after a while. You play with them, but money is not the name of the game. The end of the rainbow for the man newly promoted to management is achievement; what money a man gets for it along the way is less important than the fact that in his own eyes he is an achiever.

From time to time seminars with experts from outside the company are held at management meetings; we hope soon to conduct similar sessions in the field. Through the Principles of Professional Salesmanship (POPS) program, district managers will pass on what they learn to their salesmen in the field.

In spite of all our efforts to ease the transition from salesman to manager, we are convinced that what the new manager needs most are self-discipline and time. A manager has to discipline himself to manage and not sell. He has to learn to listen patiently, let a salesman make his own mistakes and then discuss them with him, and communicate on a very broad base with many things in mind.

It's difficult, but the men who reach the upper management levels at Levi's have developed their organizational and leadership skills on each step along the way. If they've made it this far, it's because a lot of watchful supervisors have given them high points and we have confidence in their management abilities.

SM, April 30, 1973, pp. 30–37.

How Newly Promoted Sales Managers Are Taught to Manage at Borg-Warner

Many newly promoted sales managers already know how to sell; the problem is teaching them how to manage. At Borg-Warner's Marbon Div., a major supplier of plastics, the transition is eased by a training period that actually takes budding sales managers out of the line organization for two years.

"We try to identify potential managers when we first hire them as salesmen," says Pete Whedon, manager of marketing manpower development. "Then for three or four years we keep tabs on their performance, bringing them in for occasional management seminars to indicate our interest."

If the man lives up to expectations, he'll be brought in to the home office at Parkersburg, W. Va., and given a staff job, such as advertising manager, product manager, market development manager, or sales service manager. "In these positions," Whedon explains, "he'll have budget responsibilities and a chance to work with subordinates. It's a low-risk proposition for the company because the division's top management will be across the hall, keeping an eye on him and giving him any support he needs."

Marbon has been using this plan since 1966, and Whedon is pleased with the results so far. "Three of our five sales managers have gone from salesmen to staff managers and back to field sales managers." However, some salesmen are reluctant to leave the field and spend two years in the home office. So Whedon is now considering an alternate route for prospective managers. "We're thinking of trying to teach management skills to a man while keeping him in his sales territory," he reveals. "First, we'd give him a special project, such as developing a training program for beginning salesmen. Then, we might ask him to implement that project. If he succeeds, we might give him one salesman to manage, then maybe two or three salesmen. If he clears all those hurdles, he'll be ready to take over as field sales manager."

There are problems with this approach, Whedon freely admits, such as supervision and setting up an adequate compensation formula. So he's going slow, not willing to adopt such a program until he's sure that it will truly turn out sales managers who've learned how to manage as well as they can sell.

SM, April 30, 1973, p. 37.

She's Selling Again — and Gladly

Two months ago, 30-year-old Susan Sjoberg was New Orleans district manager for Advance Schools, a Chicago-headquartered home study school (1972 revenues: $32 million) with over 500 sales representatives across the U.S. In fact, she had been promoted to that position early this year as a direct result of having outsold everyone else on the force.

She's not a district manager any more. The four full-time reps whose in-home selling efforts she supervised have a new boss, and Ms. Sjoberg is back in the field. "I didn't like the district managership," she explains, "although I appreciated the position's importance. The eight-to-five life doesn't appeal to me. I'd much rather get out and talk with people, which is what selling's all about. Then, too, I like the idea of making money roughly in proportion to how hard I work."

It's not surprising that Advance Schools, which offers courses in such fields as refrigeration, auto mechanics, electronics, and accounting, found it difficult to keep the high-earning Ms. Sjoberg as a manager. The company generally expects people to sell 10 enrollments a month to stay on the payroll. Ms. Sjoberg confesses to averaging 30 "in a good month." Last December she set the company record with 75 enrollments from the Port Neches, Texas, area.

Money was far from her most important reason for abandoning a desk, however. Advance Schools' brand of in-home selling, directed mainly at men in their early thirties who have a high school diploma, is a particular challenge. "A wife is often suspicious about her husband's committing himself to a home study course, especially one sold by a woman," Ms. Sjoberg explains. "The information I can give her as a guest in her home usually quells any doubts." Once she even invaded the labor room of a local hospital to get a wife's O.K.

Many of the qualities that Ms. Sjoberg credits with her success as a salesperson,

though, doubtless would stand any manager in good stead. "I feel capable of instilling in someone else the desire to improve himself, or at least of enlivening an existing desire," she says. "And I refuse to give up. I always make a second effort."
SM, September 17, 1973, p. 7.

Sports Champ Turns Sales Manager

Last May, when Edgar DeMeyer, national sales manager, Fischer Manufacturing, needed a sales manager for the billiard and game table marketer's new dealer sales center in Kansas City, Mo., he called on Dorothy Wise, five-time winner of the National Women's U.S. Open Pocket Billiard contest.

"I needed someone who knew our customers and knew the line," says DeMeyer, whose Tipton, Mo., company, a division of Questor, sells exclusively through manufacturers' reps. Mrs. Wise had been demonstrating for Fischer at tournaments and trade shows since 1967. Also, she and her late husband ran a string of their own family billiard parlors for 25 years. Thus she knew Fischer's reps, consumers, and the game. Luckily, DeMeyer says, the energetic grandmother, who looks at least 10 years younger than the 60 she'll be in December, decided that she wouldn't mind laying down her tournament cue stick for a selling job.

Far from being just a pretty face from the playing fields, Mrs. Wise is called upon to demonstrate the line to reps and their salesmen, to advise them on what tables and accessories sell best in department and sporting goods stores in their markets, and, frequently, to play a friendly game with them after the order is signed.

Mrs. Wise says that reps trust her advice. "Nine times out of 10 the woman makes the decision on whether to buy a billiard table," she says. "Also, few men in the business know the game like I do." Her knowledge is paying off in better quality control as well as in sales. Says Mrs. Wise, "I recently discovered the factory was putting the cloth on backwards on some of the tables."

There could be another dividend for Fischer in the future. During her lunch hours and after work, Mrs. Wise coaches the company's workmen on championship play. Should one win a title, Fischer might be in line for yet another endorsement.
SM, October 14, 1974, p. 4.

Ames' James G. Campbell

Vital Statistics James G. Campbell, president, Ames, a McDonough company . . . Ames manufactures over 5,000 types of lawn and garden tools and products, such as shovels, spades, trowels, rakes, axes, hatchets . . . 28-man field sales force sells to distributors . . . Fiscal 1974 sales $44.9 million, earnings $4.3 million . . . Campbell joined Ames as junior salesman 8/1/50 . . . Assistant sales manager 1/1/56 . . . Sales manager 1/1/57 . . . Vice president, sales and marketing 7/1/59 . . . Executive vice president 7/1/67 . . . President 7/1/68 . . . Age 59 . . . Married, two children.

While many U.S. companies are still gearing up for a Bicentennial celebration in 1976, festivities are already in full swing at Ames, a McDonough company. Founded by John Ames in Bridgewater, Mass., in 1774, the company, now located in Parkersburg, W. Va., is celebrating its 200th birthday with special promotions, special sales, print and TV advertising, and the slogan "Ames: 200 years making 'em this good." Overseeing the celebration is president James Campbell, who joined Ames as a junior salesman nearly 24 years ago.

As a junior salesman, Campbell says, he covered a nine-state territory in a two-door Chevy business coupe. It was no joyride. "One summer day in Texas," he recalls, "I put a thermometer in the car and it registered 150°. That's when I asked for an air-conditioned wagon. You couldn't get a man to work under those conditions today."

[Concerning selling, and how it has changed since those early days], Campbell says that today each of Ames's field salesmen covers, on average, "a couple of states, maybe 60 accounts. They still work with the distributor, but their thinking is more directed toward moving merchandise out of the retail store. Our field people spend 60% of their time either selling the retailer or helping the retailer sell. They may go in and actually show him how our stuff should be laid out to be sold most effectively." . . .

Emphasis on the retailer is the focal point of Ames's birthday celebration. For example, a three-page ad in the May *Reader's Digest* is "designed to direct the customer into the store," Campbell says. The ad contains discount coupons for Greensweeper rakes and for Lehigh garden shoes (made by Endicott Johnson, also a McDonough company) and announces sale prices on five Ames products.

Campbell obviously hasn't lost sight of the realities of selling as he's moved into management positions. One way he keeps up is by travelling. "If you sit in an office day after day," he says, "you lose touch with what's going on in your business. I travel 50,000 to 75,000 miles per year. I meet with the distributors, to get a feeling of what's going on. I don't sell, but I do come back with a better feeling about the business, and I pick up a lot of information."

When he's not on the road, Campbell is usually in his office from 8:00 a.m. to 6:00 or 6:15 p.m. But his workday doesn't end then. "I normally take a good bit of reading material home," he says. "I don't read novels; I read business material. Consequently, I'm not a good conversationalist when I get outside the business area. But this is what it takes to be successful."

Asked what other factors he thinks have contributed to his success in a sales career, Campbell [says,] " You must have a reasonably likable disposition, so people don't instinctively dislike you. Beyond that, I believe you can be very brilliant, but you've got to put out that perspiration. And third is the business reading—it makes you more interesting to the man you're talking with, more able to generate ideas. Reading has stimulated my thinking. But of all those things," he emphasizes, "work is the most important."

SM, June 10, 1974, p. 29.

Section 23 / Your Personal Audit: That Magic 10 Percent Plus

Electrolux's Truly Golden Jubilee

"Good morning, Tigers," said assistant sales vice president Gene Bergen: the 50th anniversary sales meeting was off in a roar of applause.

Chilling breezes and a rain-clouded sky didn't darken the spirits of some 2,000 blue-blazered salespeople walking to New York's Radio City Music Hall June 28. The cream of vacuum cleaner king Electrolux's 15,000-plus field salesmen and saleswomen, they weren't coming to see the Rockettes. They and their spouses were gathering to share the spotlight of success at the company's 50th anniversary sales meeting. And though they walked just two blocks to get there—from lodgings in the Waldorf-Astoria, Barclay, and Summit hotels—their journey had taken 18 months.

"Promoting the meeting and jubilee celebration as an incentive was a natural for us," company president Charlie A. McKee says. Because Electrolux sales volume depends wholly on direct selling, and the salesmen, who are company employees, operate as independent contractors, the company is always promoting to keep them ringing doorbells, giving demonstrations (it averages one sale for three demos), and recruiting new manpower. Regular monthly and quarterly contests culminate in all-night telephone marathons similar to election-night tabulations. McKee, sales vice president Steve Sheridan, and other top brass in the company's Stamford, Conn., headquarters man the phones to tally last-minute sales called in by 775 branch office managers. By morning, the winners' names are known throughout the organization—and the next contest begins. Thus a gigantic contest was the inevitable pièce de résistance for the company's 50th anniversary plans.

The kickoff date was January 1973. McKee sent personal letters to each salesman and "belle ringer," as women in the organization are called, inviting him or her to come, with spouse, to the jubilee sales meeting and four-day celebration in and around New York City. Travel and lodging would be free to all who attained a $37,500 annual sales volume—approximately 140 "average" sales. (Prices of Electrolux vacuum cleaners and floor polishers now range from $126.75 to $269.75, but were lower last year.) Other prizes, such as diamond rings, were thrown in to sweeten the pot. And to keep excitement at a high pitch, winners competed for the very rooms and tables they would occupy during the jubilee festival.

The company's 865 branch, division, and region managers, and its four area vice presidents (a new level of management added last year to decentralize operations and make more room at the top for really ambitious tigers) qualified for the trip by increasing sales 5% and keeping their operations profitable. Field managers, the first echelon above salesman, qualified on the basis of personal sales. They and the branch and division managers also competed against others in their own regions for the title "man or woman of the year." . . .

The result was a record-smashing year. Sales exceeded $300 million—over twice the company's annual volume in 1968, the year it became a wholly owned subsidiary of Consolidated Foods. And sales in April 1974, the month that marked Electrolux's actual 50th anniversary, were $32 million, 38% ahead of April 1973.

Roared Sheridan to the scores of "hungry tigers" eagerly packing the sales meeting: "That's a record that will last forever. Or until next April—whichever comes first."

SM, July 22, 1974, pp. 21-23.

Every Company Needs Such Salesmen

The following letter was sent by an executive of Modern Income Life Insurance, Decatur, Ill., to Addressograph Multigraph in praise of one of Addressograph's veteran salesmen. We think it's worth sharing with you.

January 30, 1975

Mr. Charles L. Davis, President
Addressograph Multigraph Corp.
20600 Chargrin Blvd.
Cleveland, Ohio 44122

Dear Mr. Davis:

I hope you will take a couple of minutes out of your busy day to read the following about one of your outstanding sales representatives.

Mr. Burrell B. Beatty of your Multigraphics Div. in Springfield, Ill., is not only a super salesman but also a super human individual. I cannot begin to tell you of all his fine qualities or of the services he has performed for our company without burdening you with a long letter. Therefore, I will try to hit the high spots.

Mr. Beatty first contacted our company when we began business in 1967. He has watched us grow to a company in excess of $6 million in assets and has upgraded our equipment from the original model 85 he sold us in 1967. He has never made a suggestion to upgrade or expand our equipment without a written proposal explaining why and the savings involved. So far, he's batting a thousand and I have learned to respect his knowledge of your equipment and to adopt his suggestions.

Our Home Office was severely damaged by fire on a Saturday in June 1971. We moved to new quarters the following Monday. By Tuesday, Mr. Beatty and your service representatives had our equipment cleaned, serviced, and back in business. By such prompt service, we saved several thousand dollars.

The most recent example was two weeks ago, when our legal department finished a proxy statement regarding our acquisition of another company. We had three days to print, assemble, and mail a 70-page statement, and one printer was out due to illness. I called Mr. Beatty and asked him to teach one of our employees to run your model 1850. He was at our company the next morning when the doors opened. After he left, Mr. Beatty contacted us several times during the day to see if any problems had developed. That night, he returned and helped us for a couple of hours, in order that our employees could take a break for dinner. I finally asked him to leave because I felt we were taking advantage of him.

By now, I'm sure you can see why we think your Mr. Beatty is such a super salesman and individual. In appreciation, the executive officers of our company have invited Mr. Beatty and his wife to join us for an all-expense-paid weekend in the Bahamas. This can in no way be compared to the savings and service given us by your company and Mr. Beatty.

Samuel W. Everett Jr.
Administrative vice president
SM, March 17, 1975, p. 12.

The [Sales] Wizardry of Og

by **Andrew Kapociunas**, Contributing Editor

He shortened his first name from Augustine to Og because he thought it sounded more interesting that way; he gained inspiration from a co-inmate in a Boston drunk tank; and he has no recollection of writing the major part of his most important book. There's another point of interest about Og Mandino: he has now sold over 1 million copies of *The Greatest Salesman in the World*, making it probably the best-selling book ever written about selling.

Mandino, 50, who is now the president and managing editor of the self-improvement magazine *Success Unlimited*, signed a contract for the book in 1966 with Frederick Fell, the New York publishing house. The book came out in 1968 and, without a penny of promotion for the first three and one-half years, has sold over 550,000 hardcover copies at $4.95 each.

Bantam bought the paperback rights for $350,000 in 1973 and issued a first printing of 540,000 last March. By last month, it had gone back for two reprints, and there are now 650,000 paperback copies in print. How was it done? By word of mouth—initially, W. Clement Stone's.

Stone is president of Chicago's Combined Insurance Co. and editor and publisher of *Success Unlimited.* With Napoleon Hill, he wrote *Success through a Positive Mental Attitude,* the book Mandino credits for his climb back from that Boston jail cell. When Mandino read the book, he applied for a salesman's job with Stone's insurance company—and lost it. But on a second try, he sold so much insurance that he was made a sales manager.

Mandino's territory extended from Fort Kent to Presque Isle, Me., and included "thousands of miles of frozen ice in between." He recalls recruiting salesmen from the farm boys and auto mechanics who lived there. "But in six months," he says, "we were leading New England in sales."

Eventually, Mandino was given a more populous territory. He wrote a sales manual and sent it to Stone; that earned him a sales promotion job at headquarters, where Stone approached him about editing *Success Unlimited.* One day, Frederick Fell asked Mandino if he'd like to do a book. The two agreed on a title—*The Greatest Salesman in the World*—and on the story line: a camel boy in the time of Christ who decides that he'd like to be a success at selling. His first assignment is to sell a robe, which he instead gives away—to the Christ child. Returning to a camel caravan, he is followed by a star. The caravan owner, sensing that boy is to be his heir, gives him a set of 10 scrolls containing the secrets of successful selling.

"All the book does is teach you how to love yourself a little more—how to utilize your potential," Mandino says. "We're all salesmen in one way or another. The book appeals to the women's lib people, and it's been picked up by the black community." *Salesman* is essentially positive thinking presented as a biblical parable. The scrolls are forceful and demand obedience, but promising "riches to the faithful," they sell.

Mandino admits he had trouble composing the scrolls. He had the basic idea for each of them: I will be loving, I will persevere, I will act now, etc., but he couldn't get beyond that stage. He says he then remembered a friend in Boston who, years before, admonished him to fulfill his potential. Mandino saw the light—and little else—for the next 24 hours as he finished the book.

He insists he has no recollection of having written anything that day and believes that he may have been writing under divine influence. The manuscript, which contained only 20-odd grammatical errors, was published intact by Fell. At Mandino's insistence, it has never been changed in its 36 editions.

Frederick Fell, says its publicity director, Charles Nurnberg, depends mostly on books it published in the 1950s. Its backlist ranges from titles like *How to Speak with Confidence* to *The Yogurt Cookbook.* Its policy on new books it publishes is "Let's see if it's worth putting any money into." Consequently Mandino's book got little promotion.

Mandino gave a copy of his book to Stone's wife, who "promptly fell in love with it," he says. She persuaded her husband to read it on a plane trip to Europe. On his arrival, Stone sent a cable to Mandino saying that he thought the book was the most inspirational he had read since *The Magnificent Obsession.* When he got back to Chicago, he ordered 30,000 copies to give to, among others, every shareholder and employee of Combined Insurance. These copies acted as seeds, with initial readers buying copies for friends, who in turn bought copies for other friends and business associates.

Mandino also wrote letters to insurance companies, offering them a free copy of the book and suggesting multiple-copy orders for their sales staffs. The book quickly became, and still is, a strong seller at such book retailers as Walden Books, Kroch's and Brentano's, Cokesbury, and Dade and Hutchinson. Fell's commissioned salesmen at Impact Marketing, Chicago, soon had their hands full keeping stores supplied with multiple-copy orders arriving from Coca-Cola, Sperry Rand, and Volkswagen.

Meanwhile, Fell began placing small space ads in the *Wall Street Journal* for the original *Salesman*. The 2" ads had a photo of the book's cover and copy stating, "This book is influencing countless lives."

By January 1973 there were 320,000 copies of *Salesman* in print, but the book had yet to appear on the New York *Times* Bestseller List (it never has). Bantam acquired paperback rights, and that further increased sales.

Fell began a major promotion for the hardcover edition that fall, and a national tour was set up for Mandino, to be tied in with ads in 80 newspapers for three consecutive weeks. Full-page ads appeared in newspapers in Washington, Chicago, Los Angeles, Dallas, and San Francisco. A huge 30-page press kit was made up, on the theory that its size alone would be impressive, and distributed to local TV and radio talk show hosts and newspaper columnists in the 22 target cities.

Meanwhile, Charles Nurnberg arranged a program of 20-second radio spots to be aired in 12 major urban markets, placed ads in the Christmas catalogues put out by Doubleday, Cokesbury, Brentano's, and Kroch's and Brentano's, and gave away 10 free copies of the book to talk jockeys who would use the book in giveaways. He also mailed 1,000 free books to the presidents and sales managers of major companies.

ON THE ROAD TO EXHAUSTION

[It has been] estimated that at the height of the campaign, 3,000 to 5,000 books were sold each week. Total sales of the book went over 400,000. The tour ended with an exhausted Mandino in a hospital in Phoenix.

Soon Bantam began heralding its forthcoming paperback edition as an "important" new title for spring 1974 and calling it "the best seller nobody knows." Mandino was put on the road, again, this time for a two and one-half week tour of the West Coast, visiting five cities. Spot ads were made up for national radio, and special display units, posters, and window streamers were distributed. Bantam's presses poured out 600,000 copies within a few months.

Esther Margolies, a Bantam vice president, says *Salesman* is one of its top 20 sellers. She expects sales to continue brisk for years because, she says, "it's a great word-of-mouth seller."

Fell isn't giving up on its hardback edition. Plans include a cassette with additional material recorded by Mandino attached to each book, plus another insurance company mailing. . . .

[Mandino has just signed a blank contract for a new book] —*The Greatest Miracle in the World*. The "miracle" Mandino refers to is the reader. All he will say about the book, other than that it will be out in 1975, is that "it's to be in the same ball-park" as the other one, and that it will be fiction.

This time, Fell has abandoned its wait-and-see marketing approach. *Miracle* will get an advertising budget from the start.

The Scroll Marked IV

I am nature's greatest miracle.
Since the beginning of time never has there been another with my mind, my heart, my eyes, my ears, my hands, my hair, my mouth. None that came before, none that live today, and none that come tomorrow can walk and talk and move and think exactly like me. All men are my brothers yet I am different from each. I am a unique creature.

I am nature's greatest miracle.

Although I am of the animal kingdom, animal rewards alone will not satisfy me. Within me burns a flame which has been passed from generations uncounted and its heat is a constant irritation to my spirit to become better than I am, and I will. I will fan this flame of dissatisfaction and proclaim my uniqueness to the world.

None can duplicate my brush strokes, none can make my chisel marks, none can duplicate my handwriting, none can produce my child, and, in truth, none has the ability to sell exactly as I. Henceforth, I will capitalize on this difference for it is an asset to be promoted to the fullest.

I am nature's greatest miracle.

SM, August 5, 1974, pp. 25–28.

The Sale That Shocked a Nation

"I rang up and asked the switchboard, 'Who is your catering manager?' " Mark Wilde, 25, contracts manager for the British sales subsidiary of Rosenthal China, Bavaria, West Germany, continues: "I approached the customer just as I would a hotel, a restaurant, or any other catering establishment. It was a completely straightforward exercise."

Not exactly. And as a result, salesman Wilde has touched off a major controversy in Great Britain, embarrassed leading figures in the government, and provided newspapers with a field day. The reason is that Wilde's prospect was John Smillie, catering manager for the House of Commons, Britain's seat of government, who promptly bought £20,000 ($46,000) worth of his china. When members of Parliament found out that they would soon be eating off plates made in Germany, the flap was on. Considering that the government is pushing a drive to "Buy British," it is something more than a tempest over teapots.

The sales contract, signed in August, was O.K.'d by the House of Commons' catering subcommittee, made up of Labour, Liberal, and Conservative MPs. One of them, Liberal Clement Freud, later said, "I don't know anything about it," adding, "It does seem rather strange, when we are told to buy British cars and goods, that an order should go to Rosenthal."

Even more surprised was Peter Shore, Britain's Trade secretary, and the man behind the "Buy British" campaign. He had made his appeal—which was broadcast nationwide—just a week before word leaked out that the sale had been made.

Most surprised of all was Richard Ware, marketing manager for Royal Tuscan's Hotelware Div., a part of Britain's Wedgwood Group, Rosenthal's biggest competitor. Wilde's sale, Ware complained, "is approximately two and a half times the volume of china we have supplied to the Commons in the past six years." Ware revealed that he personally had been trying to sell to Smillie since January. "We were arranging to have lunch," he said.

Shore and others attempted to have the sale cancelled but were surprised again— the order had already arrived from Rosenthal's Saarbrucken factory. Their sole consolation: The words "Made in Germany" have been removed from every piece of china.

About the only unruffled participant in the drama is salesman Wilde, who insists the sale was easy. He told reporters that after learning Smillie's name, he sent him a personal letter with brochures and price lists included. "I phoned a few days later and asked, 'Can I get some samples organized just to show you how good your Commons crest will look on our products?' He agreed. Some time later I met him by appointment and then, lo and behold, the order came through the mail." Government officials now admit that it was competitive prices and speed of delivery that won the order for Wilde's company.

Wilde, who joined Rosenthal's British company as a sales trainee in late 1973 and was promoted to contracts manager just last year, says, "I am not really a very experienced salesman. A year ago I was green. It takes a year to get any confidence."

Asked why he attempted to sell a prestige target like the House of Commons, he answers, "Because it was there."

SM, October 6, 1975, pp. 9-10.